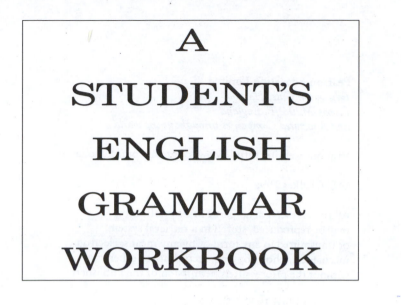

A STUDENT'S ENGLISH GRAMMAR WORKBOOK

Sylvia Chalker

being a Workbook for
A Student's Grammar of the English Language
by Sidney Greenbaum and Randolph Quirk

Longman

D0322598

Pearson Education Limited,
Edinburgh Gate, Harlow,
Essex CM20 2JE, England
and Associated Companies throughout the world

Visit our website: http://www.longman.com/dictionaries

First published 1992
Twelfth impression 2006

British Library Cataloguing-in-Publication Data

A catalogue record for this book is available from
the British Library

ISBN-13: 978-0-582-08819-1
ISBN-10: 0-582-08819-4

Set in Linotype Garamond

Printed in China
SWTC/12

Contents

Introduction

This workbook provides practice material for *A Student's Grammar of the English Language* (*SGE*) by Sidney Greenbaum and Randolph Quirk, and references to relevant sections of *SGE* are given.

The workbook should, however, prove useful to other advanced learners of English who want practice material, and simplified grammatical notes are given on points with which such students may be less familiar. Students may also find a dictionary useful.

The exercises do not have to be done in any particular order, although since the workbook follows the same general plan as *SGE*, this means that sections 1 and 2 serve as an overview, sections 3–11 deal with basic problems, and 12–19 with more complex structures. A few exercises, especially in section 2, are concerned with terminology, which is important for academic students and a useful aid to an overall understanding of the grammatical system. The majority of the exercises are, however, entirely practical. They are based on modern English, cover a variety of topics and are intended to help learners increase their own mastery of English.

There is a key to the exercises at the back, but it must be pointed out that in some cases there may be other acceptable answers. Grammar is undeniably a matter of rules and frequently of 'right' and 'wrong'; but it can also be a matter of 'right' and 'right' – a choice between two or more grammatical ways of saying something, depending on the exact meaning intended.

SC

London
1992

1 The English language

Prescriptive and disputed grammar

Although there is fairly general agreement about what you can and cannot say in standard English, there are a few 'grey areas' of DISPUTED usage where native speakers disagree. For example, can you or can you not say?

All of you will not understand.

Some people find this totally acceptable; others want to reword it as *Not all of you will understand* if that is what the meaning is, claiming that the original sentence 'really means' *None of you will understand.*

Other problems arise because of PRESCRIPTIVE rules, some of them dating from a time when people thought that English grammar should be like Latin grammar. These rules should not really apply to English at all, but many English people have heard them and (quite mistakenly) think it is wrong to break them. Examples of these doubtful rules:

Don't end a sentence with a preposition.
Say *It's I.* (Don't say *It's me.*)

Partly as a result of prescriptive rules, we often get HYPERCORRECTION – which is people seriously misapplying a rule. Thus someone who has been told to say *It's I* may get the idea that *me* is somehow ungrammatical in any position, so they say **between you and I.*

Another cause of disputed usage is natural change. Language changes all the time. People who notice changes often object to them and consider them wrong. (Perhaps in time *between you and I* will be generally acceptable.)

Exercise 1 Prescriptive rules, disputed usage and hypercorrection

Here are some authentic examples of modern English. Each sentence contains some kind of disputed usage – perhaps something that somebody would object to because it breaks a prescriptive rule, or a hypercorrection, or a newish development. Can you spot the problems?

1 I am impressed by the knowledge he and his friends show of different universities and courses … They are tapped into a network of information. It did not used to be like that.

   ....

2 It would have ended in tragedy, if it hadn't have been for the courage of the victim. (Police officer speaking on television)

   ....

3 The doctor dismissed the symptoms and suggested she take up a relaxing hobby.

   ....

4 Q: What would you have been had you not been born a sportsman?
   A: I may have followed my father into the Services.

   ....

5 I wonder if he were indeed here yesterday.

   ....

6 As for we English, we should resist the temptation to make jokes.

   ....

7 The beautiful stallions were kept to one side of the route and us spectators were kept to the other.

   ....

8 Nearly four times as many girls in Britain suffer from asthma than in the 1970s – but all those who claim to be allergic are not suffering from it.

   ....

9 Poetry needs less words. (Playwright Alan Bennett, speaking on television about poetry and novels)

   ....

10 The carbon dioxide locks in the sun's heat, like glass locks heat into a greenhouse.

   ....

11 Writing my first rugby match report a feeling of unreality hit me.

   ....

12 The world can breathe a little easier after this historic summit.

   ....

13 You use a different sort of English in a *Times* leader than in a conversation in a pub.

   ....

14 If a regular customer were to make arrangements with their own branch, it may be possible to make arrangements for speedy clearance.

   ....

15 A salesman explained that the manuals included with most computers were hopeless. They either were impossible to understand, full of mistakes, or both.

   ....

16 None of the bodies so far recovered were wearing lifejackets.

   ....

17 Sartre had one of the best educations available to a man of his generation.

   ....

18 The idea seemed far too cruel to actually carry out.

   ....

19 No sooner are one set of perils surmounted than another lot, even more intractable, take their place.

   ....

20 The Prince tests some of the inventions, including the prototype of a sports car; plus there is a review of the most successful innovations in ten years of the awards.

   ....

2 A general framework

Exercise 2 Sentences and clauses [*SGE* 2.2–3]

How much do you know about sentence structure? Complete the sentences by matching the predicates (a)–(j) to the subjects (1–10). The first answer is 1c.

1 A sentence   (a) are usually optional.
2 The subject   (b) is the most important copular verb.
3 The verb   (c) contains a subject and a predicate.
4 The predicate   (d) only occur with transitive verbs.
5 The main elements
   of sentence structure   (e) have to occur in every sentence.
6 Not all of these   (f) usually comes before the verb.
7 Objects   (g) follow copular verbs like *be* or *become*.
8 Complements   (h) are subject, verb, object, complement, adverbial.
9 The verb *be*   (i) consists of a verb and possibly other
                                                elements.
10 Adverbials   (j) has to agree with the subject.

Exercise 3 Sentence elements: forms [*SGE* 2.2–4]

Words are often joined together in groups called *phrases*. Verb phrases, noun phrases, adverb phrases and adjective phrases may consist of a single verb, noun /pronoun, adverb or adjective or of several words built around the 'head word'. Here are some examples.

verb phrases   *thinks, was hoping, may have wondered*
noun phrases   *me, someone, someone else, my home, another of*
                    those problems, a place I once visited
adjective phrases   *unusual, quite remarkable, very odd indeed*
adverb phrases   *remarkably, once, rather oddly*

Prepositional phrases are rather different because prepositions do not function on their own. A prepositional phrase must consist of a preposition + another word, usually a noun.

prepositional phrases   *in a moment, under the table, to my surprise*

Read the passage and then choose the odd form out in each set listed below.

I sat down on a stone. I was exhausted. My ankle was aching and leg muscles that I never knew existed were beginning to complain. The sun was casting long shadows and the silence worried me. There was no sign of the path, and no other trail looked at all convincing. I could not see a single house, there were no familiar landmarks, and the Indus was only a glinting trickle far below. I felt tired, miserable and slightly frightened. I sat for ten minutes without moving, unsure of what to do. All options seemed equally unappealing. Then, immediately above me, I heard gunshots. On other occasions the noise might have been sinister. Now they seemed welcoming, almost homely. I clambered upwards, and soon found a track. Following it around a bluff of rock I saw the source of the shots: a village of half-timbered huts clinging to the sheer hillside. (William Dalrymple: *In Xanadu A Quest*)

Example: a stone   my ankle   complain   no sign   gunshots
Answer: <u>complain</u> [the rest are noun phrases]

1 verb phrases	was exhausted was aching	
	were beginning to complain could not see	
	might have been	
2 noun phrases	leg muscles that I never knew existed	
	casting long shadows me no sign of the path	
	the source of the shots	
3 adjective phrases	tired, miserable and slightly frightened	
	unsure of what to do equally unappealing	
	almost homely following it	
4 adverb phrases	never far below immediately above	
	now upwards	
5 prepositional phrases	on a stone for ten minutes without moving	
	on other occasions almost homely	

Exercise 4   Sentence elements: functions [*SGE* 2.3–4]

When we talk of phrases we are talking of FORMAL categories – the way phrases are formed. When we talk of sentence elements (subjects, verbs, objects, complements and adverbials) we are thinking of the way different kinds of formal phrases FUNCTION, how the same kind of phrase can express different elements.

The verb element in a sentence must be a verb phrase, but this does not apply to other forms and functions. For example (in the passage in Exercise 3):

Noun phrases can be:
subject	*The silence* ...
object	... (worried) *me*.
object of preposition	... (on) *a stone*.
also complement	(The writer is) *a traveller*.

Adjective phrases can be:
complement	(seemed) *equally unappealing*

Prepositional phrases can be:
part of a noun phrase	(no sign) *of the path*
an adverbial	(sat down) *on a stone*

Look at the passage again (Exercise 3) and decide what function each of the following phrases has.

NPs	1	my ankle	SUBJECT
	2	leg muscles that I never knew existed	....
	3	long shadows	....
	4	a glinting trickle	....
	5	the sheer hillside	....
AdjPs	6	at all convincing	....
	7	tired, miserable and slightly frightened	....
	8	welcoming, almost homely	....
PPs	9	of the path	....
	10	for ten minutes	....
	11	without moving	....
	12	on other occasions	....

Exercise 5 Words and word classes [*SGE* 2.6–11]

How much do you know about word classes (parts of speech)?

Choose the best options. The first answer is 1a.

1 We divide words into (a) two (b) three (c) four broad categories, depending on whether these classes are relatively fixed or constantly changing.

2 Closed word classes (a) have important grammatical functions (b) often get new words added (c) consist largely of 'lexical' words.

3 The closed classes include (a) full verbs and modal verbs (b) primary and full verbs (c) primary and modal verbs.

4 The open classes (a) are constantly gaining new words (b) include mainly 'grammatical' words (c) include all verbs.

5 The terms 'generic' and 'specific' are applied to the meaning of (a) adverbial phrases (b) noun phrases (c) prepositional phrases.

6 The terms 'marked' and 'unmarked' relate to (a) inflection only (b) meaning only (c) both inflection and meaning.

7 Stative verbs (a) are mainly used in the passive (eg: *to be born*) (b) are rarely used in progressive tenses (eg: *belong, know, own*) (c) show a lack of motion (eg: *lie, rest, sit*).

8 A pro-form is (a) a special kind of pronoun (b) any word or phrase that refers to another expression without repeating it (c) a cover term for both pronouns and determiners.

9 Operator means (a) a finite verb phrase (eg: *could have forgotten*) (b) the auxiliaries in a verb phrase (....*could have* forgotten) (c) the first or only auxiliary (....*could* have forgotten).

10 Non-assertive applies to certain words that are restricted in use to (a) negative questions (b) negative statements and questions (c) negative statements.

Exercise 6 Word classes: definitions [*SGE* 2.6–11]

Complete the sentences with these words:

    adjectives adverbs conjunctions determiners nouns prepositions
    pronouns verbs

1 *Dynamic, finite, full, transitive* all describe ....VERBS...........

2 *Collective, count, genitive, proper* are used in describing ....

3 *Attributive, predicative, comparative, superlative* relate to ....

4 *Demonstrative, interrogative, personal, relative* describe different kinds of
....

5 .... often tell us how, when, where or why something happened.

6 Many .... have meanings connected with place or time. They connect
two units of a sentence together and show a relationship.

7 The articles *a/an* and *the* are special kinds of ....

8 .... join words, phrases and clauses together. Some are coordinating
and some are subordinating.

Exercise 7 More about word classes [*SGE* 2.6–11]

Choose the odd word out in each set – the word that does not belong to that
particular word class.

Example: built, door, garden, room, window
Answer: built [The other words are nouns.]

1 could	may	should	will	want
2 are	can	did	has	was
3 me	every	ours	someone	they
4 after	at	during	into	upwards
5 and	because	or	too	when
6 college	class	grammar	learn	teacher
7 angry	hungry	lonely	obviously	silly
8 cause	insist	must	persuade	suggest
9 an	how	my	no	whose
10 afterwards	badly	friendly	now	soon

3 Verbs and auxiliaries

There are three major types of verbs:
1 FULL (or lexical verbs) – eg: *believe, like, say, want* ...
   Almost all verbs are in this category, except for
2 PRIMARY verbs – *be, do* and *have*
3 MODAL auxiliaries – *can, could, may, might, must, shall, should, will, would*

Exercise 8 Full verbs: functions of the base form [*SGE* 3.2–3]

The BASE form of the verb is the uninflected form of a full or primary verb, the form that comes first in a dictionary (eg: *believe, like, be, do*. But NOT *believes, liked, being, done*).

The base is used in five different ways:

I often *come* here. [finite present tense (pres)]
Come at once! [imperative- (imp)]
They demanded that I *come* to their office. [subjunctive (subj)]
They wanted me to *come*. [infinitive with *to* (to-infin)]
I can *come* tomorrow. [infinitive without *to* (bare infin)]

Find the base forms in the following, and decide which way each one is being used.

Example: When you have nothing to say, say nothing. Who said that?
Answer: have (pres) *to say* (to infin) *say* (imp). [But not *said*, because *said* is not a base form]

1 Listen carefully.
2 If you won't listen, I'm going.
3 My parents always insisted that I listen to what they said.
4 But why am I supposed to listen?
5 Actually I always listen anyway.
6 If you can't stand the heat, get out of the kitchen. [Harry S Truman, 1884–1972, US president]
7 Who was he telling to get out of the kitchen, and why?
8 It has nothing to do with kitchens. He was suggesting to people who could not work under pressure that they get out and find other work.
9 Oh I get it!
10 I don't know whether anyone actually did get out as a result.

Exercise 9 -*ed* form: regular and irregular [*SGE* 3.3–10]

In regular verbs, the past tense and the past participle both end in -*ed*:

I *looked* [past], I have *looked* [past participle]

So the label '-*ed* form' is often used for both these parts of the verb, even with irregular verbs: He *saw*, He has *seen*.

Complete the following passage using -*ed* forms of these regular and irregular verbs:

descend   disappear   drop   give   lead   perch   populate   rise   round
say   set   stand   wrap

Example: 'That's right,' SAID the doctor. 'Look after your mother.'

My mother (1) .... me directions how to reach the dispensary, and I (2) .... off with a bottle (3) .... in brown paper under my arm. The road (4) .... uphill, through a thickly (5) .... poor locality, as far as the barracks, which was (6) .... on the very top of the hill, over the city, and then (7) ...., between high walls, till it suddenly almost (8) .... in a stony path, ... that (9) .... steeply, steeply, to the valley of the little river, ... and the opposite hillside ... (10) .... to the gently (11) .... top, on which (12) .... the purple sandstone tower of the cathedral.

Exercise 10 -*ed* form: functions [*SGE* 3.3]

The finite 'past' -*ed* form is used for:

Simple past tense: I *looked*. We *saw*.

The nonfinite -*ed* participle is used for:

Perfect: I have *looked*. They had *seen* it.
Passive: You were *seen*.
Participle clause: *Seen* from a distance, it is lovely.

Decide what function the -*ed* forms had in exercise 9, and mark them past tense (past), or nonfinite participle:

1 gave [past]   2 ....   3 ....   4 ....
5 ....   6 ....   7 ....   8 ....
9 ....   10 ....   11 ....   12 ....

Exercise 11 -*s* form: pronunciation and spelling [*SGE* 3.4–10]

The 3rd person singular of the simple present tense (the -*s* form) is pronounced in three different ways, according to the sound that it follows:

waits /s/   *weighs* /z/   *wishes* /ɪz/

Complete the following with the -*s* form of the verbs indicated. Then arrange the verbs into three lists according to the way the endings are pronounced.

Example:

1 Bad money DRIVES out good. (drive)
  /z/ – in the *weighs* list.
2 Absence .... the heart grow fonder. (make)
3 It's the early bird that .... the worm. (catch)
4 Travel .... the mind. (broaden)
5 Charity .... at home. (begin)
6 Tomorrow never .... (come)
7 He who .... is lost. (hesitate)
8 It .... belief, but it's true. (pass)
9 It .... to advertise. (pay)
10 This powder .... whiter than white. (wash)
11 History .... itself. (repeat)
12 An apple a day .... the doctor away. (keep)
13 Power .... to corrupt, (tend)
14 and absolute power .... absolutely. (corrupt)

Exercise 12 Past form: regular and irregular [*SGE* 3.5–10]

Complete the following with past tenses of the verbs given.

My mother (1 watch) ...WATCHED.. me from the kitchen doorway and I could imagine her keen eyes piercing the cloth of my blazer to where the watch (2 rest) .... guiltily in my pocket.

'Are you going on your bike, then, Will?'

I (3 say) ...., 'Yes, Mother,' and, feeling uncomfortable under that direct gaze, (4 begin) .... to wheel the bike across the yard.

'I (5 think) .... you (6 say) .... it (7 need) .... mending or something before you (8 ride) .... it again?'

'It's only a little thing,' I (9 tell) .... her. 'It'll be all right.'

I (10 wave) .... goodbye and (11 pedal) .... out into the street while she (12 watch) .... me, a little doubtfully, I (13 think) .... Once out of sight of the house I (14 put) .... all my strength on the pedals and (15 ride) .... like the wind. My grandfather's house (16 be) .... in one of the older parts of the town and my way (17 lead) .... through a maze of cobbled streets between long rows of houses. I (18 keep) .... up my speed, excitement coursing through me as I (19 think) .... of the watch and (20 revel) .... in my hatred of Crawley. Then from an entry between two terraces of houses a mongrel puppy (21 dart) .... into the street. I (22 pull) .... at my back brake. The cable (23 snap) .... with a click – that was what I had (24 intend) .... to fix. I (25 jam) .... on the front brake with the puppy cowering foolishly in my path. The bike (26 jar) .... to a standstill, the back end swinging as though (27 catapult) .... over the pivot of the stationary front wheel and I (28 go) .... over the handlebars.

Exercise 13 -*ed* form: pronunciation [*SGE* 3.5]

> The regular -*ed* form is pronounced in three different ways according to the sound it follows:
>
> *wished* /t/   *weighed* /d/   *waited* /ɪd/

Go through all the regular -*ed* forms in Exercise 12 and put them in three lists according to their pronunciation:

Example: (1) watched – like *wished*/t/

Exercise 14 Spelling rules and exceptions [*SGE* 3.6–8]

Complete the following, using -*ed* or -*ing* forms of these verbs:

develop   dye   lie   mislay   occur   offer   panic   repay   sue   whinge

It never (1) OCCURRED to me that he was (2) ...., or I wouldn't have (3) .... to lend him the money in the first place. He says he (4) .... my letter, and that's why he hasn't yet (5) .... me. He really started (6) .... when I said I'd take him to court. But I am seriously thinking of (7) .... him, because I'm fed up with his (8) .... on about how unkind I am and how unfair life is. He's a (9) .... in-the-wool scrounger if you ask me, with an over- (10) .... sense of grievance.

Exercise 15 Irregular past participles [*SGE* 3.10]

Newspaper headlines often use present tenses to report the latest news – it sounds more immediate. Imagine these headlines are in today's paper, and tell someone what has been happening. Use present perfect tenses, making any minor grammatical changes that may be necessary.

Example: Art thieves steal Gainsborough.
Answer: Art thieves have stolen a (painting by) Gainsborough.

1 Rioting spreads to city centre.

....

2 Dream comes true for octogenarian.

....

3 Boy sleeps through pit ordeal.

....

4 Tottenham lose out in a different ball game.

....

5 Thousands strike in dock unrest.

....

6 Postal charges rise again.

....

7 Madman shoots 5.

....

8 MP fights off death threat from mugger.

....

9 P&O profits fall 22 per cent at half-year.

....

10 Ferry sinks in harbour.

....

11 Refugees flee renewed fighting.

....

12 Last of the refugees fly home.

....

13 West Country bears brunt of gales.

....

14 Gun victim undergoes emergency surgery.

....

15 New pressure group swings into action.

....

16 Coup leader broadcasts to nation.

....

17 Tenor hits back at critics.

....

Exercise 16 Primary and auxiliary verbs: contractions [*SGE* 3.11–18]

Write the abbreviated words in full.

Example: Darling, they're playing our tune.
Answer: Darling, they are playing our tune.

1 There's no fool like an old fool.   ....
2 I'm only here for the beer.   ....
3 Don't call us, ...
4 we'll call you.   ....
5 It's turned out nice again.   ....
6 I'd no idea you cared.   ....
7 Who'd have thought it?   ....
8 I've arrived, and to prove it I'm here. ....

Exercise 17 Auxiliaries [*SGE* 3.11–18]

Here are twelve remarks. Show your surprise by asking a short question (using *be*, *have*, *do* or a modal auxiliary) and then add a short statement, pointing out that you differ from the speaker.

Example: I watch a lot of TV. .... DO YOU? I DON'T.

1 I don't watch the news very often, though. ....
2 I can't understand that weatherman's accent. ....
3 I missed the first programme in that new nature series. ....
4 I'd forgotten it was on. ....

5 I've been watching the tennis. ....

6 My brother's got tickets for the finals. ....

7 But he's not interested in who wins. ....

8 I'm going to watch the finals on the box. ....

9 We don't have the telly on at breakfast time. ....

10 We'll probably give up television if the licence fee goes up again. ....

11 I'd miss it terribly, of course. ....

12 We haven't got a hi-fi. ....

Exercise 18 *do*: auxiliary or main verb? [*SGE* 3.15]

> *Do* can be an auxiliary as in *Do you swim?* and a main verb as in *What can we do? What are you doing?*

Use *do* (as auxiliary or as main verb) to add negative comments or to ask questions – as indicated.

1 I enjoy my work.
   But what exactly (you). DO YOU DO? [Here the first *do* is an auxiliary and the second is a main verb.]

2 I do research.
   Oh, (you) ....?

3 I think hard work is good for you.
   Well, I suppose it .... any harm.

4 But my parents disapprove of my work.
   Oh surely, they ....

5 My brother stays in bed half the day.
   .... really?

6 He has a rather peculiar job, if you can call it a job.
   Why? What ....?

7 Well, at one time he worked in computers.
   Oh, ...?

8 But he decided to give that up.
   So what .... after that?

9 Various things. But now he plays his guitar in the streets.
   I don't believe it. He ....!

10 Awful, isn't it ?
    Well I've got friends who .... anything at all.

11 Why don't they ?
    Lazy, I suppose. They .... anything when they were at school either.

12 Maybe one day I'll join my brother – we could form a band.
    Oh, no .... You wouldn't like it.

Exercise 19 Infinitives [*SGE* 3.12. 3.17–18]

Complete the following with a suitable infinitive. Remember some verbs need a
to-infinitive and some need a bare infinitive.

1 I would...GIVE UP.......my job if I had the chance.
2 I would like ...TO TRAVEL....when I'm older.
3 I would rather .... than 4 ....
5 I may ....…....,although I ought 6 ....
7 I had better ....…........
8 I daren't ....…..........
9 I needn't ....…........ if I don't want to.
10 I don't think I'm likely ....…....
11 What am I ....…....... if they ask me ?
12 I was about ....…........ when the phone rang.

Exercise 20 *used to* [*SGE* 3.17]

> The marginal modal *used to*, referring to a past habit, can only be followed
> by an infinitive
>
> > We *used to live* in London, but we don't now.
>
> Do not confuse this with *be/get used to* (meaning *be/get accustomed to*),
> which is followed by an *-ing* form or a noun phrase:
>
> > Some people never *get used to living* in a big city. They can't *get used to
> > the crowds*. They *aren't used to them.*
>
> There is also a regular verb *use* which always needs an object:
>
> > *Use* a knife. *Use* this.

Complete the sentences 1–10 in a grammatical and sensible way by using the
endings a–j. There may be several possible answers.

1 At one time many British workers used to ....(h) BE PAID IN CASH.
2 Now most of them have got used to ....
3 This means most of the population are used to ....
4 In recent years most of us have got used to ....
5 These are a newish invention.There used to ....
6 Perhaps one day our children will have become so used to ....
7 that they will ask in amazement, 'Didn't you use to ....?
8 And did you also use to ....?'
9 I shall reply – not quite truthfully – 'We never used to ....'
10 Like everyone else I was used to ....
    A real old-fashioned cashless society!

(a) living in a cashless society
(b) having their money paid into their banks

(c) using credit cards
(d) bartering goods for other goods
(e) paying for things by cheque
(f) pay for things by cheque
(g) carry money around – coins and things
(h) be paid in cash at the end of the week
(i) be no such thing
(j) use money

Exercise 21 Verb phrases [*SGE* 3.19–22]

> A verb phrase may consist of a single word (*write*) or several verb forms
> *(had been writing)*. A verb phrase may be finite, and refer to time (*writes*,
> *wrote*) or nonfinite
> > He doesn't have time to *write*.
> > *Writing* isn't easy.

Identify the finite verb phrases in the following. Take each phrase as whole – do
not classify each word separately. Then find at least five nonfinite verb phrases.

Example: might seem (finite); *to plan* (nonfinite)

It might seem odd in the twentieth century to plan and carry out expeditions as a
means of making a living, yet I'd been doing just that for the past two years. I hadn't
consciously chosen such a life; it had just worked out that way.

In 1943, four months before I was born, my father died of wounds received not
far north of Monte Cassino whilst commanding a tank regiment, the Royal Scots
Greys. When I was sixteen, I decided to make the army my career too. I'd inherited
my father's title but not his brains, so the Royal Military Academy at Sandhurst
was out. However I managed to scrape through ... Cadet School and into the Greys
on a three-year short service commission, which I spent ploughing about Germany
in tanks, canoeing along European rivers ... and skiing in Bavaria. All this gave
me a taste for travel. (Ranulph Fiennes: *To the Ends of the Earth*)

Exercise 22 Subjunctive [*SGE* 3.23–24]

> The so-called mandative subjunctive is used in *that*-clauses after expressions
> (which may be verbs, nouns or adjectives) of ordering, recommending,
> intending. This subjunctive takes the base form of the verb – with no -*s* form,
> and no changes for past tense:
>
> > They suggested ⎫
> > The suggestion was ⎬ that he leave immediately.
> > It was essential ⎭
>
> Notice the negative subjunctive:
> > They ordered that he not leave.
>
> A common alternative is a verb phrase with *should*.

Rewrite the following, using the subjunctive where appropriate. Make any other changes necessary:

Example: The governor directed that all prisoners be closely supervised ...

The governor directed that all prisoners should be closely supervised at all times. He ordered that all prison officers should strictly observe the regulations. He insisted that they should not let any visitors smuggle in weapons or drugs. It was vital, he said, that all visitors should be searched.

The prison officers stated that this has always been done. But the fact is that three prisoners escaped on Saturday.

The new regulations state that it is essential that all sections of the prison should be searched more frequently and more thoroughly. They also recommended that extra staff are recruited so that no matter how skilful the prisoners are, they will not be able to escape. As if it was only a simple question of staffing!

Exercise 23 Passive voice [*SGE* 3.25–26]

> Most transitive verbs can be active and passive. The passive voice is used for various reasons. When it is used without mentioning the agent (the subject of the active verb) this may be because the agent is unknown or unimportant, or because the agent wants to avoid responsibility; or it may be to emphasize the action of the verb by having that near the end of the sentence.
>
> When the agent is mentioned with a *by*-phrase after the verb this puts the agent in the important position at the end.

Complete the following with suitable passives of the following verbs:

> advertise   affect   allow   build   give   hear   hold   inform(2)
>
> inspect   keep   notify   obtain   place   send   tell

In certain circumstances a public inquiry may (1) BE HELD into proposals put forward by the Department of the Environment or a local highway authority before a new road (2) .... When the Secretary of State for the Environment originates road proposals they (3 publicly) .... and there is opportunity to raise objections, which may lead to such an inquiry. The Inspector in charge of the inquiry will hear views of objectors and others so that Ministers may (4) .... by the Inspector of all material facts. The Inspector (5) .... all the relevant correspondence from objectors to the proposals and from other interested parties, so that he will (6 fully) .... when conducting the inquiry.

A copy of the rules governing such inquiries can (7) .... from Her Majesty's Stationery Office. The rules entitle people who (8 directly) .... by the proposals to take part.

A public announcement (9) .... in local newspapers not later than 14 days before the inquiry. People who have objected to the road proposals (10) .... individually, at least six weeks before the date of the inquiry. They will either (11) .... the Department's Statement of Reasons, or (12) .... where such a statement can (13) ....

The proceedings (14) .... as informal as possible, but the Inspector must keep order. Each person will (15) .... to put his case in his own way. After all the interested parties (16) ...., the Department's representative makes his closing remarks.

Exercise 24 Agents [*SGE* 3.25–26]

Here are some of the 'agents' who play a part in public inquiries about roads:

(a) people living near the proposed new road
(b) the Department of the Environment or local highway authorities
(c) lawyers
(d) the Secretary of State for the Environment himself
(e) an Inspector appointed by the Department of the Environment

Write out full answers to the following questions, using a passive tense and an agent.

1 Who builds new roads in Britain ?
   They ARE BUILT BY (b) THE DEPARTMENT OF THE ENVIRONMENT OR LOCAL HIGHWAY AUTHORITIES.
2 What sort of people raise objections?
   Objections ....
3 Who conducts the day to day business of an Inquiry?
   It ....
4 Does anyone represent the objectors?
   They can ....
5 Who makes the final decision?
   The final decision ....

Exercise 25 Active or passive? [*SGE* 3.25–26]

Complete the following in a suitable active or passive tense using the verbs given:

A soldier (1 shoot) WAS SHOT and critically wounded as he (2 sit) .... in his car outside an army careers office in north London yesterday. Two men who (3 believe) .... to be members of a terrorist organization, (4 approach) .... his car on a motorcycle just after 1 pm. The pillion passenger (5 run) .... towards the car, which (6 park) .... outside the office. He (7 shoot)........................ the soldier three times, then (8 run) .... back to the motorcycle and (9 flee) .... in the rush-hour traffic. The victim, a 28-year-old married man, (10 hit) .... in the chest. He (11 say) .... to be in a critical but stable condition in hospital.

Anti-terrorist detectives later (12 cordon) .... off the area. 'This attack (13 plan well) .... and it is likely that the office (14 target) .... for some time.'

A motorcycle later (15 find) .... abandoned about ten miles away, but it (16 not know) .... yet whether this was the getaway machine.

4 The semantics of the verb phrase

Time and tense [*SGE* 4.1–6]

Although verb tenses often refer to time – real time in the world – time and tense are not the same. Tense is a grammatical category, with various kinds of grammatical meaning. So present and past tenses do not always refer to present and past time.

Exercise 26 Present simple tense: what time? [*SGE* 4.3–4]

The simple present tense can refer to present, past and future time:

I *prefer* a quiet life. ⎫ [Present state –S]
They *live* in Scotland. ⎭

I usually *travel* by train. ⎫ [Habit – H]
He never *takes* a holiday. ⎭

I *regret* to say … [Instantaneous – I]

I *hear* you have got engaged. [Past – 'I heard recently' – P]

When *do you begin* your new job? ⎫ [Future – F]
Come and see us next time you *are* in town. ⎭

Decide which kind of time the present tenses in the following refer to, and mark them S(tate), H(abit), I(nstantaneous), P(ast) or F(uture).

Example: I like work. (S).

Dear Sir,

I (1) am told that you (2) organize summer 'environment' camps for people to help with conservation work, and I (3) write to ask for further details.

I normally (4) work in my vacation and I particularly (5) like the idea of working in the countryside.

Could you please let me know:
– where these camps usually (6) take place,
– when this year's camps (7) start,
– whether the current programme (8) continues to the end of the year,
    and also – I (9) apologize for asking , but I am a student –
– whether volunteers (10) receive any pocket money?

I (11) enclose a stamped addressed envelope for your reply, and (12) look forward to hearing from you. I (13) hope very much that you still (14) have vacancies for this year, and I will of course let you know as soon as possible whatever I (15) decide.

Yours faithfully,

…………………

Exercise 27 Past simple: when exactly? [*SGE* 4.1–6]

Look at all the instances of the past simple tense here and decide whether they refer to:

An event (E):	The Normans *invaded* England in 1066.
A habit (HAB):	They *built* some splendid cathedrals and castles.
A state (S):	They *enjoyed* fighting.

or whether the past tense is used for:

An attitude (A):	I *thought* that …
Indirect speech/thought (I):	…everyone *knew* about the Normans.
Hypothesis(HYP)	If William *visited* Hastings today, …

Example: (1) wondered (A) …

I (1) *wondered* ......whether you (2) *knew*...... that 1066 is the most famous date in English history?

In January 1066 the old king (Edward the Confessor) (3) *died*...... and Harold, the Earl of Wessex, (4) *proclaimed*...... himself king. But across the Channel Duke William of Normandy (5) *wanted*...... the English throne, and immediately (6) *started*...... assembling his army and fleet.

Throughout the summer Harold (7) *looked* ...... across to France, but no Normans (8) *came*...... Ships in those days (9) *needed*...... windpower, and contrary winds and storms (10) *delayed*...... William even when he (11) *was*...... ready.

And then in September, another claimant to the throne, Harald of Norway, (12) *landed*...... in northern England and (13) *captured*...... York. Medieval kings of course (14) *led*...... their own armies, so English Harold (15) *took*...... his army north.

Perhaps you wish that twentieth century armies (16) *used*...... such simple weapons as bows and arrows – which is what armies in those days (17) *fought*...... with – but they (18) *could*......inflict fatal injuries. An arrow (19) *killed*...... the Norwegian king …

Two days later William of Normandy finally (20) *landed*...... in southern England, a few miles west of Hastings on the south coast of England. Harold (21) *marched*...... his tired army south (armies (22) *walked*...... everywhere in those days). The two armies (23) *met*...... on 14 October. Harold and two of his brothers (24) *died*...... fighting. William was the Conqueror!

The battle that (25) *changed*...... the course of English history is known as the Battle of Hastings, but if you (26) *went*...... to Hastings today you would find a busy seaside town. To visit the actual battlefield you must go to the village that is simply known as Battle.

Aspect [*SGE* 4.7–12]

Aspect is a grammatical label that covers *progressive* and *perfect*. Progressive and perfect tenses look at time in a special way.

Progressive (or continuous) stresses activity, action in progress, and therefore may imply that the action is incomplete or not going to continue for long.

Perfect is concerned with action(s) or a state in a period before now (or, with past perfect, before 'then') and continuing to the present time (or until 'then').

Exercise 28 Present simple and progressive [*SGE* 4.7-11]

Complete the following using:

> Present simple tense [*I ask, he asks* ...]
>
> *or* Present progressive [*I am asking, they are asking* ...]

Indicate any places where both tenses are possible.

The increasing use of pesticides and other chemicals by farmers in recent years, (1 currently/cause) IS CURRENTLY CAUSING birds of prey to leave the countryside for urban areas.

Birds of prey (2 feed) .... on small mammals, so in the countryside they (3 pick up) .... pesticides through eating poisoned prey. In towns they (4 eat) .... the occasional 'garden bird', but the main reason they (5 thrive) .... in our streets is simply less pollution. Their presence (6 emphasize) .... the trend of wild life to move from the harassment of rural areas into cities and towns – a trend which (7 be shown) ....also by the increasing number of foxes in London.

It (8 appear) ....that there are now considerable numbers of sparrowhawks in the well wooded areas of London. But as a rule these birds (9 not attack) ....the more familiar birds which (10 nest) .... close to them.

At the same time tawny owls, which normally (11 nest) .... in trees in the countryside (12 adapt) ....to crevices in tall buildings.

The London Wildlife Trust (13 say) .... 'Birds of prey have increased in such numbers that we (14 now ask) .... for volunteer observers to help us get some idea of the size of this new population.'

Exercise 29 Present simple and progressive [*SGE* 4.3–6, also 4.10–11]

Complete the following using the present simple or present progressive. Remember that both tenses may refer to the future.

John: Can you come and help? What (1 you/do) ...ARE YOU DOING ....?

Joan: I (2 watch)........................ TV. It's Monica James. She (3 give) .... a cookery demonstration. She (4 make) .... meringues.

John: But you (5 know) .... how to do them. You (6 make) .... marvellous meringues.

Joan: Yes, but these are chocolate meringues, and you (7 know) .... the Bookers (8 come) .... next Sunday, and I'd like to do something different for them. Besides I always (9 enjoy) .... watching her. I (10 promise) .... I'll come and help the moment the programme (11 end) .... It (12 finish) .... at 3.30 actually. Please! You (13 interrupt) .... I (14 miss) .... her.

Monica James: And now we (15 whisk) .... the egg whites until they (16 stand) .... up in peaks. And a useful tip to remember here – slightly stale egg whites (17 make) .... better meringues than absolutely fresh ones. Well, that (18 look) .... right. Now for the sugar and grated chocolate. See, I carefully (19 fold) .... this into the whites with a fork. I never (20 whisk) .... it in.

Exercise 30 Present perfect [*SGE* 4.7–12]

Complete the following using either:

> Present perfect simple She *has thought* about it.
> Present perfect progressive We *have been thinking*.

David: Whatever (1 you/do) HAVE YOU BEEN DOING? You don't look too good. Is anything the matter?

Charles: Oh, I'm all right. But I (2 overwork) .... lately and I (3 not/sleep) .... properly. And I'm afraid I (4 overeat) .... too. I (5 put on) .... nearly 12 pounds.

David: You need a holiday. (6 you/book) .... anything yet? Tom (7 just/return) .... from Greece – says it's marvellous. He (8 go) .... there for years.

Charles: Well I (9 sometimes/think) .... of going to Greece again.

David: Oh you (10 be) .... there before, have you?

Charles: Yes, I (11 spend) .... some very good holidays there, but actually I (12 always/want) .... to go to the Far East. In fact, I (13 teach) .... myself Thai for the last couple of years.

David: But I (14 hear) .... you say several times you like cheap holidays in Europe.

Charles: Well I (15 save up) ...., though I (16 not save) .... enough yet really. But anyway, I (17 not have) .... a proper holiday for three years.

David: You (18 be) .... too busy, I suppose.

Charles: Well, yes, and I (19 just move) .... to a new flat. But anyway, I think I really shall go to Bangkok in October.

David: Ah. So you (20 make) .... your mind up at last!

Exercise 31 Present and present perfect tenses [*SGE* 4.1–12]

Complete the following, using a suitable present tense – present or present perfect, (both either simple or progressive) – *I learn, I am learning, I have learnt/learned, I have been learning*.

Maria (1 learn) HAS BEEN LEARNING English for several years now, but (2 only recently/start) .... to work hard at it. Now she (3 make) .... good progress, and (4 enjoy) .... it.

Ever since she started she (5 always find) .... reading English the easiest. She (6 like) .... novels best, and now (7 belong) .... to an English library, and (8 borrow) .... a new book every week. She (9 not look up) ....all the words she (10 not know) ...., but (11 try) .... to guess the meaning and she (12 say) .... she (13 get) .... much better now at doing this.

Perhaps not surprisingly for such an avid reader, she (14 like) .... spelling. 'It (15 offer) .... you a challenge', she (16 declare) .... She also (17 write) .... English quite well – unlike many students who (18 find) .... that is the hardest part and (19 forever make)............................ the same mistakes.

She (20 find) .... an English penfriend this year and she (21 already/ write) .... and (22 receive) .... two letters. 'This is the first time I (23 ever/do) .... this, though it is something I (24 always/want) .... to do,' she (25 say) .... As she (26 just/be invited) .... to visit England next year, she (27 feel) .... she (28 need) ....more conversation practice. So next week she (29 attend) .... her first 'conversation workshop'. That (30 mean) .... practical conversation work, she (31 say) ...., 'and I (32 look forward) .... to it'.

Exercise 32 Past simple or present perfect? [*SGE* 4.5–8]

Complete the following with either:

> past simple   *wrote, was, became …*
> present perfect *has/have written, has/have been, has/have become …*

Agatha Miller (1 be born) WAS BORN on 15 September 1890 in Torquay in south-west England. Better known as Mrs Agatha Christie, she (2 write) .... altogether 78 mystery novels and 19 plays.

Very few other crime writers (3 write) .... more books than this, and few (4 become) .... so immensely popular.

Ever since she (5 publish) .... her first novel, *The Mysterious Affair at Styles* in 1920, her books (6 never be) .... out of print. They (7 be translated) .... all over the world, and, perhaps surprisingly, her sales (8 actually increase) .... since she (9 die) .... in 1976. For a short time after her death they (10 fall) ...., so it was perhaps the screen that (11 revive) .... her popularity.

Two immensely successful films (12 be made) .... a few years ago, *Death on the Nile* and *Murder on the Orient Express*, and these (13 more recently be followed)............................ by television series, which (14 bring) .... two of her most successful detectives, the Belgian Hercule Poirot and the elderly English lady Miss Marple, to millions of viewers.

In 1990, the centenary of her birth, her birthplace Torquay (15 honour)

.... her memory with a special 'mystery festival' – good publicity for the town of course. In 1992 a London theatre (16 be) .... able to boast: *The Mousetrap*, now in its 40th year, (17 break) .... all records.'

There is now even a rose that (18 be named) .... after her.

People (19 enjoy) .... Agatha Christie's story-telling for years, and her popularity currently seems higher than it (20 ever be) .... It is not of course the first time that an author (21 become) .... more popular in death than in life.

Exercise 33 Past simple or past progressive? [*SGE* 4.5–12]

A past progressive tense often refers to an activity in a period that includes the time of a past simple event, as in examples (i) and (ii) below.

Two past simple tenses usually show straightforward time sequence – first one event, and then the other (iii).

Write out the details below in complete sentences, using either:

     past simple   *met, fell ...*
     or past progressive   *was/were meeting, was/were falling*

and adding *when* or *while* as suitable.

Examples:

(i)   President Kennedy *be assassinated*/he *drive* through Dallas.
     President Kennedy was assassinated while he was driving through Dallas.

(ii)   Everyone alive at the time remembers what they *do*/President Kennedy *be killed*.
     Everyone ... remembers what they were doing when President Kennedy was killed.

(iii) Kennedy *be assassinated*/Lyndon Johnson *be* sworn in as president.
     When Kennedy was assassinated, Lyndon Johnson was sworn in as president.

1 Julius Caesar *pursue* a political rival into Egypt/he first *meet* Cleopatra.
2 Julius Caesar *meet* Cleopatra/he *fall* in love with her.
3 Philip II of Macedon *be assassinated* in 336 BC/he *plan* an invasion of Persia.
4 Marco Polo (1254-1324) *begin* to write an account of his travels in China/he '*do time*' in a Genoese prison.
5 Christopher Columbus *look for Asia*/he '*discover*' America in 1492.
6 He *return* to Spain/he *receive* a hero's welcome.
7 Captain James Cook *make* his third great Pacific voyage/he *be killed* in Hawaii in 1779.
8 Cook *die*/his crew *take* his ship back to Britain.
9 The French revolutionary Marat *sit* in his bath/Charlotte Corday *rush* in and *kill* him.
10 She *assassinate* him/ she *be arrested* immediately.
11 Dr Livingstone *travel* near Lake Tanganyika (now Tanzania)/the journalist

Henry Morton Stanley *find* him in 1871.
12 Stanley *find* him/he *say*, 'Dr Livingstone, I presume.'

Exercise 34 Past simple or past perfect [*SGE* 4.5–9]

> The main use of the past perfect is for an earlier past:
> By the end of the nineteenth century Antarctic explorers *had mapped* out the coast of this forbidding continent and *[had] trekked* inland as far south as 78.50S. But it was not until 1911 that the South Pole itself was reached.

Study these notes about the final race for the Pole between Robert Falcon Scott (of Britain) and the Norwegian explorer Roald Amundsen. Then write out the story using the past simple or the past perfect.

Example: Scott already *lead* an earlier expedition to the Antarctic in 1901–4, when he *set out* on his fateful last journey.

Answer: Scott had already led an earlier expedition … when he set out …

12 October 1910 – Scott's ship reached Melbourne (Australia), where Scott received a cable from Madeira: 'Beg leave to inform you proceeding Antarctica. Amundsen.'
4 Jan 1911 – Scott reached Cape Evans on Ross Island.
11 Jan – Amundsen reached Bay of Whales, 60 miles nearer the Pole than Scott's base. Both parties laid depots as far south as they could and then waited for the Antarctic spring.
19 Oct – Amundsen's party left the Bay of Whales.
1 Nov – Scott's party set out.
14 Dec – Scott reached 2,000 feet above the sea. Amundsen reached the Pole, and raised the Norwegian flag.
21 Dec – Scott established his camp 43 at 7,100 feet. Sent back one of his support parties.
1 Jan 1912 – Scott established a depot only 178 miles from Pole. Sent back last support party. Scott now with four companions (Wilson, Oates, Evans and Bowers).
18 Jan – Scott's party reached the Pole and found the Norwegian flag. Began 800 mile return march to their base on Ross Island.
17 Feb – Evans died.
2 March – Reached Middle Barrier Depot, where hardly enough fuel oil left – because of leakage – to take them to One Ton Depot, 70 miles north. (They never reached it.)
17 March – Oates walked out of the tent to his death, hoping the others might survive without him.
21 March – Scott made final camp, only 11 miles south of One Ton Depot.

Frostbite and heavy gales prevented them from going to the depot for fuel.

29 March – Scott wrote in his journal: 'The end cannot be far.'

12 Nov – Search party found the bodies of Scott, Wilson and Bowers.

1   Scott *reach* Melbourne when he *receive* news that Amundsen was also heading for the Pole.

2   When Scott *set up* his first base on 4 January 1911 Amundsen *not yet reach* the Bay of Whales.

3   Scott's party *set out* on 1 November. Amundsen's party already *leave*.

4   Scott's party only *get* 2,000 feet above sea level when the Norwegians *reach* the Pole.

5   Scott *not know* that Amundsen *beat* him to it.

6   On 1 January 1912 Scott *begin* his final attack and *send* back his last support party. The other support party *be sent* back ten days earlier.

7   Scott *reach* the Pole on 18 January 1912 only to discover Amundsen *raise* the Norwegian flag there a month before.

8   They *cover* 800 miles, but they *face* the 800-mile return journey.

9   On reaching Middle Barrier Depot on 2 March they *find* that vital fuel oil *leak*.

10   On 17 March Oates *died*. Evans *died* four weeks earlier.

11   They *be defeated* by the appalling weather conditions before they *manage* to reach One Ton Depot.

12   Scott and his companions *be* dead over seven months when they *be discovered* by a search party in November 1912.

Future time [*SGE* 4.13–20]

There is no inflected future tense in English, but there are several ways of talking about the future.

Exercise 35 Future time: present progressive or *will*?
[*SGE* 4.13–20]

The present progressive is often used for future events arising from present plans or arrangements – *We are meeting tomorrow*.

The 'will future' is sometimes neutral – *I will be 21 next birthday*, but also has meanings of prediction, intention, willingness [4.27]

Complete the following using either the present progressive or the 'will future'

Celia: I hear you (1 go) ARE GOING on holiday soon.

Helen: Yes, we (2 go) ....to Italy. A package tour actually.

Celia: Oh, you (3 love)......................... Italy. When (4 you leave) .... ?

Helen: Well, we (5 fly) ....to Rome on the 15th.

Celia: That (6 be) ....nice.

Helen: Yes, it should be. We (7 go) ....on a coach tour actually.

Celia: (8 you not get)......................... tired sitting in a coach all day ?

Helen: Well, it certainly (9 be)........................ tiring, I suppose. But we (10 visit) ....Siena, Florence, Assisi and Rome.

Celia: You (11 get) .... cultural indigestion but it sounds marvellous. How long (12 you stay) ....in Assisi?

Helen: Unfortunately we (13 only have) ....a quick stop there. Maybe we (14 actually stay) ....there another year.

Celia: It sounds a good tour. But you (15 come) ....home exhausted.

Helen: No, we (16 not)........................ We (17 have) ....a second week in Sorrento, and we (18 just relax)........................by the sea.

Exercise 36 *going to* or *will*? [*SGE* 4.13–20]

> The *'going to'* future usually means the future as a result of present intentions – *We're going to be married.*
> or the future as a result of an existing, present cause – *It's going to rain. I think I'm going to be sick.*

Complete the following with *going to* [do] or *will*.

1 I hear you ARE GOING TO go on a coach tour. I thought you didn't like road journeys?
   Well if I take travel sickness pills I .... be all right.
2 What's all that gear for? .... you .... take up snorkelling?
   Well, I .... try.
3 My suitcase has broken.
   Don't worry. I .... lend you mine.
4 Have you got traveller's cheques?
   Heavens, I'd forgotten. I .... phone the bank tomorrow.
5 I've bought a phrase book, because I .... try to speak Italian.
6 When you're in Rome, ... you .... do something for me?
7 Why have you bought so many films?
   I .... take lots of pictures of everything.
8 We're a bit worried about leaving the house empty.
   We .... keep an eye on it if you like.
9 .... you .... send me a postcard from Sorrento, please?

Exercise 37 Things are hotting up! [*SGE* 4.13–20]

Choose the best tense forms to express the future in the following.

Scientists say that the level of carbon dioxide in the earth's atmosphere is increasing at an alarming rate, and they forecast that it (1) (a) continues (b) is continuing (c) WILL CONTINUE to rise while we (2) (a) continue (b) will continue (c) will be continuing to burn fossil fuels. They believe that this build-up of carbon dioxide (3) (a) causes (b) is causing (c) will cause a marked rise in the earth's temperature in the twenty-first century. If they (4) (a) are (b) are being (c) are going to be proved right, we (5) (a) see (b) are seeing (c) will be seeing unprecedented climatic change in the next century. Because when the earth's temperature (6) (a) rises (b) will rise (c) will have risen   ice caps will melt and seas will rise. And as the seas (7) (a) rise (b) will rise (c) are going to rise,   there will be widespread flooding.

A report some years ago suggested that in the third quarter of the next century, the concentration of carbon dioxide in the atmosphere (8) (a) is doubling (b) will have doubled (c) will have been doubling.   If this massive build-up of carbon dioxide (9) (a) occurs (b) is occurring (c) will have occurred   the average earth temperature will increase by several degrees and while this (10) (a) is happening (b) has happened (c) has been happening,   the sea level (11) (a) rises (b) is rising (c) will be rising   by as much as a metre.

Another report claims that these serious climatic changes (12) (a) actually begin (b) are actually beginning (c) will actually begin   rather sooner. It says as the changes (13) (a) take (b) have taken (c) will take   effect, some northern areas – New York for example – could become semi-tropical. This report also says that the growing season (14) (a) becomes (b) will become (c) has become   longer in some areas, but that in the south drier conditions (15) (a) decrease (b) are decreasing (c) will decrease   crop yields.

Nothing that we (16) (a) do (b) are doing (c) will do   in the next few decades will make much difference, it seems, unless we (17) (a) stop (b) are stopping (c) will be stopping   burning fossil fuels. I only hope the scientists (18) (a) manage (b) are managing (c) will be managing   to come up with a solution. If they (19) (a) don't (b) won't (c) haven't,   then there are global problems ahead. Perhaps we'll only realize the extent of the problem when we (20) (a) leave (b) are leaving (c) have left   it too late.

Modal auxiliaries [*SGE* 4.21–24]

Most of the modal verbs can be paired into present and past forms (eg: *will/ would*). But, as with other verbs, tenses have various meanings besides time:

There's the phone. I'*ll* answer it. [Future (F)]
It *will* be Mother, ringing about the children. [Present (Pres)]
We *would* often swim before breakfast when we were young. [Past (P)]
I realized it *would* soon be my tenth birthday. [Future in the past]
What *would* you do if you won the pools? [Hypothetical future]
Would you like some more coffee? ['Social' usage (here for politeness) referring to the present]

Exercise 38 Modals – what's the time?

Decide what time is broadly being referred to by the modals in the following. Mark each sentence Past, Present or Future – or Future in the past. (We are not concerned in this exercise with whether the event is real or hypothetical.)

1 Come early and we *can* have a picnic. ....FUTURE........
2 *Can* there be life on Mars? ....
3 It *may* well rain tomorrow. ....
4 You *may* be old, but that doesn't excuse you. ....
5 If you *will* eat so much, no wonder you're fat. ....
6 *Shall* we ever discover the truth? ....
7 The sea *could* be very rough that winter. ....
8 My cousin *could* be over there, but you're in the way. ....
9 You *will* be paid. ....
10 Children *will* do these things. ....
11 She hasn't telephoned – she *might* be ill. ....
12 Try as he *might* – he was unable to open the safe. ....
13 He *might* still come. ....
14 It's so cold – it *could* be the middle of winter. ....
15 I *could* telephone later if you like. ....
16 6 into 5 *won't* go. ....
17 All he *would* do was accept £5. ....
18 It was late in the year. Soon it *would* be Christmas. ....
19 I *should* think it's much too expensive. ....
20 I telephoned so that they *shouldn't* worry. ....
21 I'm sorry you *should* think so. ....
22 Jane *ought* to be in New York by now. ....

Exercise 39 Modal meaning [*SGE* 4.21–34]

Modal verbs have various kinds of meaning, such as:

Ability	I *can* see perfectly well without glasses.
Permission	You *can/could/may* borrow my car.
Possibility	Anyone *can* make a mistake.
	Come early, and we *can* talk.
	Adam *may/might* know the answer.
Obligation	I *have got to/must/should/ought to* pay these bills.
Logical necessity	There *must* be some mistake.
Tentative inference	The weather *ought to/should* be better soon.

Decide what is the meaning of the modals in the following, and mark them A(bility), Per(mission), Poss(ibility), Ob(ligation), Logical necessity (LN), Tentative inference (TI).

A personal computer word processor

Before you (1) can start using your PCW for word processing, your PCW (2) needs to be set up.

The printer (3) must be connected to your PCW.

You (4) need to prepare copies of the supplied discs. You (5) should only ever work with copies of these discs.

A 5 amp fuse (6) must be fitted to the plug. The colours of the wires in the mains lead (7) may not correspond with the coloured markings in your plug.

There are many different kinds of computer disc, so you (8) should always check that you are buying the right sort. Labelled discs from any leading manufacturer (9) should give good service.

I (10) can't make the thing work. It surely (11) can't be broken – it's a new machine. If I press this key I (12) ought to be able to start a new document, but nothing happens. There (13) ought to be a simpler instructions book.

(14) 'May I say something ?' 'Yes.' 'You (15) might do better if you pressed the key marked ENTER – you have got to do that most of the time, I find.'

1 Poss 2 .... 3 .... 4 .... 5 .... 6 .... 7 .... 8 ....
9 .... 10 .... 11 .... 12 .... 13 .... 14 .... 15 ....

Exercise 40 Modals [*SGE* 4.21–34]

Choose the best answers.

How (1) (a) CAN (b) may (c) need I lose weight? At one time I made a big effort – I (2) (a) must (b) should (c) would go for days without even looking at butter or potatoes or cakes. But I (3) (a) hadn't to (b) couldn't (c) mightn't   give up chocolate. I just (4) (a) had to (b) must (c) ought to   eat it in secret between meals.

Well if you (5) (a) can (b) will (c) would   eat chocolate, you're making things difficult for yourself. You (6) (a) need (b) should (c) would give up all sweets and chocolate for a start, and you (7) (a) must (b) need (c) would   cut down on sugar. And you (8) (a) couldn't (b) might not (c) mustn't   eat between meals.

Surely I (9) (a) may not (b) must not (c) need not   cut out all sweets, (10) (a) may (b) must (c) need   I?

Well I think you (11) (a) may (b) ought to (c) shall,   you know.

But I get so hungry. (12) (a) Can't (b) May not (c) Needn't   I eat anything between meals?

Well perhaps you (13) (a) could (b) have got to (c) would   eat an apple if you're desperate.

An apple! I (14) (a) can (b) will (c) need starve! You are saying that I (15) (a) have got to (b) need (c) would   starve.

No, rubbish ! You (16) (a) mightn't (b) shouldn't (c) wouldn't   starve if you eat sensibly. But you (17) (a) will (b) may (c) might   try eating less. That (18) (a) must (b) needs to (c) should ˙ get your weight down.

(19) (a) Ought it to (b) Should it (c) Would it   be a good idea to take vitamin tablets, do you think?

No, that (20) (a) couldn't (b) shouldn't (c) needn't   be necessary if you eat plenty of fruit and vegetables.

And what else (21) (a) may (b) shall (c) will   I do ?

(22) (a) Will (b) May (c) Would   I tell you something to give up? Stop thinking so much about food.

Exercise 41 Modal perfect infinitives [*SGE* 4.34]

Complete the following using a suitable modal perfect infinitive, eg: *may have forgotten, could have done*, that keeps close to the meaning of the sentences given.

We tried to get tickets for *The Mousetrap* last Saturday evening, but the theatre was sold out.

1 Oh what a pity – I like the idea, but it's too late now.
  Oh what a pity – it WOULD HAVE BEEN fun.
2 It was possible to buy tickets for Friday, but we didn't.
  We .... tickets for Friday.
3 We thought you had perhaps made other arrangements.
  We thought you .... other arrangements.
4 Well Friday would have been impossible for us.
  Well, we .... on Friday.
5 It was a mistake leaving it so late.
  We .... so late.
6 The sensible thing would have been to book weeks ago.
  We .... weeks ago.
7 Next weekend is a problem, because Mother is coming to stay and it is possible she will be here by then.
  Mother .... have arrived by then.
8 I was expecting her to telephone yesterday but she didn't, because I was in all day.
  She .... yesterday, because I was in all day.
9 But we shall definitely know by tomorrow night.
  We .... heard by tomorrow night.
10 Tom says he's sure she has forgotten all about it.
  He says she .... all about it.
11 I am really certain that she hasn't forgotten. That's not the sort of thing she does.
  She .... forgotten.
12 Tom went on and on apologizing about it, which was quite unnecessary.
  Tom .... I quite understand.

Exercise 42 *be able to, have to, be allowed to* [*SGE* 4.35]

Complete the following using parts of *be able to, have to*, and *be allowed to*, and any other words necessary so that the meaning is as close as possible to the sentences given.

1 When I was at school, games were compulsory.
  When I was at school, we HAD TO PLAY GAMES.
2 It was the fact that they were compulsory that I disliked.
  It was .... play games that I disliked.
3 But football wasn't compulsory.
  But we ....

4 Running was permitted as an alternative.
   We .... go running instead.
5 I wish I could play tennis really well.
   I'd like .... play tennis really well.
6 If you can't play games well, it's a disadvantage.
   Not .... is a disadvantage.
7 It hasn't been possible for me to continue playing tennis since I left school.
   I .... since I left school.
8 I'm sorry but I must say you don't look fit.
   I.. say you don't look fit.

Exercise 43 More modals [SGE 4.21–34]

Choose the best answers.

1 Why didn't you go to work yesterday?
   I (a) needn't have gone (b) didn't need to go (c) mustn't go (d) couldn't have gone.
2 Actually I thought you always worked on Tuesday evenings?
   I (a) might (b) must (c) would (d) used to   years ago, but not now, thank goodness.
3 In fact at one time I (a) ought to (b) had to (c) must (d) was to work two evenings a week.
4 That (a) can't have been (b) couldn't be (c) mustn't be (d) shouldn't have been very pleasant.
5 Oh it wasn't so bad. I had lots of friends there. We (a) might have (b) will have had (c) would have (d) would have had   lots of fun.
6 Looking back, I find it odd that (a) I would enjoy (b) I would have enjoyed (c) I should have enjoyed (d) I ought to have enjoyed   evening work so much.
7 But now, am I right? You (a) may not (b) mustn't (c) needn't (d) used not to work evenings.
   That's right.
8 Of course. You did tell me. I (a) could remember (b) may have remembered (c) should have remembered (d) might remember.

Exercise 44 The *Mary Celeste*: mixed tenses [SGE Chapter 4]

The mystery of the *Mary Celeste* is one of the great mysteries of the sea. An American sailing ship, the *Mary Celeste* set sail from New York on 5 November 1872 – bound for Genoa in Italy, with a cargo of 1,700 barrels of commercial alcohol. Use suitable tenses, including passives if necessary, to find out more.

A month later – on 5 December – she (1 sight) .... east of the Azores, in the eastern Atlantic, by a British ship, the *Dei Gratia*. By an amazing coincidence the master of the British ship, Captain David Reed Morehouse, and the master of the *Mary Celeste*, Captain Benjamin Spooner Briggs, (2 dine) .... together in New York the night before the *Mary Celeste* (3 set sail) .... So Morehouse (4 realize) ...., that the *Mary Celeste* (5 sail) ....in

the wrong direction. What could the ship be doing, he (6 wonder) ....?
Having hailed his friend's ship and got no reply , he (7 go) .... to
investigate. There (8 be) ....nobody on board. Captain Briggs, his wife
and two-year-old daughter (9 all vanish) .... The last entry in the ship's
log was for 25 November, on which day the *Mary Celeste* (10 be) ....
within six miles of the Azores.

An enquiry (11 hold later) ....in Gibraltar, but to this day the mystery
of the *Mary Celeste* (12 never solve) ....

Exercise 45 What do you think happened?

There were, and have continued to be, various theories about the fate of the *Mary
Celeste*. Rewrite the following theories using modal perfect infinitives [*SGE*
4.34]. Alternatives are sometimes possible.

Example: Perhaps the crew mutinied and murdered the Briggs family.
Answer: The crew may have/might have/could have mutinied and murdered the
    Briggs family.

1 No, that's impossible. The crew had vanished too.
   No, the crew .... done that, or
2 they.. found on the ship.
   [but they were not found on the ship.]
3 I am convinced that the crew got drunk, murdered the family and then escaped.
   The crew ....
4 Another possibility is that pirates boarded the ship and killed everyone.
   Or pirates ....
5 But what reason do you suggest these pirates had?
   But why .... that?
6 No, obviously that did not happen.
   No, that.. been what happened.
7 I feel certain the cargo of alcohol exploded.
   Obviously, the cargo of alcohol ....
8 Then possibly Captain Briggs decided – I'm only guessing – to get everyone
   into the lifeboat – on a tow rope, of course.
   Captain Briggs ....
9 If he did that, it was a mistake to do so.
   Well he .... that.
10 And then, obviously, a wind caught the *Mary Celeste*, the rope broke and
   everyone was drowned.
   A wind...................................., the rope ....
   and everyone .... drowned.

5 Nouns and determiners

Count and noncount nouns [*SGE* 5.1]

Some common nouns are count (countable) nouns – like *book*, *girl*, *problem*; and others are noncount (mass) nouns, eg: *rice*, *importance*. The distinction is partly related to meaning, but is also very important grammatically, because the usage of determiners with them is different.

Exercise 46 Count and noncount nouns

Count nouns must have a determiner (*a*, *one*, *my*, *this* ...) in the singular, though this is not necessary in the plural. Noncount nouns do not need a determiner.

Underline all the words that without further alteration can fit into the following sentences. If necessary, consult a good dictionary.

Example: Tom is always offering <u>advice</u>/<u>assistance</u>/idea/suggestion. [*idea* and *suggestion* are count nouns. We could say: *He is always offering ideas/ suggestions*. But not **He is always offering idea/suggestion*.]

1 You shouldn't judge him on one achievement/failure/progress/success.
2 It was difficult for him to find career/employment/job/work.
3 His new job is something to do with advertisement/advertising/publicity/ marketing.
4 Buy now – it's a real bargain/saving/savings/reduction.
5 There is a/an fortune/income/money/wealth to be made from computers these days.
6 I need a new clothes/clothing/suit/underwear.
7 Modern ammunition/arms/equipment/weapons/weaponry is sophisticated.
8 You'll have to get a leave/pass/permission/permit to get into the factory.
9 Did you have a good experience/fortune/luck/time while you were away?
10 One scene/scenery/view/countryside particularly stays in my mind.

Exercise 47 Count and noncount usage

Many nouns have both count and noncount usage. Sometimes the difference is between unit meaning and more general meaning: *a chicken* = a bird; *chicken* = the meat from it. Sometimes there is a greater difference: *a sight* = something seen; *sight* = eyesight.

Complete the pairs of sentences below, using the following words, once as a count and once as a noncount noun.

business   cheese   dinner   experience   glass   ice

life   noise   painting   paper   pleasure   worry

Use a good dictionary to help you if neccessary.

1 Where can I get A PAPER? I want to know what's happening. I also need PAPER to wrap up some parcels with.

2 Do you sell ....? I mean, could you cut a piece so that I could replace a broken window? Also I'm hoping to find .... to replace one I broke when I was washing up.

3 Shopping in this huge store is quite .... They sell everything, but some of the sales staff are very young and lack ...., so they don't know where anything is.

4 Still, I find it .... to shop here. I mean I don't exactly shop for ...., but I like the atmosphere.

5 I shall have to come back another day and go to the art department. Tom and Molly have asked for .... as a wedding present. I don't think they like (modern) .... much,

6 so it's .... to know what to choose. Silly, isn't it? Choosing a picture shouldn't be a cause for ....

7 Did you hear ....? Of course, there's a lot of ...., but I heard something that sounded like a bomb.

8 They did have a terrorist bomb go off here some years ago, but they were open next day. '............ as usual.' I've sometimes thought I'd like to start .... but it must be a nightmare these days.

9 Oh, I must go to the food department. They sell (very special) ...., made from goat's milk, one I can't get in my local grocer's. You don't like ....? You don't know what you're missing.

10 And what am I going to cook for .... this evening? I think something simple, because tomorrow we're going to .... organized by Bill Brown's family to celebrate his ninetieth birthday.

11 He's led (very active) .... and climbed almost every mountain you can think of. But now, poor old chap, he can hardly walk. Still, that's ....!

12 Well, I think we've just time for the restaurant. I'm going to have .... What about you? Are you going to have tea, or will you have your favourite gin and tonic with ....?

Determiners [*SGE* 5.3–10]

Count and noncount nouns are partly distinguished by the determiners they can take. *A great deal of* and *much* only go with noncount nouns:

The tourist office didn't have a great deal of/much information.

a lot of goes with noncount or plural nouns:

They gave us a lot of advice/a lot of brochures.

Exercise 48 Nouns and their determiners

Underline all the words that fit the following sentences without any other alterations. If necessary, consult a good dictionary.

1 Not a great deal of experiments/investigations/<u>work</u>/<u>research</u> has been done on this.
2 Almost every detail/explanation/information/news he gave us seemed inaccurate to me.
3 You see a lot of bad behaviour/conduct/custom/manner at football matches.
4 Does it do much damage/harm/hurt/injury?
5 That picture isn't of much importance/price/value/worth.
6 They have such terrible climate/storms/temperature/weather.
7 Each bag/baggage/luggage/suitcase should be labelled.
8 Neither computer/equipment/machine/machinery is suitable.
9 There's not enough fun/joke/joy around these days.
10 – but plenty of complaint/courage/patience.

Exercise 49 *some, any, no* [*SGE* 5.5]

Complete the following, using *some, something, any* or *no*.

1 Tom should be here ANY minute now. He says he forgot before.
2 That's .... excuse at all. He's terribly inconsiderate.
3 He certainly knows what he's doing. He's .... fool.
4 .... child can see that: it's elementary.
5 You've given yourself quite .... problem, promising to help him like that.
6 Well, ... days you win;
7 and .... days you lose.
8 I'd be grateful for .... help you can give.
9 I'll meet you .... time you like, to discuss it.
10 There's .... time like the present.
11 Some people always want .... for nothing;
12 but I believe there's .... free lunch!

Exercise 50 Central, pre- and post-determiners [*SGE* 5.3–10]

> When more than one determiner can be used together, there is usually a special order they have to be in.

Unscramble these sentences.

Example: 1 been have months very all few last these trying
Answer: All these last few months have been very trying.

2 are complaints matter alone one about more several this there

....

3 both every second these two day surgical dressings be changed have to

....

4 amount food needed people times for of all that those three they

....

5 take hours tablet a every four half

....

6 all few first the those worse were rest than days

....

7 at because it's now disgraceful half get double a you the packet price

....

8 age husbands were Mary's both her twice two last

....

9 another other new ten the she day dresses bought

....

10 one onc ones you the dozen as for could little big same several price get

....

Exercise 51 *few, a few, little, a little* [*SGE* 5.10]

> *Few* and *little* are rather negative in meaning, and contrast with *a few* and *a little*, which are positive.

Rewrite the following using *few*, *a few*, *little* or *a little* in place of the underlined words, making any other changes necessary.

Example: Not many people arc exactly the weight they would like to be.
Answer: Few people are exactly the weight they would like to be.

1 Hardly any women nowadays want to spend hours cooking, and even fewer want to spend all day in the kitchen.
2 Some people say they're not interested in food, and a small number actually mean it.
3 Crazy starvation diets offer hardly any prospect of success.
4 It is all right to have some butter, but try to cut down the amount.
5 Some people do overeat, but not as many as you might think.
6 A small amount of salt is all right, isn't it?
7 There's not much chance of keeping slim, unless you stick to a diet.
8 Many people enjoy foreign restaurants, but not many people know anything about Tibetan food.

Exercise 52 Articles: *a* or *the*? [*SGE* 5.11–24]

Complete the following using *a/an* or *the*.

South Africa became (1) .... first country to declare (2) ....
great white shark (3) .... protected species when (4) .... hunting
ban within 200 miles of (5) .... coast was imposed yesterday.

(6) .... jawbone can fetch £4,000.

'If (7) .... thief is determined and professional, he's going to break into your house.' This blunt assertion is all (8) .... more alarming when uttered by PC Alan Husher, (9) .... crime prevention officer for (10) .... Metropolitan Police. More than 500 crimes were committed every hour in England and Wales last year, according to (11) .... latest figures. In (12) .... effort to persuade (13) .... public to play (14) .... greater role in tackling crime, (15) .... Home Office has launched (16) .... £4.5 million nationwide advertising campaign. (17) .... public's general attitude, according to PC Husher, is 'It won't happen to me.'

In his own part of London, many residents head for (18) .... country at (19) .... weekend, leaving (20) .... way free for committed thieves. But he says that 94 per cent of crime against property last year was largely preventable.

Exercise 53 a/an, the or zero [SGE 5.11–24]

Insert *a, an, the* (or nothing at all) as necessary.

(1) .... world wildlife is in (2) .... danger. (3) .... reasons are complex – (4) .... world's population is expanding, and increasingly (5) .... man is destroying more and more of (6) .... natural environment.

(7) .... last dodo in (8) .... world died on (9) .... island of Mauritius in (10) .... late seventeenth century. Today, (11) .... black rhino in Kenya could go (12) .... same way. There is (13) .... world-wide trade – much of it illegal – in (14) .... rare animals and birds. (15) .... particular favourite, and one severely threatened with (16) .... extinction through smuggling is (17) .... orang-utan, which only survives in (18) .... forests of Borneo and Sumatra.

(19) .... fierce argument is now raging about how to protect (20) .... most endangered species. Some people argue that (21) .... zoos, with their research work and breeding programmes, offer (22) .... best hope, and (23) .... protection from international smugglers. But some of (24) .... older zoos have (25) .... disadvantage of (26) .... cramped city conditions, though (27) .... zoo with (28) .... wide open spaces like Whipsnade Zoo in (29) .... Bedfordshire countryside north of London is seen as offering (30) .... pleasant habitat.

However (31) .... public – at any rate in (32) .... West – is less interested than they once were in looking at (33) .... captive animals, so (34) .... zoos, particularly traditional ones, lose (35) .... money.

Some zoos have sought (36) .... solution in modernising. In (37) .... recent years, (38) .... Bronx Zoo in New York, for example,

has increased (39) .... attendances by introducing (40) ....
natural habitats – (41) .... jungle world, (42) .... Ethiopian
mountain and so on. But (43) .... increased attendances must be partly
due to (44) .... fact that it opens free three days (45) .... week,
and (46) .... zoo still gets (47) .... government subsidy.

Neither (48) .... traditional zoos, nor (49) .... 'theme' zoos
appeal to all animal lovers however. Some 'conservationists' would apparently
like to see all zoos abolished, and their inmates returned to (50) .... wild.
But this could perhaps lead to some endangered species becoming extinct.

Exercise 54 Articles in fixed phrases [*SGE* 5.19–20]

Complete the questionnaire by inserting suitable prepositions, and adding *a* or *the*
if necessary. (When you have completed the questions, you could try them on a
friend!)

1 When you wake up, do you get OUT OF bed immediately?
2 Do you get dressed before or .... breakfast?
3 Do you walk .... school/work?
4 If the answer to (3) is yes, do you go .... foot, because you like the
   exercise, or because there's no suitable transport?
5 If the answer is no, do you travel .... car .... bus/or .... train?
6 When do you work best? (a) .... morning (b) .... afternoon
   (c) .... evening or (d) .... night?
7 What time do you normally get .... home?
8 If you had to work (a) .... night, could you sleep (b) ....
   day?
9 Do you ever travel .... air, as part of your job?
10 If yes, what do you do .... plane (a) read (b) sleep (c) watch the
   movie?
11 Have you ever had .... infectious disease such as (a) ....
   measles (b) .... mumps (c) .... whooping cough?
12 If so, were you .... hospital with it?
13 Do you get up at your usual time when you are .... holiday?
14 Do you prefer to have a holiday .... spring/.............. summer/
   .... autumn or .... winter?

Exercise 55 Proper nouns [*SGE* 5.25–34]

> Most names are complete in themselves, but sometimes *the* is an essential
> part of the name.

Find out about Scotland by inserting *the* wherever necessary.

Come to (1) .... spectacular Scotland for a perfect holiday! And first to
(2) .... Edinburgh, (3) .... Athens of (4) .... North!
Visit (5) .... Edinburgh Castle, perched on its rock 443 feet above sea-

level. Admire (6) .... Scott Monument, a memorial to (7) ....
Scotland's most famous novelist, (8) .... Sir Walter Scott. Wander down
(9) .... Royal Mile, a series of narrow streets linking the castle to (10)
.... Holyrood House, or (11) .... Palace of (12) ....
Holyrood House, to give it its full name. Begun by (13) .... King James
IV of (14) .... Scotland in 1501, but much restored in the eighteenth
century, (15) .... Holyrood House is where (16) .... present
Queen stays when she visits (17) .... Scottish capital.

Also not to be missed is (18) .... Edinburgh New Town, which sounds
like a modern housing estate, but actually dates from the seventeenth and
eighteenth centuries.

As a change from sightseeing, shop for souvenirs in (19) .... bustling
Princes Street. Pamper yourself by dining in (20) .... Hilton Hotel. Seep
yourself in the atmosphere by reading that fine newspaper, (21) ....
Scotsman.

If you're interested in art, (22) .... National Gallery of (23) ....
Scotland is a must. There's also (24) .... Royal Scottish Academy, which
holds an annual exhibition of work by living artists. But the highlight of (25)
.... Edinburgh year is (26) .... Edinburgh International Festival
held every year in (27) .... August and September.

But perhaps you want an away-from-it-all holiday. Then to you (28) ....
Highlands and Islands further north beckon. And how hard to choose! Heading
north-west you could drive through (29) .... Pass of (30) ....
Glencoe, see (31) .... Scotland's highest mountain, (32) ....
Ben Nevis, and take (33) .... famous Road to (34) .... Isles. Or
you could travel by train along (35) .... scenic West Highland line and
cross to (36) .... Isle of (37) .... Skye. Or you could take a boat
to those remote islands, (38) .... Outer Hebrides.

Visitors with a taste for active sports will find them in (39) ....
Highlands. (40) .... River Dee is famous for its salmon fishing; (41)
.... River Spey area is even more famous for its Scotch whisky. From the
mountain resort of (42) .... Aviemore, you can go skiing in winter in (43)
.... Cairngorms, which boast the highest restaurant in Britain.

Another sight not to be missed in (44) .... northern Scotland, is (45)
.... Great Glen (a glen is a mountain valley) stretching from (46)
.... Inverness on the east coast to (47) .... Fort William on the
west. The Glen consists of a series of lochs (lakes) linked by (48) ....
Caledonian Canal, said to be the home of (49) .... Loch Ness Monster,
a vast prehistoric beast surviving in the deep remote waters of this loch. Some
people doubt the very existence of this strange creature – others are certain that
(50) .... 'Nessie' is real.

Number [*SGE* 5.35–44] and irregular plurals

Most count nouns form their plurals by adding *-s* or *-es*, but some have
irregular plurals.

Exercise 56 [*SGE* 5.37–40]

Complete the following using the correct plural forms.

Example: I want a chocolate mouse.
Answer: We haven't any edible MICE. Sorry!

1 I want a Christmas card with a snowman on it.
   I'm afraid we're out of cards with ....

2 And I need some sort of bookshelf.
   We have some good value wooden .... at £49.99.

3 And where can I get a silk scarf and a pure linen handkerchief?
   We have some beautiful silk ...., but we only sell cotton ....

4 And can you ask your food department to send me a large plaice ?
   I don't think they've any .... at all today.

5 Oh, and I need a dozen eggs – no, make it two ....

6 And I want a story about spacecraft.
   I'm afraid there's no demand for .... about ....

7 Oh, and I need a hundred pins.
   We sell pins in packets of two .... at 99p. You do seem to want some rather peculiar things.

8 Yes, well, that's the lot. I've only got about a pound in cash, but I suppose I can pay by credit card?
   All this is rather a tall order! Give me a cheque for ninety-nine ....50p.

Exercise 57 'Foreign' plurals [*SGE* 5.41]

Complete the following. There may be alternative answers.

1 Is this the only series of children's books you stock?
   No, we have several other SERIES for older children.

2 I'm buying another encyclopaedia.
   How many .... have you got now?

3 She's busy writing an index, and the appendix to her book.
   She seems to spend more time writing .... and .... than the actual books.

4 This is a crisis.
   Oh dear, your whole life is a series of ....

5 He'll send you a memorandum.
   He's always sending ....

6 Have you got a prospectus?
   There are two .... Which do you want ?

7 He needs a stimulus.
   But he never reacts to any ....

8 What's your criterion for personal success?
   I think different people have different ....

Exercise 58 Singular or plural nouns? [*SGE* 5.43–44]

Some nouns ending in -*s* are not plural (eg: *physics*); but some nouns without -*s* are (*people*).

Collective nouns (eg: *audience*, *committee*, *family*, *team*) are singular nouns – they need a determiner such as *a*, *the*, *this* – but sometimes take a plural verb: *This team have done well this season*.

Write out all the possible alternatives in the following.

1 Some/this/these folk don't/doesn't know how to spend its/their money.
    Answers: Some folk don't know how to spend their money.
                These folk don't know how to spend their money.
                [*folk* is normally plural]

2 This/these belongings of John's was/were found in the cupboard.
    ....

3 This/these family need/needs help.
    ....

4 I paid £100 for this/these binoculars, but it/they isn't/aren't very good.
    ....

5 The police has/have a hard job to do.
    ....

6 What was/were the news on television last night?
    ....

7 There is/are a couple of people outside who/which want/wants to talk to you.
    ....

8 The Prime Minister's office has/have issued a statement.
    ....

9 The outskirts of the town is/are rather dull.
    ....

10 A majority of the strikers want/wants to return to work.
    ....

11 Our MP's majority was/were higher this time than last time.
    ....

12 Why is/are there remains of food on the table?
    ....

13 The public has/have a right to know what money is being spent in its/their name.
    ....

14 The audience was/were enraptured.
    ....

Case [*SGE* 5.48–55]

The genitive case of the noun sounds the same as the regular plural. It is written ['s] after regular singular nouns or a plural without an -*s*: *a girl's name*, *the children's mother*; and simply with an apostrophe ['] after a regular plural: *the girls' mothers*.

Exercise 59 Genitive or *of*-construction [*SGE* 5.48–55]

Use the information given to complete the sentences using a genitive. In some sentences you will have to use a noun derived from another word in the sentence.

Example: Henry behaved very badly, which upset all of us.
Answer: We were all upset by HENRY'S BAD BEHAVIOUR.

1 My parents insisted on taking the dog on holiday. This caused problems.
There were problems because of (2) ....

2 My uncle says he was educated during the school holidays.
...., he says, took place in the school holidays.

3 My aunt has her initials on all her things.
.... things have her initials on.

4 Bill has been omitted from the team. It is a great surprise to us all.
We are all surprised at...

5 Bill has been very loyal to them. It impresses me.
I am impressed by ....

6 My grandmother is always losing her spectacles, and expects us to find them.
We're always looking for ....

7 The people who advised my grandfather were not exactly helpful.
My ....

8 My mother is very disappointed – that's obvious.
.... is obvious.

Exercise 60 Genitives: London landmarks [*SGE* 5.48–55]

Use the underlined words to write sentences about where to find some famous London landmarks. Use a genitive structure as in the example when you can.

But in four cases you will need an *of*-construction instead. Remember these are names, so use capital letters.

1 a <u>corner</u> reserved for the tombs   in Westminster Abbey
  and monuments of <u>poets</u>
  Answer: Poets' Corner is in Westminster Abbey.

2 a <u>cathedral</u> dedicated to <u>St Paul</u>   in the City
  ....

3 the <u>'Houses'</u> where <u>Parliament</u>
  conducts its business   at Westminster
  ....

4 <u>the</u> famous <u>club for travellers</u>   in Pall Mall
  ....

5 a <u>park</u> in honour of <u>postmen</u>   near the General Post Office
  ....

6 an obelisk (called a <u>needle</u>) –   on the Embankment, near
  not in fact connected with <u>Cleopatra</u>!   Charing Cross
  ....

7 the <u>Royal Academy,</u> a society devoted
  to the fine <u>arts</u>   in Piccadilly
  ....

8 the waxworks museum founded by
   <u>Madame Tussaud</u>   near Baker Street station

....

9 <u>the museum</u> about childhood   in Bethnal Green

....

10 The most famous <u>tower</u> in <u>London,</u>
    begun in the eleventh century   at Tower Hill

....

11 A <u>column</u> commemorating Admiral <u>Nelson</u>   in Trafalgar Square

....

12 a <u>gate</u> through which <u>traitors</u> used to be
    taken to prison (and often execution)   at (See question 10!)

....

6 Pronouns

Exercise 61 Personal pronouns [SGE 6.2–16]

Complete with suitable personal and reflexive pronouns.

1 They told us to help OURSELVES to anything we needed. But the trouble is they frequently get into difficulties .... and then expect us to help .... out.

2 I spoke to the children for nearly an hour, trying to talk to .... as simply as I could about the situations which would confront .... as they passed through life. I could not have had a more lively audience, and when I had finished they broke up into groups to talk over between .... the points I had raised.

3 She dreaded dinner. At dinner, she thought, the conversation must be serious. She took Art seriously .... and believed that others must want to talk seriously about .... too.

4 I might go up there for a few days in the holidays. Perhaps you would like to come with .... and watch a bit of parachuting, or jump .... even!

5 We lost control of the boat and within an amazingly short space of time found .... in mid-river. Eventually we got .... back to the bank we had left and some girls from the opposite bank came and rescued ....

6 I think he works .... too hard, but I wish .... all success and unhesitatingly recommend .... for the position.

7 Some people do not seem to mind living by ...., but I .... find it rather lonely.

8 If you're going camping, take a torch with .... I can't lend .... mine, because I need it .... So I'm afraid you'll have to buy .... one.

Exercise 62 The pronoun *it:* What does *it* mean? [*SGE* 6.9]

> Sometimes the word *it* is used as a grammatical subject, and the meaning subject comes later:
>
> *It* is very sad *that you have lost your job.*
>
> But sometimes *it* has no meaning but is used as a 'dummy' because there is no other subject:
>
> *It* is raining.

Distinguish these two different uses by underlining what *it* refers to, if anything.

Example: It's better <u>to have loved and lost</u> than never to have loved at all.

1 It's no use crying over spilt milk.
2 I've never known it rain so much.
3 It really is a problem sometimes to know what to do.
4 You've had that long enough. It's my turn.
5 We consider it important to keep our options open.
6 It says here that there are no performances on Sunday.
7 Who's calling? It's me, your cousin, and I want to ask you a favour.
8 Does it matter if I'm late?
9 I hate it when you talk like that.
10 Can you imagine what it's like having nothing to do?
11 It's not for me to tell you what to do.
12 As it happens, I already know.

Exercise 63 *it*

Sometimes the word *it* is used in rather idiomatic phrases with rather special meaning. Find the *it*-phrases in the following sentences that mean:

(a) (something) is finished/worn out;
(b) there's no alternative;
(c) hurry up;
(d) combine two apparently exclusive choices;
(e) live at a fast and enjoyable pace;
(f) deliberately do something by oneself;
(g) put up with primitive conditions;
(h) to want to hurt or upset (someone).

Example: 1(c) [step on it = hurry up]

1 Step on it – or we'll miss the train.
2 Well, if the last train's gone, there's nothing for it. We'll have to walk.
3 This car's certainly had it. I've got to get a new one.
4 You can't have it both ways – either do the job properly, or resign.
5 Your trouble is you just live it up all the time. You shouldn't have so many late nights.
6 Why have you got it in for me? What have I done to annoy you?

7 When his partner left the firm, he decided to go it alone.

8 I don't mind roughing it – but I'd like something a bit more comfortable really.

Exercise 64 *it* again! [*SGE* 6.9]

Sometimes the word *it* stands for a whole sentence or clause:

I asked *who had told him*, and *it* turned out to be the neighbours.

Sometimes we use an *it*-sentence with two verbs [a 'cleft' sentence] for extra emphasis:

It was only yesterday that we learnt the truth. (We only learnt the truth yesterday.)

Rewrite the following in the way indicated to show clearly what the word *it* refers to.

1 He failed the exam. It was a great blow to his pride.
His FAILING THE EXAM WAS A GREAT BLOW TO HIS PRIDE.

2 It's all those late nights that were the trouble.
All ....

3 'Do you think he should try again?' 'I'm all for it.'
I'm all in favour ....

4 Perhaps I shouldn't say it, but I think he's lazy.
I'm afraid ....

5 Well, let's face it. He's not going to take our advice.
We have to face the fact ....

6 I think he resents advice. At least it appears so.
He appears ....

7 It's all his talk of poverty that really annoys me.
What ....

8 He may ask for a loan, though I doubt it.
I doubt ....

9 Quite! I could lend him some money, but I'd rather not risk it.
I'm not keen on the idea ....

10 If it hadn't been for your help he would be in a worse mess.
If you ....

Exercise 65 *Wh*-interrogatives and relatives [*SGE* 6.17–18]

Relative and interrogative pronouns are similar, but not quite the same.
     relative pronouns   *who, whom, whose, which, that* and 'zero'
     interrogative pronouns   *who, whom, whose, which* and *what*

Whose, which and *what* can also be determiners.

The police are discussing a crime. They have some clues, and they ask themselves some questions. Write out the questions, using *wh*-question words.

1 Someone helped them.
   WHO HELPED THEM?
2 They got inside help from somebody.
   ....
3 They were looking for something.
   ....
4 We have some clues already.
   .... so far?
5 We are likely to get some help from the staff.
   ....
6 One of the thieves left his jacket behind.
   ....
7 They used someone's key.
   ....
8 This jacket belonged to somebody.
   ....
9 They entered by one of the doors.
   ....

Now complete these phrases about who the police want to interview and what the police are looking for.
Use relative pronouns (*who, whom, whose, which* or *that*):

10 someone .... had a grudge against the Museum
11 someone to .... money would be important
12 anyone ....car is missing
13 everyone .... has a key to the building
14 everyone to .... the mysterious telephone caller spoke
15 anything .... could help solve the mystery
16 someone .... family is hiding them

Exercise 66 *this* and *that* [SGE 6.19–20]

Complete the following using *this, that, these* or *those* (sometimes they are pronouns, and sometimes determiners).

Example: In THOSE far-off days, life was less stressful.

1 May I introduce you? .... is Henry and Elaine.
2 What's .... I hear about you two getting engaged?
3 I hope ....who can help, will.
4 We were talking of .... and .... – nothing in particular.
5 I wonder if .... odd-looking couple over there can help?
6 It's been one of .... days. Nothing's gone right.
7 Perhaps one of .... fine days you'll realize the world doesn't owe you a living.
8 .... is my luggage here – where's yours?

9 Could you please pass me .... cushion behind you?

10 .... are worrying times we live in.

11 I say. What do you think of ....? It says here that beer is coming down in price.

12 Will ....of you who want tickets please raise your hands.

Exercise 67 Indefinite pronouns [*SGE* 6.21–28]

Complete the following with:

> anything   everything   nothing   something
>
> *or* anybody/one   everybody/one   nobody/no one   somebody/one

Example: ANYTHING you can do I can do better!

1 Don't just sit there – do ....

2 Why should I? It's .... to do with me.

3 .... somewhere would like a letter from you.

4 .... has to lead their own life.

5 Not .... can be boss, though.

6 .... is obviously worrying him – but what?

7 I've no idea – it's .... 's guess.

8 I'm always the last to know. .... tells me anything.

9 Somebody must know ...., but who?

10 Hardly .... would agree with you.

11 If you can believe that, you'll believe ....

12 .... in their right mind would do such a thing.

13 Money isn't .... – but it helps.

14 Every little helps – it's better than ...., I suppose.

Exercise 68 *both, either, neither, each, all, half* [*SGE* 6.23–28]

Complete the following using *both, either, neither, each, all* or *half* (as pronouns or determiners).

Among medically recorded multiple births, the highest where (1) .... the children have survived are several cases of sextuplets (six at a time). In 1974 a Mrs Rosenkowitz gave birth to six children in Cape Town, South Africa. (2) .... were boys and (3) .... were girls.

In the UK, (4) .... six Walton girls born in 1983 survive, as do the Coleman sextuplets born in 1986. (5) .... of them are girls, and (6) .... are boys. (7) .... mother had any previous experience of sextuplets!

Perhaps the most famous twins in history were the 'Siamese' twins born in 1811. (8) .... were male – Chang and Eng Bunker. (9) .... of them can have had any privacy as they were joined at the chest. If (10) .... of them wanted to go anywhere, (11) .... had to go. In 1843 they married sisters, and (12) .... couples had children. (13) .... couple fortunately produced 'Siamese' twins. (14) .... brothers died in 1874 – within three hours of (15) .... other.

Exercise 69 Television and children [*SGE* Chapters 5 and 6]

Complete the following with suitable pronouns and determiners.

Anyone who has thought about (1) IT will have concluded that too much sex and violence on television cannot be good for children. (2) .... is perhaps more likely to deaden (3) .... minds than to turn (4) .... into sex maniacs or gangsters, but no matter. In so far as a report published yesterday repeats common sense opinions, (5) .... is unexceptionable.

Yet if (6) .... looks closer at *TV and Children*, one finds a certain moral priggishness and authoritarianism, (7) .... is perhaps no less dangerous than the sex and violence (8) ......all deplore. (9) .... authors of (10) .... report seem to have (11) .... identikit picture of society. Judging by (12) .... criticism of *Dallas*, (13) .... ideal society would be anti-materialistic. Elsewhere (14) .... complain that homosexuals, blacks, (15) .... disabled and old people are not represented or else shown in (16) .... bad light.

Well, no doubt (17) .... are called minorities do not always receive 'sensitive treatment'. But (18) .... of us has not been outraged to see some group of people dear to (19) .... brutally satirized in some fatuous programme?

The merits of television lie in (20) .... diversity. (21) .... really is for parents to guide (22) .... children away from tastelessness. Moreover (23) .... should not assume that children have absolutely no judgement of (24) .... own. (25) .... is better that (26) .... should be free to choose within certain bounds than be assaulted by the kind of boring uniformity, calculated to make (27) .... into better and more useful citizens that (28) .... authors of (29) .... report have in (30) .... mind's eye.

7 Adjectives and adverbs

> **Adjectives [*SGE* 7.1-26]**
>
> Most adjectives can come in attributive position before a noun (a *lovely* house) and in predicative position after a verb such as *be, become, seem* (The house is *lovely*).

Exercise 70 Attributive and predicative [*SGE* 7.3, 7.17–22]

A few adjectives usually only come before a noun, and a few normally only follow a verb.

Decide about these adjectives, and use them to complete the definitions grammatically.

> afraid   ashamed   content   elder   glad   inner   main
>
> maximum   occasional   only   outdoor   ready

Examples: A traveller who has nobody with them is A LONE TRAVELLER. (not *lone)
When people are by themselves they are ALONE. (*alone people)

1 If a person is embarrassed at having behaved badly, s/he is ....
2 A child that feels frightened is ....
3 An event that does not happen very often is ....
4 Strength that comes from within a person's character is ....
5 A party held in the open air is ....
6 If a child has no brothers or sisters s/he is ....
7 A person who is really pleased about something is ....
8 If you have several worries about something, but one that worries you more than all the rest, that is ....
9 If a person is adequately satisfied, s/he is ....
10 If the top speed allowed is 70 mph, then that is ....
11 If lunch is all prepared and cooked, it is ....
12 If your brother is older than you, he is ....

Exercise 71 Adjectives and participles [*SGE* 7.5–6]

Rephrase the sentences, using *-ing* or *-ed* participles from these verbs instead of the words in italic, but keeping roughly the same meaning. Make any other small changes necessary.

> annoy   astonish   bore   disappoint   exhaust
>
> frighten   interest   puzzle   surprise   worry

1 The play had an absolutely *(incredible)* plot.

The play had an absolutely ASTONISHING plot.

2 The way the murderer behaved was really (*scary*) ....
3 But I was (*sad*) .... that my favourite actor wasn't in it that night.
4 Some people get really (*angry*) .... when they have come specially
   to see a particular actor.
5 I also thought the first scene was rather (*dull and tedious*) ....
6 I mean, who (*really takes an interest*) .... in spiders?
7 But the last act was really (*unexpected*) .... – brilliant.
8 Incidentally, the increase in seat prices is (*a cause for anxiety*) ....
9 It is (*difficult to understand*) .... why more people don't complain,
10 but I suppose they (*have no energy left*) ....

Exercise 72 Adjective position [*SGE* 7.7–8]

Adjectives that can follow a verb can also follow a noun, often as a sort of
reduced relative clause: *nothing* (that is) *important*. So there are three main
positions for adjectives.

Rewrite the following, using these adjectives to replace the words in italic. Make
any other changes necessary. You will need some of the words more than once.

absent   certain   concerned   conscious   elect

involved   late   present   proper

1 Our *newly elected* chairman takes over immediately.
   Our chairman ELECT takes over immediately.
2 because our *former* chairman resigned suddenly last September for health
   reasons.
   ....
3 Most of the people *who were there* at the meeting are delighted,
   ....
4 but *some* people (*that I'm not going to name*),
   ....
5 people who were *not at* the meeting, have telephoned to say that they should
   have had postal votes.
   ....
6 They say the only *correct* thing to do now is hold another election, which is
   ridiculous.
   ....
7 One of our difficulties is we do not always have the *up-to-date* addresses of all
   our members.
   ....
8 The secretary is *aware* of the problem.
   ....
9 We once wrote to a member saying his subscription was *overdue*,
   ....
10 and we had a letter from a very distressed lady saying her husband, *who had
   died recently*, had always paid on time.
   ....

11 We are now making a *deliberate* effort to bring our records up to date.
....

12 The secretary has spoken to all the people *who have anything to do with the matter*
....

13 and is *confident* that we will get it right.
....

14 But it could be a long and *complicated* business.
....

Exercise 73 Adjectives with prepositions [*SGE* 7.9, 16.38]

Some predicative adjectives are often followed by a particular preposition.

Use words from the table to rephrase the sentences as shown. Use the words in the first and last column once each. You will need to use two of the prepositions twice.

answerable		satisfactory references
glad	about	the opportunity
grateful	at	the difficulties
different	for	any aspect of the work
aware	from	the board
dependent	of	coping
subject	on	negotiation
good	to	your remarks
bored	with	all my previous jobs
worried		my last job

1 The job is yours provided your references are satisfactory.
    The job offer is DEPENDENT ON SATISFACTORY REFERENCES.
2 I welcome the challenge.
    I am ....
3 I realize it won't be easy.
    I am ....
4 It's unlike anything I've tackled before.
    It is ....
5 Is there anything about the job that worries you?
    Are you ....
6 Can we discuss salary?
    Is the pay ....
7 We have every confidence in your ability to manage.
    We're sure you'll be ....
8 I appreciate what you've just said.
    I am ....
9 I've just left a very dull job.
    I was ....
10 You'll have to report to the directors.
    You'll be ....

Exercise 74 Discontinuous adjective phrases [*SGE* 7.8–9]

> It is not usually possible to put a long adjective phrase in front of a noun (**a better for this problem solution*). What we can do is make the phrase discontinuous with the adjective before the noun and the rest of the phrase after it – *a better solution for this problem.*

Rewrite what you say in the following situations, in such a way that the adjective phrase is discontinuous.

1 You want a camera that would be suitable for a child.
   You say: I want A SUITABLE CAMERA FOR A CHILD.
2 You think the camera that you are shown looks impossible for a beginner.
   That looks ....
3 The next model the assistant shows you looks similar to the last one.
   And this looks ....
4 You ask if this camera is easy to use.
   Is this ....
5 You ask if he has any makes that are different from these two.
   Haven't you ....
6 You like the next camera because the size is more suitable for a child.
   Oh, that looks ....
7 You ask for a bag that is big enough to carry spare films in.
   I'd like ....
8 You ask the assistant if he has any bags that are cheaper than these.
   Have you ....
9 You also want an album that is as big as possible.
   Oh and I want ....
10 The assistant thinks that you are a customer who is hard to please.
   This is ....

> ### Adverbs [*SGE* 7.27–37]
>
> Adverbs sometimes belong to the verb or the whole predicate:
>
> He *often goes for long walks.*
>
> But sometimes they just belong to another adverb (*very* strangely); to an adjective (*fairly* stupid); to some other word: *halfway* through the afternoon, *too* many, *rather* a mistake; or even form part of a phrasal verb (think *out*).

Exercise 75 Adverbs: functions [*SGE* 7.31–37]

Identify the single word adverbs in the following, and then decide in each case which word or phrase the adverb belongs with.

Example: This is not particularly difficult.
Answer: particularly [= adverb]; <u>particularly difficult</u>.

1 Richard Long walks round in circles.

....

2 He also walks in straight lines.

....

3 He has been on some very long walks – in Britain, Spain, Mexico, the Sahara, Nepal.

....

4 Sometimes he 'rearranges' the landscape and photographs the result.

....

5 In one photograph that he took halfway up the highest mountain in Mexico,

....

6 you can make out a circle of stones that he made.

....

7 Long once described a ten-mile walk in Britain as a ten-mile sculpture,

....

8 though whether sculpture is quite the word everyone would use is arguable.

....

9 But Long is an artist – a highly talented one in some people's eyes,

....

10 rather a joker to others.

....

11 He 'works' with stones and rocks and mud, fairly

....

12 quickly creating great circles and other shapes on the walls and floors of art galleries.

....

13 He has had well over a hundred and thirty one-man shows.

....

14 This sort of 'art' does not seem technically difficult.

....

15 Long agrees in a sense that almost anyone could do what he does.

....

16 But nobody has previously done this and called it art!

....

17 'For me it's enough to gather the materials together', he is quoted as saying,

....

18 'If I made them into my own shapes it would be too much.'

....

Exercise 76 Adverb pairs

Many adjectives have a corresponding -ly adverb (as in A careful driver drives carefully.) But there are also some pairs that look like this, where the word without -ly can be an adjective or an adverb, so that there are in fact two adverbs, often with different meanings.

All the following words can be adverbs. Complete the exercise, using adverbs from among this list. Do not use any word more than once. Use a dictionary if necessary.

first firstly hard hardly high highly just justly last lastly

near nearly late lately right rightly wrong wrongly

There has been an unfortunate increase in burglaries (1) LATELY which the police – (2) .... or (3) .... – attribute to the carelessness of many householders. So, if you value your property, you should think (4) .... about the problem, and not (5) .... hope for the best.

(6) .... , make sure that all your outside doors have secure locks.

Next, check the windows. (7) .... all casual burglars get in through an insecure door, even a window left open.

So, whenever you go out, lock up. It (8) .... makes sense to invite burglars into your home!

Then, if you're likely to get home (9) ...., leave a light on.

Next, consider some more sophisticated measures. Many householders today have infra-red outside lights – somewhere not too (10) .... on a wall – which go on automatically if someone comes (11) .... Other people think (12) .... of alarm systems, which are also set off by an intruder.

(13) .... don't just think about it. Act now (14) – .... away!

Exercise 77 Adjective and adverb pairs

As well as regular adjective/adverb pairs like *careful/carefully* and sets like *hard* (adj), *hard* (adv), *hardly* (adv),

there are pairs where both have the same form without -*ly* (eg: *fast*), pairs where both adjective and adverb end in -*ly* (*early*, *daily*), and some -*ly* words that are adjectives only (*unfriendly*). Here, to make an adverbial, we have to use a phrase, eg: *in an unfriendly way/manner*.

Write explanations as indicated, using adverbs or adverb phrases. Consult a dictionary if necessary.

Example: If you are a heavy smoker, you smoke heavily.

1 If you are a hard worker, you work ....

2 If you are the last person to hear about some news, you hear it ....

3 If you are the first person to arrive somewhere, you arrive ....

4 If you do something cowardly, you act ....

5 If you are early for an appointment, you arrive ....

6 If you are late, you arrive ....

7 If a plane is very high in the sky, it may be flying too ....

8 If you have a leisurely lunch, you have lunch ....

9 If someone is your near neighbour, they live quite ....

10 A just judge is a judge who acts ....

Exercise 78 Comparison of adjectives [*SGE* 7.39–43]

There are three types of comparison:

Equal:	The rat was *as* big *as* a cat!
(Not equal):	A rat is *not as/so* big *as* a cat.
More:	Cats are bigger than rats.
Superlative:	Augustus is *the* biggest of my cats.
	Augustus is *the* biggest cat *in* the road.
	Notice – X is the ...*est* OF (all the Xs)
	but X is the ...*est* IN (some place).

Complete the following using: (the) highest (in/of), higher (than), (as/so) high (as)

Example: How HIGH is Mount Everest?

For 135 years, from 1852 to 1987, nobody disputed that Mt Everest was (1) ....mountain (2) .... the world. The accepted height was 8,840 metres (29,002 ft), until in 1973 the Chinese announced that it was actually (3) .... at 8,848.2 metres.

There were of course other impressively (4) .... peaks in the Himalayas – for example K2, also known as Chogori, but this was not (5) ...., being a mere 8,611 metres. Everest remained (6) .... all the Himalayan peaks.

Then, in March 1987, the US K2 expedition claimed that K2 was in fact (7) .... had previously been estimated. They said it was possibly (8) .... 8,908 metres, making it, not Everest, (9) ....

However, in August 1987 the Chinese reaffirmed their estimates – of 8,848 metres for Everest and 8,611 metres for K2, maintaining that K2 was not (10) .... Everest. Then in October of the same year, the Research Council in Rome announced new satellite measurements. Everest, the Council said, was actually 15 metres (11) .... the Chinese estimate, at 8,863metres, while poor K2 was less at 8,607.

Everest, it seems, remains (12) .... all mountains.

8 The semantics and grammar of adverbials

Exercise 79 Adverbials: formal realization [*SGE* 8.9]

> An adverbial is one of the five major elements of sentence structure, along with subject, verb, object and complement. [*SGE* 2.3]
>
> An adverbial is often a simple adverb: *everywhere, always, very, just*. But adverbials can also take other forms:
>
> Noun phrase: (We go) *every day*.
> Prepositional phrase: (Come) *into the garden*.
> Verbless clause: *If possible*, …
> Nonfinite clause: *Thinking about it*, ……
> Finite clause: *When I realized*, ……

Pick out the adverbials in the following passage – there are twenty-two altogether – and group them as shown.

There were piles of papers on the stairs and piles everywhere in the room. He kicked a tidy heap with his toe. 'That pile,' he said, 'has been there for ten years. The trouble is I work all the time. There isn't time to sort things. I would get around to buying cupboards if I could be bothered. Somehow life is full of objects that suddenly take over. One week the place is tidy; and the next week it is too late. Now I can't throw things out.'

Hearing his explanation, I just smiled. I have always thought that it is best, whenever possible, not to criticize other people. And there was something very impressive about all that chaos.

single adverbs (12)   everywhere   ……………   ……………   ……………
                      ……………   ……………   ……………   ……………
                      ……………   ……………   ……………   ……………

noun phrases (3)   ……………   one week   ……………

prepositional phrases (4)   on the stairs ……………
                            ……………   ……………

verbless clause (1)   …………… possible

nonfinite clause (1)   ……………

finite clause (1)   ……………

Exercise 80 Adverbials of space and time [SGE 8.2–3, 8.16–26]

Rewrite the following in the most straightforward word order.

1 The prizefight ....
   on 22 April/will be held/in Glasgow/at St Andrew's Sporting Club
   Answer: The prizefight will be held at St Andrew's Sporting Club in Glasgow
   on 22nd April.
2 'I ....
   until Thursday/again/so I can relax and practise a bit/don't play,'
3 said ....
   later/the defending snooker champion/at Sheffield's Crucible Theatre where
   the championships are being held
4 This ....
   for some years/in London/may be the last time an IAAF competition is staged
5 According ....
   in a minor road race/to her coach/Rosa Mota's most impressive performance
   was/last summer
6 She ....
   only two days after a 10 km mini-marathon in New York/10 km/at Boulder,
   Colorado/ran
7 Hull saw Wolves skipper ....
   from near the line/in the closing seconds of the game/Ron Hindmarch clear the
   ball
8 Nottingham Forest ....
   at City Ground/beat Chelsea 7–0/yesterday
9 Golfer Fred Couples of the USA ....
   in Paris/at la Boulie/led the field in the Tournois Perrier de Paris/today
10 The talented young Yugoslav tennis player hit 22 aces.......................
   ....
   last year/on clay/to beat Becker/at the French Open
11 Bjorn Borg won ....
   five times/between 1976 and 1980/the Wimbledon tennis championships
12 After retiring in 1983, he ....
   on 23 April/returned to tennis/1991/in the Monte Carlo Open

Exercise 81 Intensifying and focusing adverbs [SGE 8.32–39]

> Adverbs that do not affect the meaning of the verb or the whole predicate,
> but that have some sort of subordinate or marginal function are sometimes
> called subjuncts. There are various kinds, with various meanings, including:
>
> Emphasizing and intensifying: It was *just/really/simply* wonderful!
>   We *fully/totally/utterly* agree.
> Focusing: I *only/merely/simply* asked.

Many words can be used both as subjuncts and as other adverbs, so the position
in the sentence is important. Compare:

She was wearing a dark blue jumper *exactly like* Laura's.
[subjunct – how *like*?]

It was an odd experience, though it is hard to *describe exactly*.
[manner adverb – *describe* in what way?]

Add the adverbs below in the best places in the sentences to produce the meanings that are indicated in the brackets.

Example:

amazingly: *He manages to dance well with his metal leg.*

(a) (It is a surprising fact that he can dance.)

Answer: Amazingly, he manages to dance well with his metal leg.

(b) (very well indeed).

Answer: He manages to dance amazingly well with his metal leg.

1 *badly*:
   (a) *I need your help.* (very much) ....
   (b) *They organized the meeting.* (not at all well) ....
2 *even: I don't try to understand the rules.*
   (a) (There's no point in trying.) ....
   (b) (You may be surprised that I of all people don't.) ....
3 *just: I sat and waited for ten minutes.*
   (a) (That's all I did.) ....
   (b) (for ten minutes exactly) ....
4 *kindly:*
   (a) *Explain what on earth you had in mind.* (I am cross.).......................
   ....
   (b) *I'll tell you if you speak to me.* (be kind) ....
5 *only: I have come because I think you can help.*
   (a) (I have no other reason for coming.) ....
   (b) (Nobody except you can help.) ....
6 *possibly: The guide told us we could not get to Aseila next day.*
   (a) (I am not sure what the guide told us.) ....
   (b) (He said there was no possibility of our getting there.).......................
   ....
7 *really: I enjoyed it.*
   (a) (very much) ....
   (b) (in fact, I admit) ....
8 *simply: Please try to explain what it is you want.*
   (a) (Don't try to do anything else.) ....
   (b) (Don't use such long words!) ....
9 *still: I don't have permission to use the library.*
   (a) (I am still waiting for permission.) ....
   (b) (My library ticket is out of date.) ....
10 *very much:*
   (a) *He looked like his father except that he was fat.* ....
   ....
   (b) *To tell you the truth I haven't thought about it at all these last few months.*
   ....

Exercise 82 Disjuncts – and other adverbs [*SGE* 8.40–42]

Disjuncts are a special type of adverb that have a sort of superior role to the rest of the sentence. There are two main kinds: either they indicate how the speaker is speaking – *frankly*, *personally* – or they comment on the content – *perhaps*, *certainly*, *foolishly*, *quite rightly*. Again, many of these words can also function as other sorts of adverbs, so position is important to indicate meaning.

Add the adverbs shown, in the best places to give the meanings indicated.

1 *understandably*: She was very upset. (I can understand that).
    SHE WAS UNDERSTANDABLY VERY UPSET *or*
    UNDERSTANDABLY, SHE WAS VERY UPSET.

2 *frankly*: It isn't easy for some people to talk to their friends and families about their problems. (They find it difficult to discuss their feelings.)
    ....

3 *frankly*: I don't know why I sit here drinking with you. (If I say what I think, that's how I feel.)
    ....

4 *truthfully*: He had tried to write a letter that described what it was like here. (He wanted the description to be fair and accurate.)
    ....

5 *truthfully*: It was fairly obvious that he didn't want me any more: and I didn't want him any more either. (I am telling the truth when I say I didn't want him.)
    ....

6 *honestly*: I'll go if you like. I don't mind. (It is really true that I don't mind.)
    ....

7 *honestly*: Dealing with feelings, on the other hand, can help bring the family closer together. (The discussions need to be honest.)
    ....

8 *generally*: Scarcely three centuries have elapsed since it has been accepted that, indeed, the Earth does move. (Before that only a few people took this view.)
    ....

9 *generally*: The poor have been in favour of greater equality. (Well, they usually have!)
    ....

10 *generally*: They felt they had to watch the film before it was shown. (Before it was shown to the public.)
    ....

11 *generally speaking*: A simple answer to the question would be that we do dream in colour. (On the whole we do!)
    ....

12 *literally*: All I had to do was take it out of the box. (I am speaking literally when I say this.)
    ....

13 *literally*: We were really poor so that often by Wednesday we didn't have anything to eat. (I mean that – I am not exaggerating.)

....

14 *literally*: These two chemicals when mixed together explode. (That is a scientific fact.)

....

15 *literally*: She was so excited her eyes danced. (Well not literally really – I am using the word for emphasis.)

....

16 *personally*: He wants to see you. I'll tell him you're here. (He wants to see you himself.)

....

17 *personally*: That girl was murdered. No, I didn't know her. I knew who she was. Didn't I tell you that? (I'd never actually met her myself.)

....

18 *personally*: I think oysters are overrated. (Speaking for myself...)

....

Exercise 83 Conjuncts [*SGE* 8.43–45]

> Conjuncts are a special kind of adverb that connect two parts of a sentence, or even two sentences, by expressing a meaning relationship between them. They are sometimes also called connectors. Examples: *however, moreover, nevertheless*.

Complete the following passage, with these conjuncts and linking words:

    anyhow   but   first   further   hence   however   secondly

    similarly   so   then   though   thus (2)   as a result   by contrast

    for example   in fact   in other words

    on the contrary   on the other hand

For years we have taken the health of the earth for granted. (1) BUT today it is under threat. It is fashionable to blame the industrialized nations, and they certainly are responsible for many environmental problems. Factories, (2) ...., may not only pollute the air we breathe; they often pour poisonous waste into our seas and rivers. (3) .... fish and other marine life may die. (4) ...., the general public in developed 'consumer societies' also cause pollution with their cars, central heating, refrigerators, air travel and vast amounts of household waste.

If we do nothing, we are told, (5) .... the planet will die. (6) .... the rise of the environmental movement, and the 'green' message that if we will only return to the simple life all will be well.

(7) ...., many observers point out that, (8) ...., really simple lifestyles can cause appalling environmental damage. Cutting down trees for firewood, a common practice in much of the Third World, usually loosens the soil,

(9) .... causing soil erosion and ultimately famine. It might be better if they had nuclear power!

(10) .... many people in the developing world want more industrialization and consumerism, which are not going to go away. (11) .... how can we minimize their bad effects?

Enter 'green economics'. Economists are generally viewed as people concerned only with money and industrial growth. Environmentalists, (12) ...., are pictured as rejecting materialistic values. (13) ...., economists are baddies and environmentalists are goodies. The truth, (14) ...., is not so simple. (15) ...., one important part of economics is concerned with the balancing of costs and benefits. Building an airport near a city gives users the benefit of quick travel. (16) .... the noise nuisance for the city's inhabitants may be too high a cost. 'Green economists' try to weigh up the conflicting arguments.

Over the past few years, two ideas have met with some measure of agreement. (17) .... that decentralizing solutions are often better than direct controls. (18) .... it is usually more efficient to control industrial pollution by taxing offending industries rather than insisting on particular equipment. (19) .... economists have come up with the idea of 'sustainable development'. It is not sustainable to use up finite resources such as oil and minerals without replacing them with alternative assets for future generations to enjoy. (20) .... it is not sustainable to allow species of animals or plants to become extinct.

Green economists are not starry-eyed but realistic. It is to be hoped that their views will be heard.

Exercise 84 The Loch Ness Monster: mixed adverbials [SGE Chapter 8]

Complete the following, putting the words indicated in a suitable place.

Example:

Many people state that a prehistoric monster could not exist
today.   possibly

Answer: Many people state that a prehistoric monster could not possibly exist today.

1	To those who have not studied the facts	still
2	the Loch Ness Monster is one of those silly stories beloved by newspapers.	merely
3	Such an attitude is understandable.	entirely
4	It is not suggested that we should accept the existence of an unknown creature	for a moment
5	without considering the evidence,	with great care
6/7	but it is not much to hope	surely/too
8	that people should have open minds?	reasonably
9	There are strange things in the world	after all
10	which we now accept, but which were	once

11	considered very dubious.	indeed
12	News of the famous Scottish monster hit	first
13	the headlines of the world's press,	in 1933
14	although stories about a strange animal	in this remote lake
15	had circulated for many centuries.	locally
16	One of the most widely reported 'sightings' – in December 1933 – turned out to be a hoax.	unfortunately
17	The *Daily Mail* newspaper arranged for a big-game hunter to track 'Nessie', and	down
18/19	he and his photographer found footprints.	within four days/ on the shore
20/21	He gave a talk about it.	even/on the BBC
22	But the footprint had been made with the stuffed foot of a hippopotamus.	sadly
23	This did not stop other monster hunters and numerous sightings have been reported.	over the years
24	Photographs and cine films (of the animals)	allegedly
25	have been produced.	in evidence
26	Divers have descended,	into the lake
27	and boats and a miniature submarine have searched.	with echo- sounding equipment
28	In 1975 new underwater photographs were shown to MPs, scientists and journalists.	in the Houses of Parliament
29/30	A famous naturalist stated that large animals existed.	in the lake/ undoubtedly
31	The British Museum (Natural History) disagreed.	strongly
32	In a book published	in 1991
33	author Stuart Campbell examines all the alleged photographs and 'sightings'.	painstakingly
34	His verdict – a blow for Nessie fans – is that she does not and cannot exist.	sadly

9 Prepositions and prepositional phrases

Exercise 85 Deferred prepositions [SGE 9.2]

> Prepositions usually come before their noun (or pronoun): *after the war,* people *with money,* look *after this,* we talked *about my problems.* But sometimes they are 'deferred', that is, they come after their noun or pronoun:
>
> They are looked *after,* What did you talk *about?*

Complete the sentences below with suitable prepositions.

Example: John is afraid OF *spiders.*

Then practise using prepositions after their complements by asking *what*-questions about John's brother Andrew.

Example: WHAT IS ANDREW AFRAID OF?

1 John is very interested .... all sorts of sport.

  ....

2 He's good ....athletics.

  ....

3 He's keen .... football.

  ....

4 He worries .... his progress.

  ....

5 He had to contend .... a back injury last season.

  ....

6 He is currently suffering .... exhaustion.

  ....

7 He's hoping .... an improvement in his game.

  ....

8 He is fond .... tennis.

  ....

9 He objects .... the commercialization of the game.

  ....

10 But he believes .... sponsorship.

  ....

11 He depends .... help from his family.

  ....

12 He longs .... the day when he can turn professional.

  ....

> **Complex prepositions**
>
> Most prepositions consist of just one word (*at*, *in*, *without*) but there are also complex prepositions consisting of two or more words: *because of*, *in addition to*, *by means of*.

Exercise 86 Two-word prepositions [*SGE* 9.3]

Use the words from the first column (once each) plus a word from the second column to make complex prepositions, and then use them to complete the passage.

according	for
along	
apart	
as	from
because	
contrary	
except	of
instead	
irrespective	to
out	
prior	
thanks	with

Is global warming a serious problem? (Compare exercise 37)

(1) ACCORDING TO a recent report, there may be no need to worry about 'global warming'. (2) .... the popular belief that (3) .... rising temperatures, the polar icecaps are about to melt, flooding vast areas of the world, it is now estimated that (4) .... the west Antarctic ice sheet, the world's ice sheets are safe.

Even if the earth warmed up by 6°C, it would take 10,000 years to melt the Greenland icecap. (5) .... the east Antarctic, that would need temperatures to rise by 20°C before it melted.

Quite (6) .... these estimates, there is another more startling prediction. This is that (7) .... getting warmer, the world may actually be getting cooler. (8) .... to our own century, there was a Little Ice Age, that lasted intermittently from the sixteenth century. The cause was reduced solar radiation – less heat came (9) .... the sun.

Many astronomers – (10) .... other scientists – believe that something similar could happen again. The twenty-first century, (11) .... changes in the sun, may be colder than the twentieth. So, (12) .... where you live, you may soon be needing warmer clothes.

Exercise 87 Three-word prepositions [*SGE* 9.3]

Can you complete these sentences as they were originally written? Use the following three-word prepositions:

> in case of   in spite of   in comparison with   in touch with
>
> by means of   by way of   on behalf of   on account of
>
> for the sake of   in exchange for   in addition to   with reference to

1 IN CASE OF fire, break the glass.
2 Dear Sir, ... your query of 24 September, my daughter will not be accompanying me, as she is currently in her third year at university.
3 It is particularly .... this part of my experience, which I take to be relevant to the work, that I am applying for the position.
4 I should like to point out that .... this experience, I also have the necessary paper qualifications.
5 It hardly seems worth while sacrificing so much that is exciting or amusing .... what is dull, indecisive and boring.
6 The division into older and newer parts is made largely .... clarity, and does not imply actual chronological succession.
7 If .... all your precautions you do have a burst pipe, it is safest to get a plumber in immediately.
8 The disadvantages are really quite small .... the very real advantages.
9 Do not hesitate to get .... us if you have any problems.
10 We aim to inform, educate, publicize, demonstrate and advance the aims of the Association .... exhibitions, lectures, films and meetings.
11 I enclose a copy of my CV .... application.
12 We act .... the above company, which has consulted us on various matters involving you and our client.

Exercise 88 Prepositions mainly of place and time [*SGE* 9.4–11]

Complete the following using suitable prepositions.

Off the Rails

*A $299 rail ticket took Ted Botha (1) .... a six-week tour (2) ....
America*

Doug, (3) .... Goshum, Indiana, could have been a character (4) .... the book (5) .... his side. It was a novel called *Chili Dawgs Don't Bark* (6) .... *Night*. He was a parks and recreation expert (7) .... his way (8) .... a conference (9) .... Phoenix, Arizona.

   He had brought (10) .... him countless brochures (11) .... the places we were going to pass (12) .... We met (13) .... the two days it took the Southwest Chief to go (14) .... Chicago (15) .... Los Angeles.

   Doug only had four days to reach Phoenix, attend the conference and return home, but he loved travelling (16) .... train. My journey was less hurried, more extensive. (17) .... $299 I'd bought one (18) .... Amtrack's tickets that allowed you to spend six weeks criss-crossing the country. You could cover, as I did, 7,721 miles (19) .... leaving the country.

I had begun my journey (20) .... Penn Station (21) .... New York (22) .... a warm day (23) .... September.

We passed places (24) .... Sugar Creek, Missouri, where Jesse James had his headquarters, and Maxwell, New Mexico, named(25) .... Lucien B Maxwell, a famous hunter and trapper.

Most places were indistinguishable (26) .... one another. (27) .... the absence (28) .... much to do, food became important. Hours were determined (29) .... meals. The last call (30) .... breakfast had hardly been made when the first lunch call went up.

In (31) .... meals, there were video showings (32) .... the lounge car. It was strange watching a video (33) .... 65 mph. You never knew whether to watch the story (34) ....screen or the one unfolding (35) ....the window.

(36) .... the time we reached Albuquerque it was mid morning. Gary, a Navajo joined us. He told us (37) .... the Indian reservations, and pointed out a plant which is used (38) .... medicinal purposes, and the snakeweed, used (39) ....an antidote (40) .... snakebite (41) .... sheep.

People got on (42) ....stations (43) .... the middle (44) .... nowhere, (45) .... papers tucked (46) .... their arms. There was a huge T-shirted father (47) .... huge arms who carried his two sons everywhere he went. There was an old lady whose aunt had fallen (48) .... a ladder and ever (49) .... then couldn't remember anyone's name (50) .... her brother's. And then of course there was Doug.

Exercise 89 Prepositional phrases

Rewrite the sentences below by using the right preposition + the word indicated. In some cases you will need to make other changes. If necessary, consult a dictionary.

Example: I realized immediately that something was wrong. (once)
Answer: I realized *at once* that something was wrong.

1 I don't know them to speak to, (though I've seen them). (sight)
2 He never arrives punctually. (time)
3 But on this single occasion he did. (once)
4 Their children seem quite uncontrollable. (hand)
5 What I want more than anything is peace and quiet. (all)
6 I think you are partly right. (point)
7 I didn't mean to break it. (purpose)
8 What are you doing these days? (present)
9 I'm not doing anything special this evening. (particular)
10 I'll be with you very soon. (minute)

11 No way. It just cannot even be considered. (question).
12 We must allow for the fact that he's very old now. (all)
13 Everything is neat and tidy and ready. (order)
14 Incidentally, have you seen Andrew lately? (way)
15 If you go on trying, you'll manage eventually. (end)

Exercise 90 Sayings

Match the meanings (a)–(n) to the incomplete sentences, using them to help you
fill in the gaps with these prepositions. If necessary, consult a dictionary.

at (3)   for   in (3)   like   of (3)   on   out of (2)   over   with   without

1 OUT OF sight, ... mind. [f]
2 It's no use crying .... spilt milk. [......]
3 Marry .... haste; repent .... leisure. [......]
4 The grass is always greener .... the other side .... the fence.
   [......]
5 There's no smoke .... fire. [......]
6 Rome was not built .... a day. [......]
7 There's no time .... the present. [......]
8 The best things .... life are free. [......]
9 Variety is the spice .... life. [......]
10 There's no accounting .... taste. [......]
11 You can't take it .... you. [......]
12 Charity begins .... home. [......]
13 Possession is nine parts .... the law. [......]
14 A cat may look .... a king. [......]

   Meanings:

(a) Great achievements take time and effort.
(b) Our first responsibility is to family and friends.
(c) You should enjoy life while you can, and not be too concerned about
    accumulating money and possession.
(d) Anyone is entitled to criticize people in power.
(e) Now is the best time to do whatever you're planning to do.
(f) Someone (or something) no longer present is soon forgotten.
(g) New and different experiences make life interesting.
(h) There's always some basis in truth for rumour and scandal.
(i) If you marry too quickly, you'll have a long time to regret it.
(j) Other people's likes and dislikes are impossible to explain.
(k) Regretting something that's happened is a waste of time.
(l) Many activities and so on that cost nothing are more worth while than things
    requiring money.
(m) Being in possession of something is a great advantage if you're trying to prove
    ownership.
(n) Some people always think that everyone else is luckier than they are.

‚ Exercise 91 Nouns + prepositions

Certain nouns are almost always followed by the same one or two prepositions. Fill in the gaps here with the right ones. If necessary, consult a dictionary.

The Research Defence Society say that the (1) case FOR using animals in medical research is overwhelming, and that such (2) experiments .... animals make an important (3) contribution .... the relief of suffering.

But there are of course (4) arguments .... such research, and there is fierce (5) opposition .... it from various animal rights groups, who say there is no possible (6) justification .... inflicting pain on animals. They maintain that there must be (7) alternatives .... such methods, and that (8) cures .... human diseases should be sought elsewhere. Their (9) anger .... what they regard as deliberate cruelty and their (10) sympathy .... the animal kingdom is commendable, but in the more extreme activists this is accompanied by an almost total (11) disregard .... their fellow human beings.

There have been numerous (12) attacks .... universities and research laboratories involved, and people thought to have a (13) connection .... the work have been singled out for attacks.

Animal rights campaigners have also targeted fur shops – so succesfully that falling fur sales have had a devastating (14) impact .... communities, such as the seal hunters of northern Canada, whose (15) dependence .... the fur trade was their main source of livelihood.

In so far as animal rights campaigners have raised our (16) awareness .... the moral issues involved in our (17) dealings .... animals, well and good. There should be no (18) quarrel .... that. But there is no (19) excuse .... the violence and the (20) threats .... human life which we have seen. The people responsible must not be allowed any (21) escape .... the (22) consequences .... their actions.

Exercise 92 Putting prepositional phrases in the right place

> Prepositional phrases have various functions in a sentence. Sometimes a prepositional phrase is adverbial:
>
> > He is going to plant a tree *in the front garden*. [This tells us *where* he is going to plant a tree.]
>
> Sometimes it follows a noun phrase, and is rather like a relative clause:
>
> > The tree *in the front garden* is two hundred years old.
>
> So there are sometimes problems if a prepositional phrase gets separated from the word(s) it really belongs to.

Think about the prepositional phrases underlined in the following authentic newspaper reports, and move them or rewrite the sentences – to bring out the probable meanings.

Example: The man accused of the 'bodies in the car' murders confessed to killing his girlfriend and her flat-mate <u>while in prison awaiting trial</u>, the court heard yesterday.

Answer: The man accused of the 'bodies in the car' murders confessed, while in prison awaiting trial, that he had killed his girlfriend and her flat-mate.

Or: While in prison awaiting trial, the man …

[The meaning must be that he confessed, rather than killed, while he was in prison. So the original sentence reads awkwardly.]

1 Since then there have been no reports of the growing tension <u>in the official media</u>, although the new China News Agency quoted the head of Nanking's Hehai university yesterday as calling on foreign students to return to class.

....

....

2 An earlier report that he had seen Terry Waite, the Archbishop of Canterbury's special envoy kidnapped in January 1987, was described as a misunderstanding <u>by Lambeth Palace</u>. [news item, 1990. Lambeth Palace is the Archbishop's London home. Terry Waite was freed in 1991.]

....

....

3 The third [man], a nephew of the Senator, has not made himself available <u>on the advice of his lawyer.</u>

....

....

4 He was forced to abandon his attempt to be the first person to sail the Atlantic both ways <u>on Monday afternoon</u>.

....

....

5 Detectives arrested the girl's father after watching the Pennsylvania flat he had rented <u>for two days</u>.

....

....

6 Advice to backache sufferers: Don't pick up heavy weights like groceries or children <u>with straight legs.</u> [you will have to rewrite this completely]

....

....

10 The simple sentence

Exercise 93 Clause structure [*SGE* 10.1–4]

> There are basically seven types of clause – combining the elements of S(ubject), V(erb), O(bject), C(omplement) and A(dverbial) in various ways.

Identify the sentence types that the following sentences belong to as SV, SVO, SVC, SVA, SVOO, SVOC or SVOA.

1 I felt very tired. SVC [*I* = S; *felt* = V; *very tired* = C.]
2 My feet hurt. ....
3 The receptionist handed me my key. ....
4 I wanted food. ....
5 I placed my coat over a chair. ....
6 I ordered myself something to eat. ....
7 It seemed sensible. ....
8 I lay on the bed. ....
9 A waiter brought coffee and sandwiches. ....
10 He set the tray on a table. ....
11 I was yawning. ....
12 I found the bed rather hard. ....
13 The thick curtains extended to the floor. ....
14 But the hotel was situated on a busy street. ....
15 The traffic noise kept me awake. ....

Exercise 94 Verbs with two objects [*SGE* 10.5]

Rewrite the following SVOO sentences, putting the indirect object after the direct object, and using *to* or *for*.

Example: She bought the children ice creams.
Answer: She bought ice creams for the children.
Example: He wrote his mother a letter.
Answer: He wrote a letter to his mother.

1 Why did you lend that dreadful man money?
  ....
2 He's always sending people begging letters.
  ....
3 He should have written you a proper letter.
  ....
4 Perhaps we could find him a job.
  ....

5 Why should I bother to get him work?

....

6 He has never repaid Tom that loan.

....

7 I hope they've reserved us a table.

....

8 Let me buy you a drink.

....

9 You'd think someone would bring us a menu.

....

10 They usually save me a table by the window.

....

11 Can you pass me the salt?

....

12 I wonder if they could prepare us a special pudding?

....

Exercise 95 SVOO [*SGE* 10.5]

Some verbs actually prefer SVOO word order. Complete the following using *them*
or *me* and one of the phrases from the third column

1 I asked		a lot of money.
2 Would they allow		the full price.
3 But they refused		a discount.
4 saying I'd caused	them	their self-confidence.
5 I pointed out they'd promised	me	a simple question.
6 But they insisted on charging		this reasonable request.
7 I envy		extra time to pay.
8 But it cost		a lot of trouble.

1 I asked THEM A SIMPLE QUESTION.

2 ....

3 ....

4 ....

5 ....

6 ....

7 ....

8 ....

Exercise 96 Subject complements [*SGE* 10.5, 10.7]

Some copular verbs can be followed by both adjective and noun complements.
Rewrite the following, using an adjective in place of the noun complement. Make
all other necessary changes.

Example: I felt a real idiot.

Answer: I felt really idiotic.

1 I felt a real fool.   ....
2 It sounded an excellent idea.   ....
3 But it hasn't proved a particular success.   ....
4 She looked a sensible person.   ....
5 She'll probably end up a rich woman.   ....
6 He's become a thorough bore.   ....
7 The whole thing seems utter madness to me.   ....
8 That's just selfishness.   ....
9 They've remained friends.   ....
10 It's turned out a nice day again.   ....

Exercise 97 Complements [*SGE* 10.7]

Complete the sentences with the adjectives given.

   bad   brown   calm   clear   delicious

   flat   old   open   peculiar   ready   true

Example: Stand CLEAR of the doors.

1 The leaves had turned .... It would soon be winter.
2 I felt I was growing .... too – like the year.
3 I was just getting .... to have my supper,
4 when suddenly the door sprang .... and I heard gunfire.
5 I threw myself to the ground and lay .... on the floor.
6 You have to keep .... in an emergency.
7 The coffee smelled ....
8 But I feared the meat had gone ....
9 It had tasted .... the previous day.
10 At this rate my dreams would never come ....

Exercise 98: Deverbal nouns [*SGE* 10.16 –17]

> Sometimes to give more 'weight' to the end of a sentence, we use a rather general verb with not much meaning + a noun derived from a verb (eg: *have an argument*, instead of just using the verb *argue*).

Rewrite the sentences, replacing the underlined verbs with one of the following verbs + an appropriate noun.

   do   give   have   make   take

Make any other necessary changes.

Example: I sighed with relief.
Answer: I gave a sigh of relief.

1 He rushes around madly underlined(photographing) everywhere.
2 Some of them are very good. underlined(Look!)
3 But one of these days he'll underlined(injure) himself.
4 I'd like to underlined(arrange) for him to see a psychiatrist.

5 He doesn't need you <u>advising</u> him.
6 Perhaps a holiday would <u>be</u> good for him.
7 He <u>lectures</u> me about interfering.
8 I've never <u>harmed</u> anyone.
9 I <u>cried a lot</u> but I still felt miserable. (use *good*)
10 He <u>is not interested</u> in anything else these days.
11 He <u>looks</u> at me in such a funny way.
12 I wish we could <u>talk</u> about it.
13 But he just <u>gets offended.</u>
14 How can one <u>excuse</u> that sort of behaviour?
15 Oh well, it's time we <u>got moving.</u>

Exercise 99 Subject–verb concord [*SGE* 10.19–27]

> Singular subjects grammatically need singular verbs, and plural subjects
> need plural verbs. But sometimes notional concord is used – concord
> according to meaning rather than strict grammar.

Choose the best words in the following.

1 The global total of homes with TV <u>was</u>/were estimated to be over 500 million
   by 1987.
2 But in 1988 the Chinese News Agency said the number of TV viewers in China
   alone was/were 600 million, watching 100 sets.
3 600 million is/are a lot of viewers.
4 The greatest number of episodes of any TV programme ever sold was/were
   1,144 episodes of *Coronation Street.*
5 In 1971 the complete series at that date was/were sold to a Canadian company.
6 *The Winds of War*, about the Second World War, was/were the most expensive
   television production ever.
7 1.6 billion people – or a third of the world's population – are/is said to have
   watched Bob Geldof's original Live Aid concerts.
8 This pop star and fund raiser are/is now world famous.
9 Actually Billy Graham – as well as Bob Geldof – was/were behind these
   concerts.
10 Around one in ten UK households was/were without colour TV in 1988.
11 But more than one in two households in the UK has/have two or more sets.
12 Having two or three sets seem/seems unnecessary to me.
13 25 hours 21 minutes are/is said to be the average UK viewer's weekly 'fix'.
14 A majority of viewers worldwide probably watch/watches news programmes
   regularly.
15 News of disasters reach/reaches a huge audience.
16 What you both see and hear has/have an enormous impact.
17 So many people being killed in earthquakes and cyclones are/is tragic.
18 So-called programmes of entertainment are/is not always entertaining.
19 But apparently the audience for 'sit-coms' and 'soaps' are/is large.

20 Too much sex and violence are/is shown in my opinion.
21 Swearing – and bad language in general – are/is also prevalent.
22 A number of concerned individuals protest/protests.

Exercise 100 Other types of concord [*SGE* 10.28–30]

> The pronoun *they* is frequently used as a 3rd person singular pronoun (*Everybody knows this, don't they?*), though some people consider it wrong or at any rate colloquial.

Complete the following with a suitable word in colloquial style.

At one time everyone with a telephone paid for Directory Enquiries – regardless of how often (1) THEY used the service. Now a British Telecom customer only has to pay when (2) .... actually (3) .... it. And some people do not have to pay at all. Neither a blind person nor a person unable to use the phone books through some disability (4) .... to pay. So if you know someone who (5) .... eligible, tell (6) .... to ask BT about it.

There's another exception. No call to Directory Enquiries from a BT public payphone (7) .... anything at all.

Apart from these free enquiries, each enquiry now (8) .... over 35p.

Usually when I ring home either my father or mother (9) .... But neither of them (10) .... at home yesterday, which surprised me as neither of them (11) .... out very often. Anyway none of the people I tried to phone yesterday (12) .... obtainable.

Exercise 101 Positive and negative tags [*SGE* 10.33–36]

> Tag questions are usually negative after positive statements (*You remember, don't you?*) and positive after negative (*You haven't forgotten, have you?*) They are also positive after statements of negative meaning (*That's scarcely a problem, is it?*)

Add tag questions to these sentences.

1 There could hardly have been a sillier excuse, COULD THERE?
2 Things are seldom quite what they seem, ...
3 You rarely get everything you want in life, ...
4 People should make the best of what they've got, ...
5 You can't live for ever, ...
6 The news is rather depressing, ...
7 There have been some terrible scenes on television, ...
8 It will be difficult to get aid to all these people, ...
9 This is scarcely generous, ...
10 We have to do what we can to help, ...

Exercise 102 Responding to negative questions

Agree or disagree as indicated to the statements suggested by these negative questions. [✔] indicates the questioner's facts are correct; [✗] means they are wrong.

Example: Hasn't Leningrad been renamed St Petersburg? [✔]
Answer: Yes, it has.
Example: Isn't Mont Blanc the highest mountain in the world? [✗]
Answer: No, it isn't. [Mt Everest is.]

1 Weren't Hillary and Tensing the first people to reach the summit? [✔]
....

2 Hasn't Everest now been climbed by women? [✔]
....

3 Can't we descend to the centre of the earth with special equipment? [✗]
....

4 Why? Wouldn't people be able to survive the heat? [✗]
....

5 Haven't all the mountains of the world been climbed now? [✗]
....

6 Isn't Jakarta the capital of Indonesia? [✔]
....

7 Didn't the island of Krakatoa blow up in 1883? [✔]
....

8 Wasn't this the biggest volcanic eruption in history? [✗]
....

9 Doesn't the sun go round the earth? [✗]
....

10 Won't the year 2000 be a leap year? [✔]
....

Exercise 103 Emphasizing negation

> We sometimes emphasize a negative meaning by putting a negative adverbial at the very front of the sentence. This usually requires inversion of the subject and operator if the negative negates the whole clause.

Rewrite the following sentences with the negative or near-negative word or phrase at the front.

Example: I never imagined that anything like that would happen to me.
Answer: NEVER DID I IMAGINE that anything like that would happen to me. (inversion)
Example: I found that, not for the first time, I was wrong.
Answer: NOT FOR THE FIRST TIME, I found that I was wrong. (*no* inversion)

1 I flew to Egypt not long ago.
2 Nowadays people no longer go by sea.
3 I haven't been so impressed since I went to Mexico.
4 You won't find a more amazing building than that pyramid anywhere.

5 Unfortunately I lost my wallet – not for the first time.
6 You little realize sometimes the trouble you can cause other people.
7 I have seldom heard such an extraordinary explanation.
8 You rarely discover the whole truth in these matters.
9 The guide didn't once complain.
10 You hardly ever find such honesty.

Exercise 104 Nonassertive words [*SGE* 10.37]

> English does not usually use two or more negatives in the same clause (*I never said nothing to nobody.*) Instead we use nonassertive forms with one negative – *I never said anything to anybody.*

Disagree with the statements as indicated. Complete your remarks with these nonassertive words or phrases:

any   anyone   any longer   at all   either   ever   far   long   much   yet

plus any other words that are necessary.

Example: Somebody must know something about it.
Answer: I don't think ANYBODY KNOWS ANYTHING ABOUT IT.

1 They'll come some time.
  I don't think...
2 I've been waiting ages.
  Go on! You haven't...
3 The exhibition is probably already over.
  Oh, I doubt if..
4 We ought to wait a few more minutes.
  Oh, don't let's...
5 The weather seems a lot better.
  I don't think...
6 Tom knows a lot about art.
  I don't believe he...
7 And his mother does too.
  No she doesn't...
8 Is it a long way from here to the station?
  No, it's not..
9 This crossword puzzle is quite simple.
  I don't think it..
10 Surely someone must know the answer.
  But I doubt if..

Exercise 105 Scope of negation [*SGE* 10.38–41]

> The 'scope' of a negation usually starts with the negative word itself, so where we put the negative may affect the meaning.

Insert the words indicated in two different ways in each of the following sentences to give the meanings shown, making any other small changes necessary.

1 *I haven't got Andrew's address. (still)*
   (a) (I had it, but I've lost it.)
      I HAVEN'T STILL GOT ANDREW'S ADDRESS
   (b) (I've been waiting ages for it.)
      I STILL HAVEN'T GOT ANDREW'S ADDRESS.

2 *I advised him to complain. (not)*
   (a) (I felt strongly that it was not a good idea to complain.)
   ....
   (b) (I offered no advice.)
   ....

3 *I don't know what's happening. (definitely)*
   (a) (I am totally ignorant.)
   ....
   (b) (I have a sort of rough idea.)
   ....

4 *I don't try to understand these things. (even)*
   (a) (There's no point in trying.)
   ....
   (b) (You might have expected that at least I would.)
   ....

5 *He didn't arrive on time. (once)*
   (a) (Just on one occasion.)
   ....
   (b) (Never.)
   ....

6 *I don't like oysters. (particularly)*
   (a) (But I don't mind them.)
   ....
   (b) (I really dislike them.)
   ....

7 *I don't understand. (really)*
   (a) (It is incomprehensible to me.)
   ....
   (b) (I half do, I suppose.)
   ....

8 *That's not acceptable. (simply)*
   (a) (It is unacceptable. Totally!)
   ....
   (b) (It's more than acceptable – it's very welcome indeed.)
   ....

11 Sentence types and discourse functions

Questions

There are three main types of questions:

1 *yes–no* questions that can be answered with a straight *yes* or *no*: *Are you ready? Haven't you got enough money?*
2 *wh*-questions, beginnning with *what, where,* etc. or *how.*
3 alternative questions – where the questioner suggests alternatives: *Will you have tea or coffee?*

Exercise 106 Negative *yes–no* questions [*SGE* 11.5]

You are rather cross and surprised at the way a friend has behaved. Criticize him and make suggestions, using negative *yes–no* questions.

Example: (*You think*) he ought to apologize.
You say to him: Oughtn't you to apologize?

You think:

1 Surely he got my message.
2 He never considers other people.
3 Surely some of this worries him.
4 He isn't going to say he's sorry!
5 It seems he has no feelings.
6 He could have let me know.
7 Surely his parents will be worried.
8 I would have thought you'd be able to see how they feel.
9 It might be better to go and see them.
10 He should try and explain.
11 It would be a good idea for him to tell his father.
12 Perhaps you (both) can forget this now.

You say to him:

1 ....
2 ....
3 ....
4 ....
5 ....
6 ....
7 ....
8 ....
9 ....
10 ....
11 ....
12 ....

Exercise 107 Tag questions [*SGE* 11.6]

Complete the following with a suitable tag question.

Example: Please send us a postcard, ...?
Answer: Please send us a postcard, won't you?

1 You'd better lock the car, ... ?
2 And do remember to shut the windows, ...?
3 And you'd better not leave the radio in the car, ...?
4 You wouldn't want it stolen, ...?

5 And don't forget to put on the brakes, ... ?
6 Oh, stop treating me like an idiot, ... ?
7 I'm just checking everything, ... ?
8 Come on, let's go, ...?
9 And let's not quarrel, ...?
10 There's nothing more to be said, ... ?

Exercise 108 *Wh*-questions [*SGE* 11.9–10]

You want to know more about sport. Use a *wh*-word (including *how*) and the words given to ask questions as indicated. The answers to the questions are given in brackets.

Example: first Olympic Games/held. (At Olympia in ancient Greece).
You ask: WHEN WERE THE FIRST OLYMPIC GAMES HELD?

1 first Olympic Games/modern times/inaugurated. (on 6 April 1896)
   ....

2 other events besides running/constitute athletics. (relays, walking, field events and multiple events like the decathlon)
   ....

3 field events/include. (the high jump, the long jump, discus throwing – things like that)
   ....

4 the word decathlon/mean. (a contest in which each competitor takes part in 10 events)
   ....

5 often/Olympic Games/now held. (every four years)
   ....

6 country/host/1988 Olympic Games. (South Korea)
   ....

7 become/youngest ever player to win/men's singles championship/Wimbledon. (Boris Becker – in 1985)
   ....

8 old/the time. (He was 17 years, 227 days)
   ....

9 people/manage/finish the London Marathon/1990. (nearly 25,000)
   ....

10 older – cricket or football. (possibly football – there are conflicting claims)
   ....

11 motor racing win at Asheville, North Carolina, USA/1988/set record (Shawn Robinson's)
   ....

12 this achievement/special. (because she was the first woman to win this sort of event)
   ....

Exercise 109 *Wh*-questions ending with a preposition [*SGE* 11.10]

Practise asking *wh*-questions that end with a preposition.

Example: I don't know what you mean; ...... on earth are you talking ......
You say: WHAT ON EARTH ARE YOU TALKING ABOUT?

1 I can't afford a bicycle.   .... can I borrow one .... ?
2 I can't talk about this to my father, so .... can I discuss it ....?
3 UN means the United Nations, I know, but .... do the letters WHO stand ....?
4 I don't understand what you're trying to say; .... are you getting ....?
5 Something is making you unhappy.   .... are you worrying ....?
6 Everything is going wrong; .... have I got to look forward ....?
7 I met someone yesterday – someone you know!   .... do you think I bumped ....?
8 Do you think there's a family resemblance?   .... of his parents do you think he takes ....?
9 I've got far too many jumpers.   .... shall I get rid .... ?
10 You look as though you're expecting someone.   .... are you waiting ....?

Exercise 110 Exclamations [*SGE* 11.20]

You are in an exclamatory mood! So turn your thoughts into exclamations, using *How* or *What*. Where possible also make an exclamatory remark in the form of a negative question.

Example: (You think) This restaurant is unusual.
You say: WHAT AN UNUSUAL restaurant!
               or ISN'T THIS RESTAURANT unusual?

1 You think: The food is delicious.
    You say: .... food!
    .... delicious?
2 But the service is slow.
    .... service!
    .... slow?
3 The waiters are good-looking.
    .... waiters!
    .... good-looking?
4 (Your friend) eats quickly.
    .... eat!
    .... quickly?
5 The vegetables are expensive.
    .... vegetables!
    .... expensive?
6 They charge a lot.
    .... charge!
    .... a lot?

7 Everything is very fresh.

.... is!

.... fresh?

8 I just love food.

....

9 I really dislike dieting.

....

10 I wish I could come here more often.

....

Exercise 111 Irregular sentences; block language [*SGE* 11.21–22]

Explain the following newspaper headings by turning them into regular sentences. (There are several possible answers.)

Example: Birthday Party Murder

Answer: There was a murder at a birthday party. (i.e. Someone was murdered at a birthday party.)

1 Gangland Feud Fear By Police

....

2 Air Bomb Hoaxer Jailed For 30 Years

....

3 Surprise Pay Award For Colony Police

....

4 Bank loan man's 'secret plan'

....

5 Six die in crash

....

6 Cash Machine Ripped from Wall

....

7 Heathrow to have 5th Terminal

....

8 Six In Court After City Street Battle

....

9 Body Washed Up

....

10 Clothes Swap Inmate Flees

....

11 Train stabbing

....

12 Missing Couple Safe

....

13 30 on top of world in day

....

14 High-tech spy guards bridge

....

15 No N-weapons On Navy Ships

....

12 Pro-forms and ellipsis

There are two grammatical devices to help us avoid boring and unnecessary repetition:

pro-forms: pronouns and other words (eg: *there, then, do so*) that refer back

ellipsis: leaving out words that appear elsewhere (usually earlier) in the same context

Exercise 112 Pro-forms [*SGE* 12.1–13]

Write out in full what the underlined words refer to.

Example: Study the underlined words and say what they stand for.
Answer: the underlined words

Please read the instructions carefully. When you have read (1) them fill in the form, and have (2) it ready for collection. If you have children, (3) each should be listed separately. Your answers will be treated in strict confidence and (4) none will be disclosed to other people.

Some of the questions seem harmless, but (5) some are surely unnecessary. Better questions, but (6) fewer would have been an improvement. Questions 13 and 14 are complicated. (7) Neither is easy to answer. (8) And many are badly worded, so many people will find them difficult to answer. As for the two parts of question 11, (9) both are open to interpretation.

And what about the question that makes a woman have to state whether (10) she is single, married or remarried or whatever? Well, a man has to answer (11) that one too. But I wonder what they are going to do with this information. (12) It could all be misused.

Answers:
1 .... 2 ....
3 .... 4 ....
5 .... 6 ....
7 .... 8 ....
9 .... 10 ....
11 .... 12 ....

Exercise 113 *one, ones, that, those* [*SGE* 12.4–5]

Complete the following using *one, ones, that* or *those*.

Examples:
The house has been preserved as ONE of architectural value.
  [i.e. *a* house]

The Minister stressed the need to consider Britain's performance against THAT of the country's competitors.
  [i.e. *the* performance]

1 We've got a new pedestrian crossing; it's .... where you press a button.
2 The cities of Europe are much older than .... of America and Australia.
3 The problems are .... of considerable difficulty.
4 We are grateful, but the life of a refugee is .... of misery.
5 The position of refugees is far worse than .... of immigrants.
6 Is your new job .... with prospects.
7 I prefer the sound of a guitar to .... of a violin.
8 People who write gossip and .... who read it are equally to blame.
9 Many problems are .... of style rather than meaning.
10 Our lives then were easier than .... of young people today.
11 The message of the book and .... of the broadcast was depressing.
12 The public is fascinated by famous people's doings, particularly .... of the Prince and Princess.

Exercise 114 *one, ones* [*SGE* 12.5]

Rewrite the following sentences to show clearly what *one/ones* means in each case.

Example: We haven't got a textbook: I ought to write *one*.
Answer: I ought to write a textbook.
Example: I'm not *one* to complain, but I wish you'd be more careful.
Answer: I'm not the sort of person to complain ...
Example: The competitors were on the line. The starter said, '*One*, two, three, go!
       And away they went – all except *one*, who presumably did not hear.
Answer: The starter said 'One, two, three, go!' And away they went – all except one competitor ...

1 These little statues are part of a set. Some carry weapons, others musical instruments. One has a chair across his shoulders.
2 Daddy came to Canterbury with me last Saturday to buy me a new dress for last night. It was hopeless. I never saw one I could even tolerate.
3 He used to give talks to students on various topics. One began: 'How far can you count? One? two? three? infinity?
4 We went to Hannah's party. I thought I wasn't going to enjoy it at first, but I met some other 'young ones'.
5 I think probably what Captain Kay said was – provided it is witnessed, a will is legal even if it's on the back of an envelope. Did he say he'd personally witnessed one?
6 Houston stared at him, licking his lips. He said, 'He's not ill, or injured or anything?' 'Oh no. On the contrary. He's staying to look after the ones who are.'
7 The whole family were cricketers. One was in a Test team for England.

8 Out of about every five that start off doing general medicine and general surgery only one gets to being a consultant.
9 She was an extraordinarily able woman and never one for half measures.
10 We picked up my visa, forged another one and got some food for the journey.
(*Survey of English Usage*)

Exercise 115 *it, them, one, ones, some*

Find the sentences (a)–(f) that follow sentences 1–6, and complete them using *it, them, one, ones, some*.

1 Can anybody lend me some money?
Answer: I need SOME.   (d)

2 My CD player's broken.   (....)
3 Have you heard these two new discs?   (....)
4 Have you got a personal computer?   (....)
5 And a camera? Have you a camera?   (....)
6 Mine's very good.   (....)

(a) Oh I was looking at ...... the other day. What do you think of ...... that take instant pictures?
(b) I don't know what's the matter with ...... I think I'll buy a new ......
(c) Well I'm thinking of getting .... for home use. But I don't know which ...... would be best.
(d) I need ......
(e) I'll show you ...... Borrow ...... if you like before you buy .... with built-in flash are useful.
(f) No, I'd like to hear ......

Exercise 116 *do, do so* [SGE 12.6–8]

Choose the best option.

1 Please renew your subscription if you (a) haven't already done (b) haven't already done it (c) HAVEN'T ALREADY DONE SO.
2 The secretary thinks we need to attract younger members, and the committee (a) does too (b) does it too (c) does that too.
3 If we manage (a) to (b) to do (c) to do it,   we shall be in a much better position financially.
4 My brother belongs to two tennis clubs and (a) has (b) has done it (c) has done that   for many years.
5 He plays tennis like a professional, but I'll never (a) do (b) do it (c) do that.
6 He's just taken up golf and I'm thinking of (a) doing (b) doing it (c) doing so   too.
7 Take up golf? Nothing would make me (a) do (b) do it (c) do so.
8 Unfortunately I don't see very well without glasses. Well I (a) don't (b) don't do it (c) do that   either.
9 I suppose I could wear contact lenses. Yes, why (a) don't you? (b) don't you do? (c) don't you do it?

10 Joining a club is fun, and you'll find after (a) doing (b) doing it (c) doing so   that you make lots of new friends.

11 I joined this club five years ago, and (a) having (b) having done (c) having done so   I know that it was a good decision.

12 I've just lost my tennis racquet. Oh dear. How did you (a) do (b) do so (c) do that?

Exercise 117 *it, so, that* [*SGE* 12.6–13]

Complete the following, using *it*, *so* or *that*

Example: They're giving tickets away.
Answer: Who told you THAT?

1 'Fares are going up again next week.' 'Where did you hear ....?'
2 Is that really true?' 'I'm afraid .... '
3 If we don't buy our tickets now we'll regret ....
4 'Could I buy now, and pay later?' 'I doubt ....'
5 'Some air fares will be double!' 'How do you know ....?'
6 You won't believe .... , but they are going to abolish economy class.
7 'And there are going to be no more special offers.' 'How do you know ....?'
8 'Are train fares going up too?' 'I believe ....'
9 'We shall have to get used to higher prices.' 'I suppose ....'

Exercise 118 *so, even so, not, nor* [*SGE* 12.9–13]

Rewrite the following using phrases or clauses with *so*, *even so*, *not* or *nor* to replace the words underlined.

Example: You've forgotten your bag. Oh goodness, yes I have dropped it.
Answer: Oh, so I have.

1 Is the weather ever going to get warmer?
   Oh, I think it's going to get warmer. ....

2 You don't think it's going to snow?
   Well, I hope it doesn't snow. ....

3 I think the winters are getting colder.
   It seems that they are getting colder. ....

4 I waited hours for Tom last Saturday, and he didn't turn up.
   That's what I heard. ....

5 I know it's difficult to find a callbox, but all the same he should have tried to let us know. ....

6 Didn't he try to send a message?
   It appears that he did not try. ....

7 I would always send a message.
   Yes, I would too. ....

8 I don't like being kept waiting.
   I don't either. ....

9 You can't expect the young to feel the same as we do.
   Maybe we cannot expect them to feel as we do, but still it's annoying.
   ....

10 You have to make allowances for them.
  <u>That's what</u> people say.   ....

11 They see things differently.
  Well, perhaps <u>they do</u>.   ....

12 But I don't actually think <u>they do</u>.   ....

13 Perhaps you and I could go together next week, but if <u>we cannot go together</u>,
  what about the following week?   ....

14 Look, it's snowing.
  Oh <u>goodness</u>, it is!   ....

Exercise 119 Ellipsis [*SGE* 12.14–23]

Rewrite the following, leaving out everything you can.

Example: Could you, if you wanted to manage with less sleep, manage with less
  sleep?

Answer: Could you, if you wanted to, manage with less sleep?

Of course a baby's need for sleep is greater than an adult's need for sleep. That's
different.

  But the effects for an adult of too much sleep are not dissimilar to the effects of
too little sleep – tiredness, irritability and so on. Most healthy adults sleep between
six and a half hours a night and eight and a half hours a night. Less than 5 per cent
of healthy adults sleep more than nine and a half hours or less than five and a half
hours. But some celebrated short sleepers can manage with a mere five hours'
sleep. How do they manage with a mere five hours?

  Studies indicate that most of us could cut down on our sleep, though we cannot
perhaps cut down to five hours, if we practised cutting down on our sleep. A team
of experimental 'sleep slimmers' gradually reduced their sleep by two hours, and
research suggests that short sleepers improve the quality of their sleep.

  Short sleep, it is claimed, is the best sleep you can have, and of course if you are
not in bed when other people are in bed, think of all the things you could do.

Exercise 120 Ellipsis [*SGE* 12.14–22]

Rewrite the following, filling in all the words that have been ellipted.

Example: 'What sort of job is it?' 'I don't know.'

Answer: I don't know WHAT SORT OF JOB IT IS.

1 I meant to bring the letter and of course I forgot to.
  ....

2 How's John's job going?
  Oh, perfectly well, I gather.
  ....

3 Oh, by the way, Mary, we finally spent your book token today.
  Oh, have you?
  ....

4 Incidentally, you know about Malcolm dislocating his shoulder?
 Well, anyway, he's been back from the Lake District about a week and he can
 now drive again.
 I didn't realize he'd been.
 ....

5 They're the sort of books that you tend to pick up and look at in odd moments,
 you know, so don't sort of just stay on the shelf doing nothing.
 ....

6 I can't pronounce it.
 Oh, right! I see! No, I won't try, either.
 ....

7 'We were together when we saw these.' 'No we weren't.' 'Oh, yes, we were
 together this morning.'
 ....

8 Are you a bit interested, David?
 Well, about to the same extent as Jo, I'd say.
 ....

Exercise 121 Faulty ellipsis [*SGE* 12.14–23]

Here are some authentic newspaper items where the ellipsis or substitution is
faulty. Rewrite them correctly. There are clues to help.

Example: Tonight's stories show that children are still exposed to poverty,
malnutrition, poor education and health care. (taken from the TV page of a Sunday
newspaper 1.10.90)
 Clue: Is the health care all right?
Rewrite: Tonight's stories show that children are still exposed to poverty,
malnutrition, poor education and poor health care.
Or ...... to poverty, malnutrition, and poor education and health care. [The
sentence as written suggested that it is bad for children to be exposed to
health care – which is presumably not what was meant.]

1 [A past president of the club] took me aside and said that, although the remark
 was made, it was quite awful to see it in print. The offending words were thus
 deleted from the final draft [of the club annual report], but perhaps, bearing in
 mind present behaviour, we were wrong to do so. (*The Sunday Telegraph*
 28.4.91)
 Clue: What did the president and committee do wrong?
 ....
 ....

2 If you're retired (or just about to) you know full well that peace of mind only
 comes from having the confidence and security of a high regular income and
 capital growth.
 Clue: You are about to what?
 ....
 ....

3 So the latest idea is red routes, which will certainly fail if they are not efficiently enforced and work better than double yellow lines and other No Parking restrictions have done. (*The Sunday Telegraph* 11.11.90)

   Clue: Red routes, like yellow lines, are all part of a scheme to control traffic in towns and cities. What is the big 'if'?

   ....

   ....

4 A shooting campaign is under way to wipe out Tasmanian masked owls introduced in the 1920s to eradicate the rats, but instead developed a taste for the Lord Howe island woodhen, one of the world's rarest birds, found only on the island. (*The Daily Telegraph* 27.7.89)

   Clue: Who or what started eating the rare woodhens?

   ....

   ....

5 The decision sets a precedent which will encourage owners to protect their listed buildings against decay, or risk much larger bills if a property must be rescued by compulsory emergency action later. (*The Daily Telegraph* 23.5.91)

   Clue: A listed building is a building of historic importance (and put on an official 'list'). Is this new decision going to encourage risk?

   ....

   ....

13 Coordination

Exercise 122 Coordinators and subordinators [*SGE* 13.1–13]

When a main clause and a subordinate clause are joined, it is sometimes possible for either clause to come first:

When you are ready, you can begin.
You can begin when you are ready.

But clause coordinators (eg: *and*, *or*, *but*) must come at the beginning of the second clause.

Rewrite those sentences in which the clauses can be reversed with no other changes. For example (1) cannot be rewritten as the result is unacceptable: *And they do so consciously, people everywhere make gestures.* (Ignore the fact that rewriting may upset the flow of the context.)

1 People everywhere make gestures and they do so consciously.
2 People may wave to others to attract attention, or they may point at something to call attention to it.
3 So signalling is universal, but individual signals mean different things in different cultures.
4 We need to be aware of these differences, so that we don't offend people.
5 A signal may be perfectly friendly in one culture, yet the same signal may be rude in another.
6 Unconscious gestures can be even more revealing, for we do not censor our unconscious body language.
7 We are often unaware that we are gesturing, so that we don't realize that we are sending out signals.
8 A famous murderer, Dr Crippen, was brought to justice, because his girlfriend, Ethel le Neve unconsciously betrayed herself with her body language.
9 Crippen had killed his wife and was sailing to America with le Neve, when the captain of the ship realized who they were.
10 Ethel le Neve had feminine body language, although she was disguised as a man.
11 She always crossed her legs, whenever she sat down.
12 The captain was convinced that the couple were Crippen and le Neve.
13 The captain telegraphed the authorities, so the police were waiting for the ship's arrival in New York.
14 It was the first time that radio-telegraphy was used to catch a murderer. (Crippen was executed in 1910.)

Exercise 123 Coordination and subordination [*SGE* 13.3–13]

> When two coordinated clauses have the same subject, the second can be omitted:
>
> Some people are fascinated by crime and [they] read a lot of crime novels.
>
> But when one of the clauses is subordinate, this cannot happen:
>
> They read a lot of crime novels because they are fascinated by crime. [not* *because are fascinated by crime*]

Omit the subjects in the following wherever possible.

Example: Some people look forward to retirement, and [they] are glad when they no longer have to work and [they] can find time to pursue other interests.

1 They enjoy their work, yet they will be glad to give up.
2 Other people recognize that they will have to retire, but they fear boredom once they no longer have a job.
3 Others again look forward to retiring, but when they do they find they long for the companionship and they miss the stimulus they had at work.
4 If people stop work and they have no mental stimulation or they feel they are of no use to society they may rapidly decline physically.
5 Most retired people will be physically fitter if they stimulate their brains and they will be mentally fitter if they take some physical exercise.
6 Some people of course take plenty of exercise; they walk, they play golf, they work in their gardens.
7 Other older people want more mental pursuits, so they go to classes of one sort or another.
8 They learn to handle computers or they study some area of music or art they have never explored before and they suddenly find out all sorts of things.
9 Sometimes a group of people start their own class because they discover a shared interest and they cannot find an existing class.
10 A new skill acquired at the age of sixty plus is perhaps not particularly likely to lead to a new career, although it could.
11 A sixty-year-old grandmother recently won a prize when she published her first novel.
12 She had not had time to write before while she brought up a family and she pursued a career.

Exercise 124 Correlatives [*SGE* 13.14–16]

Join the following pairs of sentences using *either ... or*; *neither ... nor* or *both ... and*. Make any other small changes necessary.

Example: The blue whale is the largest mammal in the world.
    The blue whale is the heaviest mammal in the world.
Answer: The blue whale is both the largest and the heaviest mammal in the world.

1 We must protect the world's wildlife. If we don't, some species of animal will

die out.

....

2 The panda is in danger of extinction. The black rhino is in danger of extinction, too.

....

3 Some species have been nearly wiped out by man for food. Other species have been nearly wiped out for sport.

....

4 I personally do not like snakes. I personally do not like bats. But I don't want to see them disappear.

....

5 Many people do not understand what the problem is. Many people do not appreciate what the problem is.

....

6 People admire tigers as beautiful animals. People fear tigers as man-eaters.

....

7 Rhinoceroses are not the most valuable animals in the world – in cash terms. Tigers are not the most valuable animals in the world – in cash terms! (Racehorses are!)

....

8 Elephants are found in Africa. Elephants are found in Asia.

....

9 The African elephant is not the largest mammal in the world. The African elephant is not the heaviest animal in the world.

....

10 Some species spend most of their time eating. When they are not eating they are sleeping.

....

Exercise 125 Simple coordination [*SGE* 13.17–26]

Ellipt as much as possible – as shown in the first sentence.

If someone asked me what to see in Australia and [if they asked me] how to get there, I'd say: Explore the Outback in your own vehicle, and [explore it] slowly.

Driving through the Outback in an ancient Land-Rover enabled us to enjoy the changing scenery, and enabled us to appreciate the desert's changing moods. I do not think that I have ever felt so close to nature or that I have ever felt in a sense so carefree. Occasionally, when the desert's silence fell upon us we would consider our isolation and we would consider our vulnerability; we would gaze in wonder at the vast empty plain, and we would watch the birds of prey circling overhead.

The road itself was narrow but the road was smooth. So the driving was easy except when we had to pull aside for one of the 'road-trains' – huge linked lorries which stir up great clouds of red dust and which are definitely lacking in road manners!

The other hazard of driving in the Outback is the wildlife, resilient to the extreme environment, but not resilient to the motor car. At dusk unsuspecting kangaroos, cows and buffalo would wander on to the road, attracted by the glare of car headlamps. It was curiosity which would often lead the kangaroo to its untimely end, and would often lead the car to the nearest garage.

With rusting cars lying abandoned at the roadside, and with dead animals lying abandoned at the roadside, you experience moments of anxiety. So when you finally reach Ayers Rock, when you finally reach the largest monolith in the world – you get a wonderful sense of achievement.

But this is not the end. You start photographing it from every angle, you start gazing at it in wonder, and you start touching it, or you start walking round it. Finally, you climb it.

Exercise 126 [*SGE* 13.22–23]

> Noun phrases linked by *and* may express two rather different meanings: *John and Mary have won a prize* may mean *They have won a prize between them* (together) or *They have both won a prize* (a prize each – separately).

Rewrite the sentences where *and* has, or could have, this second, separate, meaning by using *both ...and* or *neither...nor*.

Example: John and Mary have won a prize.
Answer: Both John and Mary have won a prize.

1 John and Mary are two young people.
   ....

2 John and Mary don't look after themselves properly.
   ....

3 John and Mary have always liked one another.
   ....

4 In fact, John and Mary are on very good terms.
   ....

5 In some ways John and Mary are very much alike.
   ....

6 John and Mary are thoughtful and caring.
   ....

7 John and Mary do not like going around alone.
   ....

8 John and Mary go almost everywhere together.
   ....

9 John and Mary did not share the first prize.
   ....

10 John and Mary did not go in for the competition!
   ....

11 John and Mary are not yet thirty.
   ....

12 John and Mary are not the same age, though.
   ....

13 John and Mary are mutually supportive.

....

14 John and Mary often help each other.

....

15 John and Mary are good friends of mine.

....

Exercise 127 Complex coordination [*SGE* 13.27–29]

> When we coordinate clauses we normally avoid too much repetition by omitting words that can be grammatically understood (ellipsis).

The following sentences are all acceptable sentences. But can you insert the words that have been omitted?

1 Most people would like, but don't know how, to read faster.
   Most people would like [TO READ FASTER], but don't know how, to read faster.

2 They are wasting, and not efficiently using, their time.

3 Some people imagine that to improve their reading skills they must train their eyes to make 'good movements' and their lips to make no movements.

4 Slow reading should not however be attributed to wrong eye movements, nor efficient reading to good ones.

5 Slow readers are using, or at least many of them are using, habits more suitable to young children.

6 There is some evidence that mouthing the words with your lips can, and that pointing at the words with a finger does, slow the reading process.

7 It is important, by the way, to realize that efficient reading is not exactly the same as, and must not be confused with, quick reading.

8 Sometimes we read to get a general outline, but sometimes to find specific information.

9 Quick skimming may be more suitable for some kinds of materials and more careful reading for others.

10 Reading 170–200 words a minute is generally considered slow, and 550–700 exceptionally fast – except for skimming-reading.

11 There are several skills that once acquired will help most people to improve dramatically, and everyone to improve a bit.

Exercise 128 Quasi-coordination [*SGE* 13.32]

> Usually when the subject of a sentence is two coordinated nouns or pronouns, the verb must be plural. But there are also phrases that look like coordination but are not really: with this 'quasi-coordination', the verb must be singular if the real subject is a singular noun phrase. For example:
>
> Adam, along with Andrew, was involved.

Choose the best answer.

Example: The nature of intelligence – as much as some other human attributes –
   (a) are (b) is   not entirely understood.

Answer: (b) is

1 It seems that nature, in addition to 'nurture', (a) affect (b) affects   what a
   person is like.
2 In other words, what your parents and grandparents are like, as well as your
   upbringing, (a) has (b) have   an effect upon you.
3 As well as (a) study (b) studying   twins brought up together, pychologists
   have studied identical twins separated in childhood.
4 Results show that identical twins, in addition to (a) look (b) looking   alike,
   have very similar intelligence, whatever their upbringing.
5 This, with another very different study, (a) do (b) does   seem to show that
   intelligence is not just a matter of education.
6 Unrelated children brought up together in a children's home, with an identical
   environment, (a) show (b) shows   different levels of intelligence.
7 All this suggests – rather than entirely (a) proves (b) prove (c) proving – that
   heredity, ancestry, is important.
8 Perhaps for this reason, intelligence testing, along with other forms of testing,
   (a) are (b) is   challenged by some teachers.
9 They say an IQ test is unreliable and unfairly labels children, rather than (a)
   help (b) helps (c) helping them.
10 Sometimes a headteacher, or most of the staff, (a) refuse (b) refuses   to use
   such tests.
11 Intelligence tests certainly raise as well as (a) solve (b) solving   problems.
12 Perhaps they should be used with caution, rather than (a) abandon (b)
   abandoned (c) abandoning   altogether.

14 The complex sentence

Exercise 129 Matrix clauses [*SGE* 14.1–2]

A complex sentence contains at least one matrix clause (called the main clause by some grammarians) and at least one subordinate clause. For example:

You will understand/when you do the exercise.
    [matrix]   [subordinate]

All you need/is practice.
[subordinate] [matrix]

Underline the matrix clauses in the following. Omit all subordinate clauses however they are functioning.

Example: <u>I'll lend you some money</u> if you don't have any money on you.

1 New traffic lights have been developed because the existing ones are difficult to see in strong sunlight and sometimes appear to be 'on' when actually they are in the 'off' position.
2 The flat-lensed signals that are used for green filter arrows can be 'washed out' when reflected light obscures the signal, so they can appear white.
3 It is claimed that the new signals overcome these problems and that they can contribute to road safety.
4 The new signals will look similar at a distance, but close up the driver will notice a pattern of holes.
5 When the new light is off, it will look a lot blacker.
6 The main change is in the lens, which in the new lights consists of small 'lenslets' that channel the reflector's light through 2000 holes in a mask.
7 The lenslets make the best use of available light and form an intense light beam that can be seen from a distance and a more diffuse beam that can be seen at wider angles closer to the signal.

Nonfinite and verbless clauses

As well as finite subordinate clauses, that is, clauses with a finite verb, there are also:

Nonfinite clauses: *Carrying my luggage*, I headed for Customs.
                            Met by friends, I felt safe and happy.
Verbless clauses: *With my luggage in the car*, I relaxed.

Exercise 130 Nonfinite and verbless clauses [*SGE* 14.3–6]

Rewrite the following, using nonfinite or verbless clauses. Use the words indicated, and keep the meaning as close to the original as possible.

Example: When you arrive at Customs, you will find you have a choice.
Answer: On ARRIVING AT CUSTOMS, YOU WILL fiND YOU HAVE A CHOICE.

1 If you have nothing to declare, you may follow the green signs.
With ....

2 If you think that might mean you'd be doing something illegal, you should go through the red channel.
Rather than ....

3 Provided that all is well, you will not have to pay any duty.
All ....

4 Some people of course are carrying dutiable goods, but don't realize it.
....without ....

5 But it is best if people declare anything they are uncertain about.
It is best for ....

6 If they go through the red channel, they stay on the right side of the law.
By ....

7 Some people go through the 'Nothing to Declare' channel although they know they are wrong to do so.
Despite ....

8 The Customs officers are looking for drugs. And they are also looking for smuggled pets.
Besides ....

9 Smuggling pets is a serious offence, because there is a danger of rabies.
Because of ....

10 People who are caught trying to smuggle anything illegal face heavy fines and even imprisonment.
If ....

11 Unless they are prepared to risk this, they should stay within the law.
If not ....

12 If you are asked to take something through Customs for someone else, you should always refuse.
If ....

Exercise 131 Nonfinite and verbless clauses [*SGE* 14.3–6]

Rewrite the following using verbless or nonfinite clauses wherever this is possible.

Example answer: Rewrite the following using verbless or nonfinite clauses *wherever possible*.

1 Whether it is sensible or not, many people carry a lot of money on them.
2 Though this is understandable, it is risky.
3 Wherever it is at all possible, you should pay by cheque or with 'plastic'.
4 Particularly when you are on holiday, you need to take care of your money.
5 If they are obtainable in your country, money belts are a good idea.

6 You'll feel safer if your money and passport is in a money belt. [Use *with*]
7 While you are on holiday, you should eat sensibly.
8 When you are in a climate you are not used to, try to dress sensibly.
9 Whenever it is possible, learn at least a few words of the language.
10 Do not point your camera at people as if you are about to photograph them.
11 Never wave your arms around as though you are about to hit somebody.
12 Although you may sometimes be understandably annoyed, never, never shout!

Exercise 132 Nonfinite and verbless clauses [*SGE* 14.3–6]

Rewrite the following, using nonfinite or verbless clauses in place of the italicized finite clauses, and making any other small changes necessary.

Example: *As we village people had no regular newspapers and of course no radio or TV*, we were the inheritors of an oral tradition.

Answer: Having no regular newspapers and of course no radio or TV, we village people were the inheritors of an oral tradition.

1 *If they were given a book*, my grandparents were likely to turn it over in their hands, cough loudly, and lay it aside.
....

2 My mother however *had learnt to read*, and she would read to us on winter evenings from her 'Penny Readers'.
....

3 *When I was lent my first book by a rich old neighbour*, I thought she was off her head.
....

4 Then one day the old lady *stopped me in the street*, and asked me how I was enjoying the book.
....

5 *I had not even thought of reading it*: I had used it as a tunnel for my clockwork train.
....

6 *If I had been told that one day I would be a writer*, it would have astonished me.
To ....

7 *While I was still at the village school* I read several famous English 'classics', which I had bought at a jumble sale.
....

8 Then *when I reached the age of 12* I was sent to the school in the town.
....

9 Here *I was made to read novels by Sir Walter Scott*, and have managed to avoid him since.
....

10 But *I was not put off reading*, and developed a passion for out-of-school reading.
....

11 Then one day, *as I walked through the town*, I discovered the free public library.
....

12 *Because I didn't know what to choose*, I started with the books near the door.

....

Exercise 133 Subordinate clauses of future time [*SGE* 14.11]

> Subordinate clauses referring to the future, especially clauses of time
> (*when ...*) and condition (*if...*), usually use a present tense, because the verb
> in the main clause is sufficient to indicate the future meaning.

Join the pairs of sentences together, using the words given and making any other
small changes necessary.

1 I'm going to be sixty soon. I'm going to retire. (when)
   I'M GOING TO RETIRE WHEN I'M SIXTY.

2 I'm going to retire. I shall go round the world. (as soon as)

....

3 I shall let my house. I shall be away. (while)

....

4 Perhaps I shall live to be a hundred. There won't be time to do everything I want
   to do. (even if)

....

5 I can hardly wait. I'm going to be sixty. (until)

....

6 I will keep my health. I hope. (that)

....

7 I shall go round the world. But it could be too late. (unless)

....

8 You should retire yourself. Or you could be too old. (before)

....

9 Our health could fail. Then what would we do? (suppose)

....

10 What will be happening in ten years' time? I do wonder about this. (–)

....

Exercise 134 Subjunctive [*SGE* 14.13, also 3.23]

> There are three kinds of subjunctive:
> - mandative subjunctive [see note at exercise 22]
> - *were*-subjunctive [used formally in hypothetical conditions:
>   *If I were you ... If Churchill were alive today, he would ...*]
> - formulaic subjunctive [found in a few fixed expressions:
>   *Come the summer* = when the summer comes;
>   *truth be told* = if the truth is told]

Rewrite the following, changing the verbs that are in the subjunctive mood into the indicative mood, with or without *should*, and making any other changes that are necessary. All except the first two are from newspapers.

1   Glodstone said nothing. If his aunt chose to draw such crude conclusions it was far better that she do so than suspect the *true* nature of his enterprise. (Tom Sharpe: *Vintage Stuff*)
Answer: ... it was far better that she should do so than that she should suspect ...

2   A minute later, a frail hand touched my arm. The bus conductress was asking that I take her seat. (Colin Thubron: *Behind the Wall*)
....

3   The Prince's predicament is common to all those, be they princes or peasants, who find themselves educated beyond their station in life.
....

4   This is my idea of what a pretty female robot should look like; some sort of feminist-radical group had signed petitions demanding that it not be shown.
....

5   It remains one of my favourite restaurants, with its hard-seated chairs and rough red wine. This is the Cote d'Azur I knew and loved. Still do, truth be known.
....

6   He ordered that Potohar Plateau, then used for military exercises, be transformed into a new federal capital.
....

7   I am full of admiration for his courage, but I would much rather he were safely on dry land and the search and rescue forces not engaged in looking for him.
....

8   Come Christmas, she will have even more opportunity for concentration.
....

9   Be it never forgotten though, that oil is a commodity with some special characteristics.
....

10   The show judges insisted that a broadcast of her music be turned off because it was upsetting the animals.
....

11   Next morning a senior aide to Mr Hart telephoned the executive editor of the *Washington Post* ... and asked that the woman's name not be published.
....

12   The boy will not be returning to school after the headmaster asked his parents that he 'not be allowed to come back'.
....

Exercise 135 Putative *should* [*SGE* 14.14]

A verb phrase with *should* is sometimes used in a *that*-clause when we are commenting emotionally on a situation that we think exists or perhaps commenting rather personally about plans. For example:

I am sorry *that you should be upset*. [I think you are upset.]
They've arranged *that I should join them later*. [that is their plan]

Rewrite the following with *should*, wherever possible.

1 I understand that you do not intend to accept the job.

....

2 Everyone regrets that you have made this decision.

....

3 What I don't understand is why you are embarrassed.

....

4 It is only natural for you to have considered the pros and cons.

....

5 I am most anxious that this won't affect your future career.

....

6 It is possible of course some people will blame you.

....

7 But it will be a scandal if they do so.

....

8 I am certainly glad you felt able to come to the decision you did.

....

9 It is definitely preferable that people make up their own minds.

....

10 It is a shame some of the committee are so difficult.

....

Exercise 136 Mixed tenses [*SGE* 14.11–16, also Chapter 4]

Complete the following using suitable tenses. Use the passive mood where necessary.

Example: The first flight around the two Poles (make) in 1971, when Captain Elgen M Long (cover) 62,597 km (38,896 miles) in 215 flying hours.

Answer: The first flight WAS MADE in 1971, when Captain Elgen M Long COVERED 62,597 km ...

1 Man (dream) .... of flying since the world (begin)
....

2 Leonardo da Vinci (1452–1519) designed a flying machine but (die)
.... before he (achieve) .... his ambition of
seeing his dream become reality.

3 The first controlled power-driven flight (occur)........................ when
Orville Wright (fly) .... for about 12 seconds at a height of 8–
12 feet in 1903.

4 No one (fly) .... the English Channel when Louis Bleriot (fly)
   .... from France to England in 1909.
5 When Alcock and Brown (fly) .... the Atlantic non-stop in
   1919 they (be)........................ the first to do so.
6 The American, Captain Lindbergh (become) .... the first man
   to fly the Atlantic solo when he (fly) .... from America to
   France in 1927.
7 By that date seventy others (fly) .... the Atlantic since Alcock
   and Brown (make) .... their record flight.
8 After these pioneers (lead) .... the way, many many records
   (break) .... in the years that followed.
9 When the Second World War (break out) ...., jet-engined
   flight already (occur) ....
10 The first supersonic flight (achieve) .... in 1947 over an
   airforce base in the USA when Charles Elwood Yeager (fly) ....
   in a rocket plane at 1,078 km/h (670 mph).
11 The supersonic *Concorde* first (fly) .... – by a test pilot – on
   2 March 1969 and regularly (use) .... on passenger services
   since January 1976.
12 It (fly) .... on passenger services for over 14 years when it
   (set) .... a New York to London record of 2 hours 54 minutes
   in April 1990. It normally (cruise) .... at 1,450 mph (2,533
   km/h).

Exercise 137 Direct and indirect speech [*SGE* 14.17–21]

The following examples of direct speech are taken (with added details of who is
speaking) from *Difficulties with Girls* by Kingsley Amis. Change these into
indirect speech.

Example: Jenny: A very funny chap came to the door just as I was leaving.
Answer: Jenny said a very funny chap came/had come to the door just as she was
   leaving.

1 Patrick: Did he mention a wife?
   J: No. No, nothing about that, I'd have remembered. Nor a girl-friend.
   P: Oh... Did he give his name?
   J: Yes, but I forgot straight away, although I remember thinking it couldn't be
       right. Anyway, he said he'd be back.
2 P (to J): Unless you feel like another of those [i.e. a drink] I suggest we move.
   With Saturday shopping there may be a bit of traffic and I want to be there
   on the dot.
3 JLR Sebastian: So you're nothing to do with books, or anything like that? May
   I ask what you are to do with, Mrs Standish?
   J: I teach in a hospital, so I suppose I am a bit to do with books.
   JLRS: Oh, how splendid. Tell me, what's your, what's your field?
   J: I haven't really got one, I just go in in the mornings in the week, and teach
       the long-stay children, some of the younger ones. I used to teach in a
       proper –

4 J: Sorry. I'm just popping round to the hospital. One of the little girls had a
            minor op yesterday … so I thought I'd look in for a few minutes, going for
            a breath of air really.
    P: Fine – do you want me to come with you?
    J: No, I'll be there and back in a second.

Exercise 138 Indirect into direct speech [*SGE* 14.17–21]

Turn the following into direct speech – the words probably said. There may be
several ways of doing this.

1   He said he'd like to ask me a few things if I didn't mind
    I'D LIKE TO ASK YOU A FEW THINGS IF YOU DON'T MIND.
2   [The barman] asked Jenny if she had come to live round there… and told her that
    [his wife] was out shopping at the moment but would be only too delighted to
    give her the benefit of her local knowledge any time, but meanwhile the dry
    cleaners in the block had tried to get away with losing his topcoat for him last
    winter.
    ....
    ....
3   She no longer went round saying to herself he was the best-looking man she had
    ever met.
    ....
4   Francis thought to himself that if they were just going to stay there all the
    evening talking he would get very hungry.
    ....
5   Tom begged us not to tell anybody, explaining that he did not want his
    neighbours to find out. We promised him we would say nothing to anyone, but
    we did advise him that it might be better to apologize. And I offered to help him
    write a letter. However he refused, suggesting rather rudely that I should mind
    my own business.
    ....
    ....
    (Kingsley Amis: *Difficulties with Girls*)

Exercise 139 Free indirect speech and free direct speech
[*SGE* 14.22]

Sometimes people report what somebody has said in a way that mixes indirect and
direct speech.

Write out what people actually said or thought.

1   He introduced me to his friend who asked me with a speculative eye where I came
    from. A country called England, I said. Oh yes, he said, England; would that
    country not be near Kabul? (Peter Levi: *The Light Garden of the Angel King*)
    The friend: ....
    Levi: ....
    The friend: ....

2 Shall I go after them? he asked … Nina advised against. Perhaps it wasn't opening time yet. It would be best if they waited for Olga. (Beryl Bainbridge: *Winter Garden*)

He: ....

Nina: ....

3 My waiter alone is splendidly unperturbed. Would Sir like his coat checked, a drink, a menu, perhaps the wine list? (*The Daily Telegraph* 5.2.88)

The waiter: ....

4 When Alan Stripp was in his first year at Trinity College, Cambridge he was invited to an interview. The questions asked of him were unusual: did he play chess, could he read music and how good was he at crosswords?

The interviewer: ....

5 He knocked aside protesting travellers in his eagerness to get to the bookstall. Did they have a copy of *The Faerie Queene* by Sir Edmund Spenser? No, they did not. Not even the Penguin edition? Not in any edition. Did they realize that *The Faerie Queene* was one of the jewels in the crown of English poetry? There was not much call for poetry at Heathrow. Sir could, if sir wished, try the other bookstalls in the airport, but his chances of success were slim. (David Lodge: *Small World*)

He: ....

Bookstall assistant: ....

He: ....

Bookstall assistant: ....

6 He called me one day and said would I come up to see him because he had an idea. He was writing a show … and he wanted me to appear in it. 'Was I prepared to leave Paris?' he wanted to know. (*The Sunday Telegraph* 2.6.91)

He: ....

7 Has he ever been in danger? 'Not so far.' In his travels what has he learned? Lewis answers in his measured voice. 'I'm gradually coming to the conclusion that the Ancient Britons lived a more satisfactory life than we do' … 'Does this depress him?' The sun comes out and his attention is drawn to a bank of extremely rare fritillaria [flowers]. 'I can't say that it does actually.' (from an interview with writer Norman Lewis, *The Sunday Telegraph* 2.6.91)

Interviewer: ....

Lewis: ....

Interviewer: ....

Lewis: ....

Interviewer: ....

Lewis: ....

8 The two detectives remained, and so did the two policemen. They were exceptionally nice to her, and Jack Noonan asked if she wouldn't rather go somewhere else, to her sister's house perhaps, or to his own wife who would take care of her and put her up for the night.

No, she said. She didn't feel she could move even a yard at the moment. Would they mind awfully if she stayed just where she was until she felt better? She didn't feel too good at the moment, she really didn't.

Then hadn't she better lie down on the bed? Jack Noonan asked.
No, she said, she'd like to stay right where she was, in this chair. A little later perhaps, when she felt better, she would move. (Roald Dahl: *Lamb to the Slaughter*)

Noonan: ....

Woman: ....

Noonan: ....

Woman: ....

Exercise 140 Transferred negation [*SGE* 14.23]

> We sometimes transfer a negative from a subordinate clause where semantically it belongs to the matrix clause. Thus we may say *I don't think it will rain* instead of *I think it won't rain*.

Give negative answers to the following sentences. Use transferred negation wherever possible.

Example: Did he appear to understand what you were saying?
Answer: No, he didn't appear to.

1 Did you expect that he would be surprised?
   ....

2 Did you hope he would change his mind?
   ....

3 Did he seem to be listening?
   ....

4 Do the two of you believe he is stupid?
   No, we ....

5 Do you suppose he has other plans?
   ....

6 Do you consider he should complain?
   ....

7 Do you imagine his parents can help?
   ....

8 Would you have thought it was possible?
   ....

9 Does it look as though he will succeed?
   ....

10 Do you feel there's any point in going on?
   ....

15 Syntactic and semantic functions of subordinate clauses

Subordinate clauses can be finite and nonfinite, and can have various functions:

nominal	like a noun or noun phrase (as subject, object, complement or in apposition)
adverbial	like an adverb
relative	relating to a noun or noun phrase
comparative	after a comparative phrase (eg: *more*, *-er*, *as*)

(Students are advised to read Chapter 15 of *SGE* carefully before attempting exercises 141 and 142.)

Exercise 141 Functions of subordinate clauses [*SGE* 15.2]

Study the subordinate clauses in the following (underlined for you) and decide whether their function is nominal, adverbial, relative or comparative. With a nominal clause, decide whether it is functioning as subject, object, in apposition or complement.

1 Where I go is my business.
   Answer: nominal (subject)

2 I don't want to tell anyone where I go. ....
3 Otherwise everyone will go where I go. ....
4 The place where I go is quiet and unfashionable. ....
5 Some people say that I hide from the world. ....
6 Why shouldn't I have some secrets that I hide from the world?
   ....
7 Actually the idea, that I hide from the world, is absurd. ....
8 I don't mind admitting a desire for solitude. ....
9 A hotel offering peace and quiet is my idea of bliss. ....
10 I usually go away when there's not much work to do. ....
11 I don't really know when would be the best time. ....
12 I am wondering if you'll be in town. ....
13 If you're in town, do ring me. ....
14 I go away as often as possible. ....
15 But I don't go away as often as my sister. ....
16 You never seem to relax enough to enjoy yourself. ....
17 The main thing is to enjoy yourself. ....
18 Don't you ever go away just to enjoy yourself? ....

Exercise 142 Finite nominal clauses [*SGE* 15.3–12]

Identify the *finite* nominal clauses in the following sentences and state their functions – subject (including extraposed subject), direct object, subject complement, appositive, complement of adjective, complement of preposition. Ignore other clauses.

Example: *Born Free*, Joy Adamson's story of Elsa the lioness, shows how truth is sometimes stranger than fiction.

Answer: *how truth is sometimes stranger than fiction* – direct object (of *shows*)

1 It was reported to George that this animal [a man-eating lion], accompanied by two lionesses, was living in some nearby hills.

2 This was why we were camping far to the north of Isiolo among the Boran tribesmen.

3 Suddenly I heard the vibrations of a car; this could only mean that George was returning much earlier than expected.

4 George, who was most distressed, told me what had happened. [He and another game-warden had killed one of the lionesses in self-defence, and then discovered her three cubs.]

5 He blamed himself for not having recognized earlier that her behaviour showed that she was defending her litter. (two finite nominal clauses here)

6 Whatever trick I tried to make them swallow diluted unsweetened milk only resulted in their pulling up their tiny noses and protesting.

7 The average number of cubs in a litter is four, of which one usually dies soon after birth and another is often too weak to be reared. It is for this reason that one usually sees only two cubs with a lioness.

8 [Even in their second year cubs are unable to kill on their own and] have to rely for their food on what may be left over from a kill by the full-grown lions of the pride.

9 [The Adamsons appointed Nuru, their garden boy, as 'lion-keeper in chief'.] The post pleased him for it raised his social status; it also meant that when the cubs got tired of romping ... and preferred to sleep under some shady bush, he was able to sit near them for long hours, watching to see that no snakes or baboons molested them. (two finite nominal clauses)

10 Soon they showed us that they only required three-hourly feeds.

11 [The Adamsons already had a small wild animal, Pati, (a rock hyrax) as a pet, and this little animal played with the growing cubs] I was very touched that she [Pati] should continue to love the little rascals even though they diverted our visitors' attention from herself.

12 [Elsa was the weakest of the cubs and could not get her share of meat when the Adamsons started them on solid food, so Mrs Adamson] used to take her on to my lap for meals. She loved this; rolling her head from side to side and closing her eyes, she showed how happy she was.

13 It was hard to accept the fact that we could not keep for ever three fast-growing lions.

14　Regretfully we decided that two must go and that it would be better that the two big ones, who were always together and less dependent on us than Elsa, should be the ones to leave. (three clauses)

15　As to Elsa we felt that if she had only ourselves as friends she would be easy to train.

Exercise 143 Subordinate questions [*SGE* 15.4–5]

Join the following pairs of sentences into one sentence each, making any minor changes that seem necessary. Remember that subordinate questions follow normal word order (without inversion of subject and auxiliary).

Example: What first impelled prehistoric man to travel? We do not know.
Answer: We do not know what first impelled prehistoric man to travel.

1　Was it the need for food or perhaps some natural disaster? We do not know.

2　What, in historical times, inspired men to risk their lives in search of the unknown? Perhaps it is easier to understand this.

3　Was it trade or the desire for land or for gold – or perhaps a mixture of motives? Do we understand?

4　Why do some people even today undertake difficult and dangerous journeys? Who can explain?

5　Are they seeking adventure? Or a challenge? Is it perhaps the case?

6　What are the emotions of space travellers as they gaze down on the earth? Can we who have never travelled in space imagine this?

7　When did Christopher Columbus 'discover' America? Doesn't everybody know?

8　Could he have been mistaken in thinking he had reached India. Columbus did not ask himself this.

9　Where did he actually make landfall? Do you know?

10　Was it what we now call the Bahamas? Do you think that?

11　Which is the remotest place in the world today? Can you say?

12　Who first sailed round the world? Tell me.

13　How long did Magellan's fleet take on the voyage? Do you remember?

14　Where was Magellan killed? I can't remember.

15　Who made the second circumnavigation of the world? Well, do you know that?

Exercise 144 *if* and *whether* [*SGE* 15.5]

Complete the following with *if* or *whether*. State where both are possible.

Example: Have you ever wondered WHETHER/IF left-handedness is simply a disadvantage in a right-handed world, or WHETHER/IF it is an actual defect?

1　Well, some 'experts' have recently claimed it is a physical defect, though they do not know .... to attribute it to mothers who drink during pregnancy or to mothers who smoke!

2　Left-handers probably don't know .... to laugh at this theory or .... to get angry.

3　These wretched experts don't seem to have wondered ....left-handedness could in fact be neither a disadvantage or a defect – simply a difference.

4　Actually .... or not left-handedness is felt as a disadvantage depends very much on the individual.

5　.............. the experts think that Leonardo da Vinci, Jacob Einstein, George Bush or Prince Charles are defective is not clear.

6　.............. they even know that many famous people have been left-handed seems doubtful.

7　And they don't seem to have considered .... or not left-handedness could even be an advantage in some sports.

8　They could have asked Navratilova or McEnroe – or their opponents – .... it is a disadvantage or not in tennis.

9　Surely it can be positively useful for some people – .... difficult for others.

10　But anyhow, ... an advantage or a disadvantage, why worry !

Exercise 145 *to*-infinitive or *-ing* clause? [*SGE* 15.9–10]

Complete the following using a *to*-infinitive or an *-ing* form.

Example: It is no good merely (talk) about (preserve) the world's wildlife. You've got *(do)* something.

Answer: It is no good merely TALKING about PRESERVING the world's wildlife. You've got TO DO something.

(1 talk) .... won't save anything. But (2 act) .... is (3 cause) .... things to happen, and though the objectives of the wildlife lobby – (4 save) .... endangered species – is admirable, there have been some unforeseen and not totally welcome results.

In fact one surprising result has been (5 endanger) .... the human species – at least to the extent that there is now a greater risk of (6 be) .... attacked, if not killed, by wildlife.

A law was passed a few years ago (7 protect) .... seals off America's west coast. Naturally the result of not (8 cull) .... the seal populations was more seals (9 swim) .... around inshore. So far so good. But though to us seals are beautiful wild creatures, to sharks they are food. (10 provide) .... more food for sharks naturally results in more sharks. And it is no use (11 expect) .... a shark (12 distinguish) .... between a seal and a human swimmer. Result – several swimmers killed and a lot more savagely attacked. Of course you could say (13 swim) .... is an unnecessary pastime. But (14 swim). .... or not swimming isn't the only question.

On the other side of the world, in India, (15 kill) .... tigers has been stopped. Quite right, you say. For that noble animal (16 become) .... extinct would be a world disgrace. But you might feel differently if you were an Indian farmer living near the jungle's edge – and your crops, your animals, even your family were in constant danger. The intention of the regulations – (17 preserve) .... the tiger – is admirable. But part of the outcome

– (18 endanger) .... members of the human species – makes us realize that few issues in this world are simple.

Exercise 146 *to*-infinitive clauses [*SGE* 15.9, 15.14–27]

> *To*-infinitive clauses can have various nominal and adverbial functions and meanings, and can even follow a noun in a noun phrase (*a book to read*).

Rewrite the following using *to*-infinitive clauses where possible. Use the structure *for X to* ... [*SGE* 15.9] if it is important to mention the subject of the infinitive clause.

Example: *When people say* that tourism is a major threat to the environment, this is no exaggeration.

Answer: To say that tourism is a major threat to the environment is no exaggeration.

1 Nobody nowadays can hope *they can visit* a famous 'sight' without being part of a huge crowd.
2 It is a rare pleasure indeed *if you find* a deserted beach.
3 And *when you see* the enormous crowds wandering around Venice, you wonder how that great city has not already sunk into the sea.
4 It would be foolish *if any of us imagined* that we can stop people wanting to travel.
5 If we do nothing about this, there will soon be nothing left *that we can preserve*.
6 But we urgently need measures *that will protect* both historic buildings and the countryside.
7 One possible solution is *that governments should set up new bureaucracies* with armies of officials ...
8 ... *who could direct* visitors to 'suitable' sights.
9 Another possibility, *that we should rely on the price mechanism*, would probably be simpler.
10 People will just have to pay more *if they want to see* the more popular tourist attractions.
11 Already some English cathedrals charge tourists admission – *so that they can repair* some of the damage caused by trampling feet and wet breath.
12 Serious tourists would not be the only ones *who would benefit* from smaller crowds.
13 The local people who live in or near these places would be happier *if they were not overrun*.
14 If we do not act soon, we shall wake up one day *and find it is too late*.

Exercise 147 Adverbial clauses of time [*SGE* 15.14]

Join the sentences together, using the conjunctions shown, and making any other changes necessary.

Example: I was reading. We reached Peterborough. (until)
Answer: I was reading until we reached Peterborough.

 1 I was on my way to Edinburgh by train recently. I had an odd experience. (while)
 2 I reached Paddington station. My train was leaving. (just as)
 3 I had to wait half an hour. The next train left. (before)
 4 I walked all along the train. I found a seat at the front. (until)
 5 I put my case on the rack. I settled down to read my book. (once)
 6 The train stopped at Peterborough. A young man got in. (when)
 7 He sat down next to me. He began a conversation. (as soon as)
 8 I couldn't go on reading. This young man had decided to talk. (after)
 9 It was all right! I had given up trying to read. (once)
10 He too had caught the 'wrong' train. He had missed the earlier one like me. (after)
11 He had spent two years as an engineering student in York. Then he had decided to change courses. (before)
12 I told him I only knew one person in York. It turned out that he knew her. (when)
13 We reached York. We were deep in conversation. (while)
14 The train stopped. He jumped out. (the moment)
15 Alas, he left the train. He had not told me his name. (before – careful!)

Condition [*SGE* 15.17–20]

Conditions are of two major types:

OPEN (neutral) conditions. We do not know whether the condition and the outcome are true or will happen, but we feel they are possible:

> If Colin is at the meeting tomorrow, I'll tell him.

HYPOTHETICAL conditions suggest that the condition will not happen, or is not true now, or did not happen:

> If he came tomorrow, I'd be surprised.
> If he were here now …
> If only he had telephoned yesterday.

A third type, RHETORICAL conditions, look grammatically like open conditions, but are actually strongly assertive:

> If I win, I'll eat my hat. (I am sure I won't win.)

Another minor type of condition is INDIRECT condition, where the matrix clause does not actually follow as a consequence of the condition:

> I think that's a mistake, if you don't mind my saying so.

Exercise 148 Conditional clauses [*SGE* 15.17–20]

Identify the conditional clauses and decide whether they are open, hypothetical or rhetorical. Also mark any that are indirect.

Example: I'd keep quiet *if I were you*. (hypothetical)

 1 If this is justice, I am a banana. (Ian Hislop)

2 If Aristotle were alive today, he'd have a chat show. (Timothy Leary)
3 You can lose a lot of work if people think you're dead.
4 If anything can go wrong, it will.
5 If you don't like the heat, keep out of the kitchen.
6 If you ask me, that's absurd.
7 I wouldn't have asked if I didn't want to know.
8 If there is one thing a successful man should know, it is when to stop.
9 Clearly money has something to do with life. In fact, they've a lot in common if you enquire. (Philip Larkin)
10 I wouldn't have asked if I hadn't wanted to know.

Exercise 149 Hypothetical conditions [*SGE* 15.19]

Write the following as single conditional sentences.

Example: The temples at Aswan were moved. So they were not flooded when the dam was built.

Answer: If the temples at Aswan had not been moved, they would have been flooded when the dam was built.

(Use *might* rather than *would*, where this makes better sense.)

1 People are curious about the past. So archaeology exists.
2 The ancient Egyptians believed in an after-life. So they built elaborate tombs.
3 They were clever at star observations, and the Great Pyramid of Giza is accurately lined up – with north, south, east and west sides.
4 There was no coinage when the pyramids were built. So the workmen were paid with food.
5 Because the Egyptians put objects in the tombs, we know a lot about ancient Egypt.
6 The pyramids were plundered in ancient times, so later explorers did not find great quantities of treasure.
7 The first European visitors did not make detailed notes because they were not archaeologists.
8 The sands buried some treasures. Part of a wooden boat was safely excavated in 1954.
9 The Valley of the Kings, further south, was also partly protected by sand. So Tutankhamun's tomb was not discovered until 1922.
10 Tutankhamun's tomb was not found by the grave robbers, and the wonderful treasures are now in the Cairo Museum.
11 Archaeologists work carefully and painstakingly. They continue to teach us about the past.

Exercise 150 Conditionals with inversion [*SGE* 15.19]

Rewrite the following with inversion of subject and (auxiliary) verb. Your answers will begin with: *had*, *should* or *were*.

Example: If I told him, he'd probably laugh.
Answer: Were I to tell him, he'd probably laugh.

1 If you see an unidentified flying object, let me know.

....

2 If I were to see one, I should certainly inform you.

....

3 And if by any chance I met an alien astronaut, I'd inform the newspapers too.

....

4 If you were not so sceptical, you might learn.

....

5 If you had been with me last night, you would have seen the UFOs.

....

6 If you hadn't told me, I would never have believed it.

....

7 Many sightings would prove to be hoaxes, if we investigated them.

....

8 If I hadn't examined the photograph myself, I would have thought it was a fake.

....

Exercise 151 Concession [*SGE* 15.21–23]

Rewrite the following, using the conjunctions given and making any necessary changes.

Example: I don't approve of telling lies. But telling the truth can be painful. (while)
Answer: While I don't approve of telling lies, telling the truth can be painful.

1 Employers naturally want to recruit the right people, but some of their methods do seem doubtful. (although)
2 They need to find out about us, yet do they have to ask such personal questions? (though)
3 I don't mind filling in a questionnaire, but I object to some types of question. (while)
4 Some personal information may be necessary. Even so, I don't want to give it. (even if)
5 I very much wanted the last job I applied for. However, I refused to complete the questionnaire. (much as)
6 The questions may have been relevant. But they struck me as unpleasant. (as [see 15.21 note])
7 The consequences could have been anything for me. I still wasn't going to reveal my private life. (whatever)
8 So my application was a waste of time. But I did get practice at dealing with awkward questions. (except that)
9 I really disliked the questionnaire. Nevertheless, I enjoyed the interview. (even though)
10 Perhaps I'll make up the answers next time. But don't tell anyone! (only)

Exercise 152 Reason, purpose and result [*SGE* 15.26–28]

Rewrite the following, using the words given and making all other necessary changes.

Example: Some people make themselves run because they want to live to a ripe old age.

.... so that ....

Answer: Some people make themselves run so that they will live to a ripe old age.

1 Convinced that exercise is good for you, doctors are urging everyone to take more exercise.
Because ....

2 A lot of men in particular die of heart disease, so they ought to be warned.
Such a lot ....

3 Many people eat too much fat and damage their hearts.
.... because ....

4 Some doctors set such a bad example that people do not listen to them.
.... so that ....

5 We are always being told to change our habits, with the result that some people don't listen.
Since ....

6 Some marathon runners experience real pain because they train very hard.
.... so .... that ....

7 Some runners are obsessive, and consequently they injure themselves.
.... so .... that ....

8 Other people take no exercise and become really unfit.
As ....

9 Since such people often also overeat, they put on weight.
.... so ....

10 Some people really dislike exercise, and therefore make excuses.
Because ....

11 Some people say they lead very busy lives, and so don't have time.
.... that they ....

12 Some older people take up running because they want to strengthen their bones.
.... in order to ....

13 Violent exercise can damage muscles, so serious runners plan their diet carefully.
.... for ....

14 You might have a 'heart condition', so have a check-up with your doctor.
.... in case ....

15 Choose your running shoes carefully; otherwise you may damage your feet.
.... so as ....

16 You don't have to run if you want to keep fit – cycling or swimming will do.
.... in order to ....

Exercise 153 Subjects in nonfinite and verbless clauses
[*SGE* 15.34–35]

When a nonfinite or verbless clause has no subject of its own, grammatically we understand that it is the same as the subject of the matrix clause. This is called the attachment rule, but it does not have to apply in all cases.

Some of the following genuine quotations break the attachment rule. Rewrite them where this matters – in order to bring out the probable meaning.

Example: Living in Plymouth, a visit to a West End theatre is an annual trip to which my husband and I always look forward.

Answer: As we live in Plymouth, a visit … etc.

1 Once sold, you're unlikely to see such fine quality real leather boots offered at just £16.95 ever again. (advertisement)
2 Given the circumstances, there seems no point in complaining.
3 As an active supporter of the arts in Britain, I thought you would be interested to know of a service that offers you the chance to provide financial help for the arts – absolutely free. (circular letter)
4 Waiting around to sign books the other day, a bright-faced ten-year-old made a welcome appearance. (author John Mortimer)
5 The play needs to be presented with more sense of style. That having been said, there are some good performances.
6 Open for lunch and dinner, booking is advised at this comfortable and modish but very reasonable restaurant.
7 Asked much later on, what he was really up to, a wide silent smile divided his face, accompanied by an oddly youthful blush.
8 Considering she's ninety, my grandmother is amazingly active.
9 One of the wealthiest men in the world, his foreign investments are estimated at over $100 billion.
10 Once inside, the house exudes a feeling of security.
11 Up to eight inches of snow fell in large parts of the Swiss Alps, ending more than two weeks of dry and balmy weather.
12 The restaurant was full when suddenly came a terrible explosion throwing us to the ground.

Exercise 154 Comparative clauses [*SGE* 15.36–42]

Use the facts given to complete the sentences suitably.

Example: The country with the highest rate of emigration is Mexico.

Answer: Proportionately… MORE …people emigrate from Mexico… THAN… from any other country.

1 The Vatican City, the smallest independent country in the world, covers 44 hectares, compared with Monaco's 191.4 ha. Nauru, in the western Pacific (2,129 ha) is the smallest republic in the world.
    Monaco is ………………… the Vatican City, but ………………… as Nauru. Nauru ………………… any other republic in the world.
2 The most densely populated territory in the world is Macao, on the southern coast of China (over 28,000 people per km^2.) This compares with Hong Kong (5,497 per km^2). Of large countries, the most densely populated is Bangladesh (783 per km^2).
    Many people assume that Hong Kong is ……………………… any other territory in the world, but actually it is …………………… than Macao. Bangladesh of course is ……………………… as either.

3 The country with the biggest population is China. But the United Nations estimate that by the year 2050 India's population will be 1,590 million and China's a mere 1,554 million!

India's current population is .... as China's; but the UN forecast that by the year AD 2050 it .... China's.

4 In 1985 Tokyo-Yokohama was the biggest city in the world. But Mexico City is expected to overtake it by the year 2000.

Mexico City was not .... Tokyo in 1985, but by the end of the century it could be .... any other city in the world.

5 The world population is increasing at the rate of 98 million a year. The lowest rate of natural increase of any independent country was recorded in West Germany (in 1986). In Kenya the rate is twice the world average.

Natural population increase was .... in West Germany .... in any other country in 1986. In Kenya the population has been increasing more than twice .... the world average.

6 In 1981 there were estimated to be 1,006.7 males in the world for every 1,000 females. But in 1985 the USSR had 1,132.1 females to every 1,000 males.

According to estimates there are not .... females in the world .... males, although in some countries) there may be .... than men.

7 World expectation of life at birth is rising from an average of 47.4 years (in 1950–55) towards 64.5 (1995–2000). The highest expectation of life is in Japan (81.9 years for women and 75.8 for men in 1988). The lowest is in parts of Africa for men (39.4) and for women in Afghanistan (42).

Throughout most of the world people can expect to live .... their parents did. No other country's expectation of life is .... Japan's. Most records suggest that men do not on average .... women .... Even in Japan .... men .... women can expect to reach eighty.

Exercise 155 Mixed clauses [*SGE* chapter 15]

Identify the finite subordinate clauses in the following, and (a) mark their type, eg: nominal, adverbial or relative and (b) state their function, eg: nominal (object), adverbial (reason).

Example: Accident investigators are examining the possibility that a wing came off the Boeing 767 before the aircraft crashed on Sunday.

Answer: *that a wing came off the Boeing 767 before it crashed on Sunday –* nominal (in apposition to *the possibility*)
before the aircraft crashed on Sunday – adverbial (time).

1 The possibility that a surface-to-air missile had been fired at the plane was under consideration.

2 Investigators said lightning and pilot error had been ruled out.

3 Officials would not say if any of the bodies had injuries consistent with a bomb blast.

4 Helicopters widened their jungle search yesterday, but it was reported that they could not find the right wing and its engine.

5 'That is extremely strange,' said a spokesman. 'We have no idea what it implies.'

6 However other sources said the implication that the right side of the plane could have borne the brunt of an explosion had led to the theory that it might have been caused by a missile.

7 The spokesman declined to speculate on how the wing came to be detached.

8 But he ruled out the possibility that it disintegrated.

9 'The wing has a very flexible structure, so it is highly improbable that it would have broken up in small pieces.'

10 He also confirmed that his team of investigators had found no trace of detonated explosives during their two days combing the site.

11 The investigators from Boeing, who joined the investigation yesterday, similarly found no trace of a bomb blast.

12 The investigation committee will decide today about where the black box flight recorder will go for examination.

13 'In our view,' said a spokesman 'it is necessary that the examinations should be done in a country where nobody is involved.'

14 'I would be disappointed if it were the United States because the Americans are players in this. It was a US pilot and the plane was of US origin.'

15 But he said Boeing 767s were 'well constructed and well proved'.

16 The only certainty was that the aircraft had exploded at a high altitude.

17 Ten days into the investigation, which began with a mass of speculation about sabotage, drug barons and bombs, the owner of the airline confirmed that the left-hand engine had apparently gone into reverse thrust – causing the plane to break up in mid-air.

16 Complementation of verbs and adjectives

Exercise 156 Intransitive phrasal verbs [*SGE* 16.3]

Use the verbs given to rephrase the passages below:

> come about   go ahead   fool around   pass away   look back
> settle down   touch down   cry off   take off   wear off
> drop out   stand out   come on   carry on   catch on   hold on
> bear up   own up   ring up   wait up   give up   give in   fall through

Example: They *continued* (*to behave*) as though nothing had happened.
Answer: They carried on as though nothing had happened.

Tom must be 25 by now. It's time he stopped (1) *behaving irresponsibly* .... and (2) *started taking life a bit more seriously* .... You know, he went to university and then (3) *left without finishing* .... He was offered quite a good job, accepted and then (4) *said no* .... He (5) *stops trying* .... far too easily. Oh, (6) *be fair!* .... The job (7) *collapsed* ....

I'm just (8) *telephoning* .... to say please (9) *don't hang around for us to arrive – go to bed* .... Our plane was late (10) *leaving* .... (from) Moscow, and we've only just (11) *arrived* .... at Heathrow.

Oh, I'm glad you've rung. I'll (12) *confess* .... – we (13) *continued* .... and had dinner.

Oh, that's good. Actually it was a bumpy flight and I'm feeling a bit sick and...

Oh, (14) *be cheerful!* .... That sort of feeling will (15) *disappear* ....soon.

Would you like to speak to Marjorie? ... (16) *Don't ring off* ...., I'll get her.

When I (17) *think about* .... over my past life, one of the things that (18) *is really noticeable* .... is the way things often (19) *happen* .... quite by chance. It's odd the way some of my inventions have really (20) *become popular* .... – the public love them. But with other things I've just had to (21) *accept defeat* .... Not that I ever really accept defeat. I shall go on working until I die – or as some people would say (22).....................

Exercise 157 Prepositional verbs [*SGE* 16.5]

Turn the following into the passive if the result is acceptable English.

Example: Someone broke into the house while we were on holiday.
Answer: The house was broken into while we were on holiday.
Example: Someone got into the house while we were out.
Answer: (Passive unacceptable – *The house was got into…)

1 Nobody has paid for the tickets, have they?

....

2 BBC stands for British Broadcasting Corporation.

....

3 We'd better see to the car or we'll have an accident.

....

4 A dreadful thought has just occurred to me.

....

5 Somebody really ought to look into this problem further.

....

6 The house belongs to a very old lady.

....

7 We've already referred to some of the problems.

....

8 Some people objected strongly to some of the proposals.

....

9 The car is old, but the owner has really cared for it well.

....

10 No one is ever going to account for that missing money.

....

11 Has everybody finished with these library books?

....

12 Nobody is to interfere with these boxes.

....

13 Everyone must adhere to the rules.

....

14 They seem to have looked after the house quite well.

....

15 People argue over some things for ages – with no result.

....

16 We've disposed of the problem now.

....

17 Basically my flat consists of three rooms.

....

18 The work will amount to £500 when it's finished.

....

19 I think we can rely on David to help.

....

20 Why are people always laughing at me?

....

Exercise 158 Phrasal or prepositional verbs? [*SGE* 16.2–7]

Respond to the sentences below by completing the responses using pronouns. Remember that the word order here may be different.

Example: Fill in your name please.
Answer: I've already FILLED IT IN.
Example: Do you believe in ghosts?
Answer: No, I certainly don't BELIEVE IN THEM.

1 I've been running in my new car.
   Surely you're not still ....

2 He took in his parents completely.
   How sad! How did he...?

3 Why don't you confide in your mother?
   I always do ....

4 I've invested in some electricity shares.
   Why have you ....?

5 I cashed in all my other shares.
   You mean you ....?

6 You can rely on your sister.
   Of course I can ....

7 The dog turned on the postman.
   Why did it..?

8 The police were trying to move on a lot of demonstrators who had brought the traffic to a standstill.
   And did the police manage to ....?

9 They insisted on silence.
   How could they ....?

10 Please pass on this notice when you've read it.
   Who shall I .... to?

11 The government needs to win over the floating voters.
   But do you think it can ....?

12 I can't get over his terrible behaviour.
   I can't .... either.

13 You should stand by your brother.
   I always have ....

14 He's bad at putting across his ideas.
   He's always been bad at ....

15 I came across this antique clock quite by chance.
   But where did you ....?

16 How can I keep out these wasps?
   Why do you want to...?

17 Marie takes after her father.
   Oh, I don't think she ....

18 Why did you turn down my offer of help?
   I didn't ....

19 Look up words you don't know in your dictionary.
   I always do ....

20 Could we put off our meeting?
   Why do you want to..?

Exercise 159 Phrasal-prepositional verbs [*SGE* 16.9]

Match the responses to the sentences.

Example: I keep meaning to sort out all my papers.
Response: (a) Well, you'd better get on with it.

1 I don't really want to, but I've promised to help.   ....
2 We're going to Turkey on holiday.   ....
3 I'm fed up with her rudeness.   ....
4 We've no food in the house.   ....
5 I suppose I eat too much fat.   ....
6 I haven't been getting enough sleep.   ....
7 The real difficulty is it's so expensive.   ....
8 I never pay any income tax.   ....
9 Robert's studying law.   ....
10 I've got a terrible problem.   ....

Responses:

(a) Well, you'd better get on with it.
(b) Couldn't you cut down on it?
(c) You can't get out of it now.
(d) I thought it would come down to cost in the end.
(e) Everyone comes up against difficulties sooner or later.
(f) You won't get away with it in the long run.
(g) You're always running out of things.
(h) I don't know why you put up with it.
(i) You must be looking forward to that.
(j) I thought of going in for that when I left school.
(k) Well, you can catch up on it at the weekend.

Exercise 160 Verbs: transitive or not? [*SGE* 16.11]

> Some verbs are always intransitive (*Jane has come*) and some can be intransitive or have an object, with little change of meaning (*Jane is cooking/Jane is cooking food*). Some can be both, but the meaning changes more:
>
> *You haven't drunk your tea/coffee/orange juice* etc.
> *Don't drink* [= don't drink alcohol] *and drive*

Omit the direct objects if this is possible without seriously changing the meaning.

Example:
I'm afraid we've just eaten [our meal].
But I think Andrew is still cooking [something] in the kitchen.

Will you have something to drink?

Oh, thanks, I'd love something. [Not *I'd love.]

Well, there's whisky, red or white wine …

I don't really drink [alcohol]. There isn't any coffee, is there? I'm afraid I drink coffee all day long. [Not *I drink all day.]

Of course you can have some coffee. [Not *you can have.]

1 Please answer my question.

Well, stop criticizing me. Why can't you help me?

I'm asking whether you are still borrowing money from the bank. You really should stop spending money the way you do. At your age I saved money regularly. You seem to spend a fortune on rubbish.

That's not true. I don't accept that. I need a lot of things – a car for a start.

Oh, come! You don't need a car. You mean you want a car. I think you should write a letter to your bank manager and …

If I don't get a new car, you won't be able to borrow it, will you?

2 I arrived hot and tired. I'd been driving the car all day and then I had a job trying to park it. After I'd unpacked my suitcase, washed myself and changed my clothes, I lay on the bed reading a book until it was time for dinner. Next morning I went out looking for a bank, because I needed to change money. But I couldn't find a bank anywhere.

Exercise 161 Middle verbs [*SGE* 16.15]

> Most transitive verbs can be turned into the passive (with the object of the active verb becoming the subject of the passive – see also Chapter 3). But there are some middle verbs that have objects, but are not used in the passive (or not in certain senses.)

Rewrite the following in the passive where this is possible.

Example: When they weighed her in the hospital, she only weighed 98 pounds.

Answer: When *she was weighed* in the hospital, she only weighed 98 pounds.
   [but not *98 pounds was weighed by her]

1 Has anyone costed these repairs in advance?

   ....

2 Well, I think they'll cost at least £1,000.

   ....

3 When my brother's tailor measured him for a new suit, he told him that he'd put on a lot of weight and now measures 40 inches around the waist.

   ....

4 Do you feel you lack access to further information?

   ....

5 My new car holds three people comfortably in the back.

   ....

6 They are holding the three hostages in dreadful conditions.

....

7 The school comprises the main school building and two accommodation blocks.

....

8 Cheap clothes never seem to fit me properly.

....

9 You need to fit a new washer to that tap.

....

10 Modern art frequently resembles children's art.

....

11 The weekend they suggest will suit me perfectly.

....

12 Did Navratilova's record equal Billie-Jean King's?

....

Exercise 162 Hypothesis: the verb *wish* [*SGE* 16.20]

> The verb *wish* takes the same tenses as hypothetical conditions:
>
> If I *were* really clever ... I wish I *were* really clever ...
>
> If only you *had come* earlier ... We all wish you *had come* earlier ...

Choose a situation that you do not like from each of the following sets, and then wish the opposite.

1 You are very quick tempered/easily worried/soft hearted.
   You say [for example]: I WISH I WEREN'T so easily worried.

2 You are not a quick reader/a brilliant speaker/a good listener.

....

3 You can't spend enough time with your parents/speak four or five languages/remember everything you read.

....

4 You don't understand yourself/know what to do for the best/feel at ease with strangers.

....

5 You waste your money/watch too much TV/worry a lot. [Use *so much*]

....

6 You didn't have a holiday last year/save much money last year/work hard enough last year.

....

7 You recently watched a really nasty horror film on TV/bought a CD you don't like/bought some clothes that don't fit. [Use *this*, *that* etc.]

....

8 You haven't got an interesting job/a really understanding friend/enough time to do everything you want.

....

9 You have a lot of problems/too much to do/difficult hair. [Use *so* or *such*]

....

10 You have not been to the United States/Russia/China.

....

11 People will keep giving you advice/criticizing you/asking you for money.

....

12 You will never be able to meet your favourite film star/make a fortune/sail round the world. [use *one day*]

....

Exercise 163 Verb + *to*-infinitive or verb + *ing*? [*SGE* 16.23]

Complete the following using the correct nonfinite form of the verb given.

Example: Do you want (win) friends and (influence) people?
  I do – I don't mind (admit) it.
Answer: Do you want TO WIN friends and (TO) INFLUENCE people?
  I do – I don't mind ADMITTING it.

1 Avoid (criticize) .... people.
2 Don't hesitate (pay) .... compliments.
3 Aim (do) ,,,............... some kind action every day.
4 Don't postpone (do) .... something just because it's difficult.
5 Practise (listen) .... to what others say.
6 Resolve (be) .... a good listener.
7 Don't spend time (worry) .... about things that may never happen.
8 Carry on (try). .... You'll succeed sooner than you think.
9 Never agree (do) .... something you know to be wrong.
10 Never fail (speak up) .... in a good cause.
11 Never threaten (do) .... something unless you're prepared to carry out your threat.
12 Never stop (try)............... .
13 Be prepared to admit (make) .... mistakes.
14 Don't deny (be) .... in the wrong – if you are.
15 Learn (understand) .... other people's points of view.
16 Don't offer (do) .... more than is reasonable.
17 Try (realize) .... how the other person feels.
18 Don't even consider (stop)............... .
19 Just keep on (try)............... .
20 You will deserve (succeed)............... .

Exercise 164 Nonfinite clauses and *that*-clauses [*SGE* 16.11–37]

Explain what happened by completing the sentences with the verbs given.

Example: *He*: Why don't you try again?
Answers: He thought (THAT) I OUGHT TO/SHOULD TRY AGAIN.
    He encouraged ME TO TRY AGAIN.

  She to him: Have you seen this job advertisement? You should apply.

1 She wanted ....

2 She suggested ....

3 She advised ....

She: Well, think about it.

4 She hoped ....

5 She told ....

She: It's up to you, of course, but you will write in, won't you?

6 She knew she couldn't make ....

7 She could only propose ....

He: May I borrow the car this evening?

She: No, I'm sorry, I'm not going to lend my car to anyone – not after what happened.

8 She refused ....

9 She wouldn't allow ....

10 She wouldn't let ....

11 because she had decided .... her car ever again.

She: I'm sorry, but my mind is made up.

12 She insisted ....

She: Nothing will make me change my mind.

13 Nothing would cause ....

He: You're cross that I asked.

She: No, I'm not cross. But never, never ask again.

14 She didn't mind ....

15 But she forbade ....

Exercise 165: Complex–transitive verbs [*SGE* 16.24–30]

Complete these verb + object + complement sentences using these objects (once each).

(a) the club (b) the membership (c) the present state of the club
(d) the job (e) the bar (f) Janet (g) everyone (h) her (i) herself (j) it

1 We've appointed (f) JANET treasurer.

2 We expect her to make .... a success.

3 She called .... a mess.

4 She declared .... honoured to have been chosen.

5 She finds .... challenging.

6 She hopes to keep .... happy.

7 She plans to make .... larger, to raise subscription income.

8 She wants .... open at lunch-time.

9 We think .... a good idea to improve the bar.

10 I call .... a super person.

Exercise 166 Passive + *to*-infinitive [*SGE* 16.27]

Rewrite the following using a passive verb + a *to*-infinitive. Omit the agents.

Example: We expect that the report will be published shortly.
Answer: The report is expected to be published shortly.

1 Everyone supposes some progress has been made.
   ....

2 Everyone considers that the chairman is an expert.
   ....

3 The rumour is that some members are unhappy.
   ....

4 We understand the findings are fair.
   ....

5 People presume the recommendations are radical.
   ....

6 We believe that tempers ran high.
   ....

7 People reported that the discussions had been tough.
   ....

8 People say the results are far-reaching.
   ....

9 People think some proposals have been dropped.
   ....

10 We know that some members disagree.
   ....

Exercise 167: Verb + object + prepositional object [*SGE* 16.32]

> Some verbs take an object and then another object after a particular preposition. (I *addressed the letter* TO the Chairman).

Complete the sentences, using the information given. Add suitable prepositions, and make any other grammatical changes necessary.

Example: The hotel gives you everything except a toothbrush!
Answer: It provides you WITH EVERYTHING EXCEPT A TOOTHBRUSH.

1 She looks like my cousin.
  She reminds me ....
2 'Well done. I'm so glad you've passed your exam.'
  I congratulated her ....
3 It's wrong to keep offering people drinks.
  Don't keep plying ....
4 They said I'd borrowed the car without asking.
  They accused ....
5 I'd like to meet your parents.
  Please introduce ....

6 My aunt sent me a wonderful present.
I must write and thank .... it.
7 Some people ruin their own lives.
But you just can't prevent ....
8 £100 sounds reasonable for that camera. Have you looked at prices in other shops?
Have you compared ....?
9 It's not safe these days to make remarks about a woman's appearance.
Feminists think it is 'sexist' to compliment .... her appearance.
10 They probably find it 'degrading' if anyone wants to buy them a meal.
It is probably even more 'sexist' to try and treat ....

Exercise 168 Verbs with/without an indirect object [*SGE* 16.33]

> Some verbs which are followed by a *that*-clause need an indirect object (the person or people told):
>
>   He told *them* that ... [and not usually *He told that ...]
>
> Other verbs do not pattern like this, although they can optionally indicate the indirect object with a *to*-phrase:
>
>   He suggested that ... *or* He suggested to them/us that ...

Complete the following by inserting *us* where an indirect object is necessary. Where it is optional, add *to us*.

Example: He persuaded us that he was the ideal person for the job.
He didn't disclose [to us] that he had no experience.

1 He admitted .... his application contained errors of fact.
2 He assured .... it was all an innocent mistake.
3 Obviously he wouldn't confess .... that he had wanted to mislead us.
4 He somehow convinced .... he was well suited to the job.
5 He explained .... that he had just the right experience.
6 He informed .... that he enjoyed a challenge.
7 He didn't mention .... that he might only stay a year.
8 He predicted .... he would be a great success.
9 He reminded .... that his uncle had been in the firm.
10 He repeated .... he was well qualified.
11 He swore .... that everything would be all right.
12 He told .... he was really keen.

Exercise 169 Adjective + *to*-infinitive [*SGE* 16.40]

Rewrite the following with an adjective + *to*-infinitive phrase.

Example: Bob waited for us. That was kind.
Answer: Bob was kind to wait for us.

1 Marie always pays her bills regularly. She's careful that way.
   She is always ....

2 She always spots a mistake quickly.
   She is always ....

3 When we finally heard that David had arrived, we were very relieved.
   We were relieved to ....

4 Why have you thrown up your job? You're mad.
   You are ....

5 What I want to do is start my own business. I'm keen.
   I am ....

6 It is disappointing that we haven't heard from Molly.
   We are ....

7 We thought she would telephone. But perhaps she couldn't.
   Perhaps she was unable ....

8 Contacting her at work is usually quite easy.
   She is usually ....

9 Well, I tried to get hold of her yesterday, but it was impossible.
   She was ....

10 Can you sign the papers please? They are ready now.
   The papers are ....

11 Don't lend Tom any money. That would be most unwise.
   You ....

12 Being able to help really pleased us.
   We were ....

17 The noun phrase

Exercise 170 Noun phrases: identifying the head [*SGE* 17.1–2]

Identify the head nouns in the following passage. The noun phrases have been picked out and numbered – except for single pronouns and one-word names, which are ignored.

BBC weatherman Michael Fish's *failure* to give a warning of the great storm of October 1987 (1)
was
a spectacular example of how modern meteorology fails (2)
says
the Consumers' Association (3)
in
a report (4)
today.
   It claims that
the Met Office's near monopoly on meteorology (5)
casts
a cloud (6)
over
consumer interests, (7)
and argues for
an Office of Fair Trading investigation into the weather forecasting industry. (8)
   The association's *Which?* magazine report (9)
stresses that
forecasting (10)
is clearly improving overall, but it takes
the Met Office (11)
to
task (12)
for failing to explain
the weather (13)
in
a user-friendly way. (14)
   It says
the language of isobars and anticyclones (15)
is less important than 'whether Suffolk should put out its washing'
and calls for
better translations of what forecasts actually mean. (16)
   Which? (17)
favours

a new style of forecasting based on probability. (18)

Closer to

the science of placing a bet on a horse (19)

than

a traditional forecast, (20)

this would include

phrases such as 'there is a 70 per cent chance of rain in the South' (21)

rather than the more usual 'there may be scattered showers'.

Exercise 171 Relative clauses: *whose* [*SGE* 17.6]

Rewrite the following sentences with *whose* if possible, and see what the original writers wrote. But one sentence cannot be changed – why?

Example: They have given thousands of pounds to various pressure groups, mischief-making bodies the main purpose of which is to stir up hatred and disorder.

Answer: ... mischief-making bodies, whose main purpose is ...

1 I came to realize this through the study, not of economics – that abstract science the professors of which never seem able to agree – but of history, which is the record of cause and effect.
2 Bermondsey turns out to have been unique as the first by-election of which the result has been claimed by all party spokesmen as a victory.
3 When Dorsey decides, for plot reasons of which it takes an accomplished scriptwriter to convince you, to audition for that female part in a daytime television soap opera, he becomes overnight a cult success.
4 This is a tour the function of which is to introduce the Princess to Canada.
5 When you have 100 million dollars the value of which you must maintain against inflation, there are not many safe places to put it.
6 The decoration of Chinese neolithic pottery nearly always consisted of abstract and geometric designs, the meaning of which is not understood.

Exercise 172 Relative clauses [*SGE* 17.5–11]

Complete the passage by inserting relative words as necessary. Indicate all possible alternatives, including zero(–).

The mystery of the Bermuda Triangle is intact. American deep sea divers (1) WHO claimed last month to have found the wrecks of five US Navy planes (2) .... disappeared near Bermuda have announced that they are not the famous Lost Squadron.

The wrecks (3) .... the divers found last month in 750 feet of water 10 miles off the coast of Florida were of an earlier model of TBM Avenger than the five (4) .... vanished on training flight 19 on a hazy afternoon in 1945.

The squadron's disappearance helped build the reputation of the Bermuda Triangle, in (5) .... people, planes and boats are said to vanish without trace.

When the wrecks were found it seemed as if the myth had been shattered. But Mr Graham Hawke, (6) .... led the search, and to (7) .... fell the unenviable task of admitting a mistake, said yesterday: We are now quite certain that the five aircraft (8) .... we found are not those of flight 19.

His evident disappointment, (9) .... perhaps reflected the lost fortune (10) .... his company had stood to make from salvaging the discovery, will be matched by the pleasure of others (11) .... enjoy the mysterious power of the Triangle, the three points of (12) .... are formed by Bermuda, Puerto Rico and Miami.

Mr Ted Darcy, an archaeological adviser to The Scientific Search Project, said that the area in (13) .... the five wrecks were found was used by the US Navy as a practice range for low-level torpedo runs, and that the five planes (14) ....were found were probably lost in separate accidents over several years.

Susan Powers-Spangler, (15) .... father disappeared with the famous Lost Squadron in 1945, said: I'm sad that they weren't found, but kind of glad in a way that it wasn't them.

So the wrecks (16) .... discovery aroused such interest last month are not quite what they seemed. Incidentally, the place (17) .... the wrecks were found has also claimed many ships, and it was the hope of finding Spanish galleons that originally drew the divers to the spot.

Exercise 173 Relative clauses [*SGE* 17.5–12]

Join up the information given, so that in each case you have one sentence containing relative clauses.

Example: Some people undertake long journeys. They will remember these journeys all their lives.

Answer: Some people undertake long journeys/WHICH/THAT/– they will remember all their lives.

1 Travellers on the Trans-Siberian railway take 8 days 4 hours 25 minutes on the journey. The Trans-Siberian railway stretches from Moscow to the Pacific Ocean. During this journey there are 97 stops.

   ....
   ....

2 The 'Indian-Pacific' railway crosses Australia from Perth on the Indian Ocean to Sydney on the Pacific. Its reputation is perhaps less fearsome than the Trans-Siberian.

   ....
   ....

3 It covers a distance of 2,720 miles (4,352 km). Of these, 297 miles (478 km) across the Nullarbor Plain are dead straight. This is the longest straight stretch of railway in the world.

   ....
   ....

4 These journeys appeal to a certain type of traveller. A certain type of traveller is not in a hurry. To this type of traveller the journey, not the arrival, matters.

   ....
   ....

5 Gary Sowerby (Canada) and Tim Cahill (USA) drove a four-wheel drive pick-up truck from Ushuaia (Argentina) to Prudhoe Bay (Alaska, USA) in 1987 in just under 24 days. Tim Cahill was Gary Sowerby's co-driver and navigator. From Ushuaia to Prudhoe Bay is a distance of 14,739 miles (23,720 km). Just under 24 days is a record time for the journey.

....

....

6 They were however surface freighted over the Darien Gap. Darien Gap is between Colombia and Panama. Here the Trans-American highway does not exist.

....

....

Exercise 174 Appositive clauses [*SGE* 17.13]

> When two noun phrases are in apposition, they both refer to the same person or thing, so that one gives us more details about the other. Sometimes a *that*-clause is in apposition to an abstract noun like *fact*, *idea*, *information*.

Rewrite the information so that in each case you have a single sentence containing a noun + an appositive clause.

Example: Some people believe that we can abolish war. This seems hopeful rather than realistic.
Answer: *The belief that we can abolish war* seems hopeful rather than realistic.

1 People sometimes suggest that we are not all equal. This makes some people very angry.
  Any ....

2 Some people explain that accidents are often nobody's fault. But many people do not accept this.
  Many people ....

3 I was told that there are more scientists alive today than have ever lived before. Is that a fact?
  Is it a ....?

4 Scientists say that there are a lot of black holes in the universe. I don't understand this theory.
  I don't understand the ....

5 The universe started with a big bang. There is also that idea.
  There is also the ....

6 Of course we hope to rid the world of poverty. But can we?
  Is there any ....?

7 Neil Armstrong remarked when he stepped on to the moon, 'That's one small step for a man, one giant leap for mankind.' Everyone remembers this.
  Everyone remembers Neil Armstrong's ....
  ....

8 Shakespeare observed that 'all the world's a stage'. I'm not sure whether I agree.
  I'm not sure whether I agree with ....

Exercise 175 Postmodification by nonfinite clauses [*SGE* 17.14–18]

Rewrite the sentences by changing the finite relative clauses into nonfinite forms. Use -*ing* forms, -*ed* forms or *to*-infinitives as suitable. Mark the new noun phrases you have made.

Example: The man who wrote the obituaries is my friend.
Answer: THE MAN WRITING THE OBITUARIES is my friend.
Example: Any coins that are found on this site must be handed to the police.
Answer: ANY COINS FOUND ON THIS SITE must be handed to the police.
Example: The next train that arrived was from York.
Answer: THE NEXT TRAIN TO ARRIVE was from York.

Millions of insomniacs could benefit from a new technique (1) *which may cure sleeplessness*, (2) *which is based on 'thought-jamming'*.

The idea is that a simple word like *the*, (3) *which is repeated under the breath three or four times a second*, can block stimulating thoughts and induce sleep. This anti-insomnia technique (4) *which is being tested by researchers from Cambridge* offers pill-free hope for millions (5) *who suffer from sleeplessness*. It is based on a theory that the brain has a kind of 'memory traffic control', (6) *which has been called 'the central executive'*, and that this controls information (7) *that enters the brain*.

The Cambridge team believes that with insomniacs 'the central executive' insists on finding tasks when nothing (8) *that is particularly interesting* is happening. The team decided to look for ways (9) *in which they could provide a steady flow of information into the brain*, which would prevent it from looking for other tasks (10) *that it could do*.

The age-old technique of counting sheep as a method (11) *that may induce sleep* requires concentration and stimulates thoughts about the imaginary sheep (12) *that are being counted*. Repeating a boring little word like *the* is so dull that the only thing (13) *that most people can do* is to go to sleep.

Tests (14) *that have been specially designed to try out the theory* were carried out under controlled conditions. A third of those (15) *who were tested* had quick success. But other people stayed awake. They were able to mouth simple words while still thinking other thoughts. There is still work (16) *that needs to be done*.

Exercise 176 Postmodification by prepositional phrases [*SGE* 17.19–23]

> Prepositional phrases are frequently used to 'postmodify' nouns, that is to add information after them.

Fill in the gaps with suitable prepositions, and underline the noun phrases that the prepositional phrases are part of.

This is usually easy – (1) *a row* WITH *your family*. Notice, however, that sometimes a prepositional phrase contains another. Thus at (9) there is no noun phrase **mental well-being on physical health*. Instead the prepositional phrase *on physical health* belongs to the bigger noun phrase:

the latest study ... [*the effects* (... mental well-being) *on physical health*]

If you have a row (1) WITH your family today, you could end up with a cold by the end (2) .... the week. Research (3) .... psychologists suggest that joyless days full of irritation (4) .... a social kind can lead to a weakening (5) .... the disease-fighting immune system, and that four days (6) .... a row your system can become too weak to stop cold viruses from attacking.

The theory is the latest study (7) .... the effects (8) .... mental well-being (9) .... physical health.

Evidence (10) .... such effects has already been found for a number (11) .... serious diseases. Typically those who have problems expressing emotions (12) .... anger or who have suffered traumatic experiences after the death (13) .... a spouse appear to be most at risk.

Now a similar effect has been found (14) .... the common cold. A hundred clerical staff (15) .... a tax office (16) .... the north (17) .... England were asked to keep a diary (18) .... their health, their moods and what sort (19) .... day they had.

After ten weeks, seventeen volunteers had colds. It then emerged that four days (20) .... contracting the cold, there had been a marked drop (21) .... diary entries recording friendly relations (22) .... their spouses, and an increase (23) .... the number (24) .... social annoyances.

The researchers believe that all this shows a definite link (25) .... mood and infection. So – if you don't want a cold, don't get annoyed!

Exercise 177 Nominalization [*SGE* 17.23]

Noun phrases that correspond to verbs and other clause elements are sometimes called nominalizations.

Rewrite the following, using nouns in place of the verbs in italic, and making any other changes necessary.

Example: She *refused* to answer, which was disapppointing.
Answer: Her *refusal to answer* was disappointing.

1 I *believe* that the fire was started on purpose.
   It's my ....
2 They *corresponded* for twenty years.
   .... lasted for ....
3 Is the word cooccur ever *hyphenated*?
   Is there ....
4 They *behaved* really badly, which upset everyone.
   Their ....
5 These people *inhabit* one of the remotest places on earth.
   These people are ....
6 Everyone *competing* must put down their names.
   All the ....
7 Did anyone *survive* the crash?
   Were there ....
8 The way they *organized* the event was brilliant.
   The ....

 9 Those children were not very well *educated*.
    Those children's ....

10 You should *practise* more.
    You need ....

11 It was wonderful when the hostages were *released*.
    The hostages' ....

12 I don't like the way you continually *criticize*.
    I don't like your ....

13 Can we *arrange* to meet?
    Can we make ....

14 What do the stars and stripes *symbolize*?
    What are the .... of?

15 Perhaps we should *publicize* the club more.
    Perhaps the club needs ....

16 Have you *fed* the cat?
    Where is the cat's ....

17 It's a hotel where you can *dine* in the garden.
    It's a hotel where you can have ....

18 When offices *relocate*, the staff don't usually like it.
    Office .... usually upsets the staff.

19 I could hardly *breathe*.
    I was out of ....

20 You didn't *object* before.
    You didn't raise any ....

Exercise 178 Apposition [*SGE* 17.27]

Two or more noun phrases are in apposition when they refer to the same person or thing.

Complete these authentic quotations by adding the following appositive phrases in the right places.

Example: 5(a) He greatly dislikes the British Library building, a fast-rising blot on the Euston Road.

(a) a fast-rising blot on the Euston Road
(b) the latest word in anti-fraud know-how
(c) the police device for immobilizing illegally parked cars
(d) the willingness of academics to pay tribute to the leaders of bloodthirsty regimes
(e) those richer than himself
(f) them or us
(g) Millie

1 Three diplomatic cars were among the first 46 victims of the wheel clamp when it came into operation in London in 1983.
2 Murauchi has a low opinion of the scramble by the new rich for European art.
3 The Bushes' spaniel is the latest in a long line of White House pets.
4 It was gang warfare. We had to kill them or they would have killed us.
5 He greatly dislikes the British Library building.
6 Australia's new plastic banknote still cannot cope with earlier forms of

technology. People leaving the $10 note in trouser pockets have found that it shrinks when ironed.

7 The fêting of the dictator's wife by the polytechnic is a classic example of a peculiar phenomenon.

Exercise 179 Premodification by participles [*SGE* 17.28–33]

Complete the following, using premodifying participles + nouns – but only where possible.

Example: Some plays today disgust me.
Answer: There are SOME DISGUSTING PLAYS today.

1 The play was very entertaining.
 It was ....

2 Edward Fox's performance amazed us.
 He gave ....

3 I admire him for the way he timed his acting beautifully.
 I admire Edward Fox's ....

4 I don't like people who arrive late.
 .... are a nuisance.

5 The language of some plays rather surprises me.
 Some plays contain ....

6 One man was really shocked and left.
 One ....

7 The children behind us were talking, which was a nuisance.
 ....

8 The scene that opened the play was brilliant.
 The ....

9 We got ice-creams in the interval and ate them.
 During the interval we ....

10 I don't usually buy a programme because I won't pay the prices they demand.
 The .... are too high.

11 We always reserve our seats.
 We always have ....

12 The plot was rather complicated.
 The play had ....

13 The play ended with a 'twist' that was not unrelated.
 There was .... at the end.

14 We certainly were not expecting that ending.
 That was certainly ....

Exercise 180 Attributive nouns [*SGE* 17.35]

Make compound nouns on the pattern noun + noun.

Example: a book of cheques =
Answer: a cheque book

1 someone addicted to drugs = ...
2 insurance on people's lives = ...
3 strain on the eyes = ...

4 a bulletin of news = ...

5 the skin of a banana = ...

6 an outbreak of measles = ...

7 chairs to use in the garden = ...

8 decay in the teeth = ...

9 holes (in a jacket, shirt etc) for one's arms = ...

10 a brush for brushing one's clothes = ...

11 an intellectual whose head is said to look like an egg = ...

12 a family with two cars = ...

13 an office where you can post letters (and buy stamps etc) = ...

14 a place where you can wait for buses to stop = ...

15 someone who sits with (and looks after) babies (and young children) = ...

16 an office block of ten storeys = ...

17 a holiday arranged as a package = ...

18 control of arms (weapons) = ...

19 a shop selling dresses = ...

20 food that is really junk = ...

Exercise 181 Noun phrases in general [*SGE* Chapter 17]

Study the following passage, and then answer the questions that follow.

In November the sportsmen change their clothes. The fishing rods are put away in favour of shot guns and hunting boots. Each year the sportsman is being more closely marked by an anti-sportsman, often the shadow of himself. The anti-sportsmen are part of a loose collection of activist organizations, concerned with animal welfare, and ranging across the whole skein of relationships between human kind and the animal world.

The anti-sportsmen seek to eliminate hunting, shooting and fishing as a pastime. They adopt methods of behaviour which apart from being uncivil, if not illegal, reveal a weakness for the chase – their quarry in this instance being the sportsman and his activities – which bears a striking resemblance to the weaknesses they affect to deplore in others.

So far the campaign has prospered more against fox hunting than against shooting or fishing ... Intermittent harassment of hunts and their supporters occur throughout the winter somewhere across the country. Nevertheless fox hunting since the war has prospered ...

Opposition to field sports in Britain is almost as traditional as the field sports themselves. Both sides of the argument have literature and a culture which stretch back for centuries. Hitherto the argument has been conducted fairly; but there is evidence that a new war is now being waged with fewer holds barred by those whose purpose is to eliminate field sports from the British scene.

One disconcerting aspect of the argument is the extent to which it reveals that country habits and perspectives are becoming less and less understood or respected by city dwellers; and it is more often the city dwellers who command the money and the access to the media which gives them a better opportunity to press their arguments to successful conclusions.

(a) Premodification. Complete these noun phrases from the text with adjectives or an adjective-like participle.

1 a   loose   connection
2 ... .   skein
3 ... human   ....
4 ... .   resemblance
5 ... .   scene
6 ... .   opportunity

(b) Complete these noun phrases where the premodifier is a noun or noun-like *-ing* form:

7 ....   rods
8 shot   ....
9 ....   boots
10 ....   organizations
11 ....   sports
12 country   .... and ....

(c) Postmodification. Complete these noun phrases, where the postmodification is a prepositional phrase.

13 relationships ....
14 .... as a pastime
15 a weakness ....
16 intermittent harassment ....
17 foxhunting ....
18 the involvement ....
19 both sides ....
20 .... to the media

(d) Find the noun phrases which are completed by the relative clauses shown:

21 .... which reveal a weakness for the chase
22 .... which bears a striking resemblance to the weaknesses ...
23 .... they affect to deplore in others
24 .... which stretch back for centuries
25 .... whose purpose is to eliminate the sport ...
26 .... to which it reveals that country habits and perspectives are becoming less and less understood
27 .... which gives them a better opportunity to press their arguments to successful conclusions

(e) Find the nonfinite verbs/clauses that postmodify these nouns:

28 activist organizations ....
29 fewer holds ....
30 a better opportunity ....

18 Theme, focus, and information processing

Exercise 182 Given and new information [*SGE* 18.1–4]

> There is often more than one way of 'saying the same thing'.
> How we say it depends on several factors – the emphasis we want to give to different parts of the 'message' and what we think is the most important part. Often we begin with something already known or GIVEN, and keep the important NEW INFORMATION to the end of the sentence.

Decide which is the likeliest (unmarked) answer to each of the following questions.

Example: When shall we know what Mary's going to do?

(a) Next week we shall know.
(b) It's next week we shall know.
(c) She'll tell us next week.
(d) Next week she will tell us.

Answer: (c)

1 What have you done with your car?
   (a) We have sold our car.
   (b) We've sold it.
   (c) Our car has been sold.
   (d) The car we have sold.

2 Is there a post office near here?
   (a) There's one near here.
   (b) Near here there's one.
   (c) There's one just beyond the chemist's.
   (d) Just beyond the chemist's is a post office.

3 Where do you keep your car?
   (a) I have to park it outside the house.
   (b) Outside the house is where I park it.
   (c) It's outside that I park my car.
   (d) Park it outside is what I have to do.

4 Which newspaper do you read?
   (a) *The Guardian* I sometimes read.
   (b) *The Times* is my favourite paper.
   (c) Usually *The Daily Telegraph*.
   (d) What I read is *The Independent*.

5 What are the most popular TV programmes in your family?
   (a) Comedy programmes and the news are watched by all the family.
   (b) Comedy and the news are our favourite TV programmes.
   (c) We regularly watch comedy programmes and the news.
   (d) It's comedy and the news that are most popular with us.

6 How often do you go to the cinema?
   (a) About once a week on average I go.
   (b) About once a week on average I go to the cinema.
   (c) To the cinema I go on average about once a week.
   (d) I go about once a week on average.

Exercise 183 Theme and focus: end-weight [*SGE* 18.7–12]

Although we do not always begin a sentence with something known or
'given', the beginning is usually the THEME or topic of our sentence – what
we are going to talk about, so that we can then put the FOCUS of attention on
the new information.

   This has an important consequence for the shape of a sentence. We often
need more words for the new information than for the 'given' or the theme,
so the end of the sentence often has to be the longest part – with END-WEIGHT.
Sentences with a lot of weighty information at the beginning are much more
difficult to understand.

The sentences below have been written out here in 'unmarked' word order
(SVOCA). But they were originally written in a different order to give end-weight
(and end-focus) to the more important information. Can you reconstruct them as
they were originally written?

1 S   I
   V   had extracted
   O   the admission that, while the frontier would in effect have been closed to
        everyone else, he would, in view of my official position, in principle have
        been prepared to let me cross it, if there had been any means of getting me
        across.
   A   after an hour or two
   A   from my interlocutor
   [Begin with one of the adverbials. Where should the end-weight be?]
   ....

2 S   The Revolutionary Guards
   V   beat up and
   V   detained
   O   Mr Edward Chaplin, a British diplomat
   A   for one day
   A   in apparent retaliation for the arrest in Manchester of one of their consular
        officials on shoplifting charges.
   [Move one of the adverbials to give end-weight to the object and to the other
   adverbial]
   ....

3 S   David Sylvester
  V   argues (that)
  A   in his contribution to *Late Picasso* (£25, paperback £17.95)
  S   these pictures
  V   lay
  O   the horror of growing old
  C   naked
  [Make the adverbial the opening topic. Then emphasize the final object.]
  ....

4 S   We
  V   cannot deduce
  O   any very confident pointers towards the next general election which may
       be as much as four years hence
  A   from an election in which the don't knows and don't cares won by a
       distance
  [Give end-weight to the object]
  ....

5 S   Wild horses
  V   would not have dragged
  O   the truth
  A   from me
  [Emphasize the object]
  ....

Exercise 184 Theme and focus [*SGE* 18.5–12]

Bearing in mind that in answering people's questions we should focus on the new
information that they want, choose the likeliest answers in the following.

1 Who was the first man to walk to both Poles?
   (a) Robert Swan (GB) led expeditions to the South Pole in 1986 and to the
       North in 1989.
   (b) Robert Swan (GB), who led expeditions to the South Pole in 1986 and to the
       North in 1989.
   (c) A small expedition to the South Pole in 1986 and another expedition to the
       North were both led by Robert Swan.
   (d) Robert Swan became the first man to walk to both Poles.

2 What was the name of his South Pole expedition?
   (a) The Footsteps of Scott was the name of his South Pole venture.
   (b) It was called the Footsteps of Scott.
   (c) He led a South Pole expedition called the Footsteps of Scott.
   (d) The Footsteps of Scott was the name given to this expedition.

3 How big was this Footsteps of Scott expedition?
   (a) There were just three men.
   (b) Three men took part in the Footsteps of Scott expedition.
   (c) A three-man expedition is what it was.
   (d) Three men walked to the South Pole.

4 How long did the South Pole trek take them?
  (a) Through the worst Antarctic winter for years they trekked for seventy days.
  (b) For seventy days they trekked through the worst Antarctic winter for years.
  (c) For seventy days through a terrible Antarctic winter they trekked.
  (d) It took them seventy days – through the worst Antarctic winter for years.

5 And was the North Pole walk also a three-man expedition?
  (a) No, the international expedition had eight men.
  (b) No, it was an eight-man international expedition.
  (c) No, eight men – from different countries – walked to the North Pole.
  (d) No, there were eight men walking to the Pole from different countries.

6 Did this North Pole expedition have a name?
  (a) Yes, Icewalk it was called.
  (b) Yes, Icewalk they called it.
  (c) Yes, Icewalk was its name.
  (d) Yes, it was called Icewalk.

7 Wasn't there some connected environmental project involving students?
  (a) Yes, a connected environmental project involved international students.
  (b) Yes, twenty-two students from fifteen countries took part in some connected environmental project.
  (c) Yes, an international group of students did some interesting work.
  (d) Yes, there was a connected environmental project involving students.

8 Where did this part of the project take place?
  (a) At the polar team base on Canada's Ellesmere Island.
  (b) Canada's Ellesmere Island is where the project took place.
  (c) Ellesmere Island, where the polar base is, is part of Canada.
  (d) At the polar team base on Ellesmere Island environmental studies were carried out.

Exercise 185 Marked focus [*SGE* 18.7–12]

Read the passage. Then, in the exercise that follows, mark the stressed words in the answers that probably receive the main focus.

MFPA is not a charity but a company entirely owned by seriously disabled members of the Association of Mouth and Foot Painting Artists. Its members have all learned to draw and paint with the brush held in the mouth or with the toes.

Perhaps the best known MFPA artist was Christy Brown, who died in 1976. The Oscar-winning film, *My Left Foot*, was based on his autobiography.

Christy Brown was born with a disability, but some MFPA artists have become disabled as the result of accidents. Bruce Peardon was in the Navy when a serious road accident left him with a permanent spinal injury. During his long stay in hospital he met two MFPA artists who encouraged him to paint. He is now a very accomplished landscape artist who is well known for his illustrations of children.

 1 MFPA doesn't sound like a real company.
    – But it is a real company.

Answer: But it ɪs a company.

2 It must be difficult to paint with your mouth or feet.
   – Very difficult.
3 So the Association was founded in nineteen sixty-six.
   – No, nineteen fifty-six.
4 And do the members manage to support their families?
   – I don't know about their families, but they support themselves.
5 I saw the film about Chris Brown on television.
   – Not Chris Brown, Christy Brown.
6 Oh yes of course. The film showed him writing and drawing with his right foot.
   – His left foot.
7 He's dead now, isn't he?
   – Yes, he died in 1976.
8 I'd like to see some of Bruce Pearson's work.
   – Peardon, not Pearson.
9 How awful to have an accident after leaving the Navy.
   – No, he was still in the Navy.
10 And he's now an accomplished portrait painter?
   – I think he's mainly a landscape artist.
11 And he met some MFPA artists while he was in hospital?
   – Actually, he met two MFPA artists, who encouraged him.
12 There are plenty of able-bodied people with the use of their hands who can't draw or paint at all.
   – It's amazing to draw and paint without hands.

Exercise 186 Fronting [*SGE* 18.14–17]

Decide whether the marked fronted elements are object, complement, adverbial or predicate. Then rewrite the sentences in unmarked word order.

Example: Immature and over-enthusiastic they said I was.
Answer: [Complement] They said I was immature and over-enthusiastic.

1 That sort of remark I can do without.
2 Objective it is not.
3 Unkind I call it.
4 They'd said they weren't going to criticize, but criticize they did.
5 To them I must have seemed a child.
6 Three or four cars these people would bring in at a time for servicing.
7 (and then) about some £10 item on the bill they'd grumble and grumble.
8 Always grumbling they were.
9 Millionaires they probably were,
10 (but) generous they were not.
11 This particular law nobody can defend.
12 About the need for a libel law nobody is arguing.
13 We can accept that needed it is.
14 In its present state the law cannot be seriously defended.
15 Still, unsatisfactory though it may be, we could end up with something worse.

Exercise 187 Subject–verb inversion [*SGE* 18.16–17]

Reconstruct these sentences as the authors originally wrote them, so that the subjects follow the verbs and receive 'end-weight'.

Example: The body of Samuel Taylor Coleridge/lies/beneath this stone. (SVA)
Answer: Beneath this stone lies the body of Samuel Taylor Coleridge. (AVS – the words on a memorial stone in a north London church)

1 The new generation of Communists, revolutionaries no longer in the old sense, but worshippers of the established order, deeply suspicious of dangerous thoughts/sat/staring up at him, row upon row, smug, self-satisfied and hostile.
   ....,...

2 [Or else we would find our way barred by a sand dune.] Then/the spades, sand mats and towing ropes/came/out [and the whole dreary business of 'unsticking' would start again.]
   Then ....

3 The first of the ranges of hills, which lay between us and the coast/rose/across the valley, dark against the setting sun.
   ....

4 A chain of sand islands and black jagged rocks, sheltering the harbour from the westerly gales and squalls of the Adriatic/stretched/across the bay.
   ....

5 The collection of Egyptian pashas, Greek millionaires, exiled Princes, high-ranking British officers and cosmopolitan beauties that constituted Cairene society during the war/sat/round us at other tables.
   ....

6 Cries of terror/rose/out of the fire and smoke. (Shiva Naipaul: *An Unfinished Journey*)
   ....

7 The bare white ribs of a boat being constructed to that design unchanged since the days of Noah's Ark/could be seen/every so often along the seafront. (Robert Lacey: *The Kingdom*)
   ....

8 [In 1925 Ragamah was a simple farm and] The agreement that unified Arabia/was enacted/there. (Robert Lacey: *The Kingdom*)
   ....

9 Two retired factory workers whose faces were withered contour maps/sat/opposite me. (Colin Thubron: *Behind the Wall*)
   ....

10 A bar by which the Chairman could haul up his ageing body/ hung/above it and/a red button for emergencies/was/near the tap. (Colin Thubron: *Behind the Wall*)
   ....

Exercise 188 Subject–operator inversion [SGE 18.17]

Subject–operator inversion is needed when a negative adverbial or object (in sentence structure) is fronted:

Never had I expected this.
None of the food could we eat.

or when *neither* or *nor* introduces a 'second' clause.

Nor do I.

But this does not apply when the negative word only belongs to 'local negation':

Nothing interesting ever happens!

Rewrite the following as indicated, making any other changes necessary.

1 I have not seen a more wonderful building anywhere.
   Nowhere...

2 There are no longer regular passenger liners calling at Bombay.
   No...

3 There is nowhere that I have seen that surpasses the Taj Mahal.
   Nowhere ....

4 I don't like the heat. My sister does not like the heat either.
   Neither..

5 She doesn't like it. And I don't either.
   .... And neither ....

6 We had no sooner arrived than the storm broke.
   No...

7 I have not experienced such a storm since I was a child.
   Not..

8 I did not know what would happen, and I did not care what would happen.
   I neither..

9 Tom arrived late and started complaining.
   Not only..

10 I'll never invite him again.
    Never...

11 Nothing good will come of this.
    No..

12 This will do you no good.
    No..

Exercise 189 Cleft and pseudo-cleft sentences [SGE 18.18–20]

Cleft and pseudo-cleft are devices for splitting a sentence into two to give greater emphasis to a particular part.

Complete the following using the information given to make cleft or pseudo-cleft sentences as indicated.

Examples: Drugs worry many governments. [the increase in drug-taking]
Cleft sentence: It's THE INCREASE IN DRUG-TAKING THAT WORRIES MANY GOVERNMENTS.
Pseudo-cleft: What WORRIES MANY GOVERNMENTS IS THE INCREASE IN DRUG-TAKING.

1 What makes people experiment with drugs? (perhaps boredom, a longing for excitement)
Perhaps it's..

2 Do we find drug-taking among all age-groups? (I think mainly among the young)
I think it's ....

3 We need to make people realize that drug-taking is self-destructive.
What..

4 But some people think that all drugs should be legal.
What..

5 They say the glamour of doing something illegal attracts people.
They say it's...

6 Some governments have such tough laws about trafficking, I am surprised any people become 'couriers'.
What surprises.. when ....

7 I suppose the hope of easy money tempts them.
I suppose it..

8 Many people don't realize that ordinary drug-takers need big money to buy drugs with.
What...

9 The drug barons deliberately involve 'small people'.
What...

10 The Customs people are looking for travellers who behave suspiciously.
What...

11 Often the small people, not the big people, get caught.
It's often...

12 Most governments want to stop drugs coming into their countries.
What...

Exercise 190 Postponement: extraposition [*SGE* 18.23–26]

Sometimes for the sake of end-focus or end-weight a sentence element is postponed, and put later in the sentence. When this kind of postponement involves using a pro-form earlier in the sentence it is called extraposition. Extraposition of subjects and objects is common.

It won't take long *to do this exercise.* (=To do this exercise won't take long.)
I am sure you will find *it* easy *doing this exercise*? (=I am sure you will find doing this exercise easy.)

Rewrite the following, where possible, without *it*, and with normal S V word order.

1 It won't be easy to persuade him.
2 I find it difficult to talk to him.
3 It strikes me that it'll be difficult.
4 It seems clear that we're quite likely to fail.
5 I think it extremely odd that he says nothing.
6 I've always thought it easier writing to him.
7 It'll probably make no difference what you say.
8 I leave it to you to do your best.
9 It seems that I misjudged him.
10 I take it that you don't want to consult Geoffrey?

Exercise 191 Discontinuities [*SGE* 18.27–28]

> Sometimes in the interests of end-focus and end-weight a sentence element gets split up. This sort of discontinuity often involves noun phrases.
>
> She's a *better* tennis-player *than I am*. [and not *a better than I am tennis-player].

Underline the discontinuous noun phrases and other discontinuities in the following.

1 Several accidents have been reported recently involving passengers falling from trains.
2 Last month there was an outcry in the press about the safety of carriage doors.
3 This followed an accident in which a young man fell to his death who had been drinking for most of the journey.
4 He had, alas, drunk rather more alcohol than he should have.
5 Now a claim is being made by the young man's parents that the railway is responsible for his death.
6 Accusations have been made against the railway of negligence.
7 And yet another investigation is being demanded into safety standards.
8 Railways clearly have a duty at all times to ensure that doors and windows are not faulty.
9 But it is surely up to passengers not to consume more alcohol than is good for them.
10 A lot of nonsense is talked these days about 'human rights'.
11 And the idea has got about that there is always someone to blame for an accident, who should pay compensation to the victims or their families.
12 But there is, alas, no absolute 'human right', as some people would have us believe, to survive a journey.
13 It is a fact of life that journeys – at any time – by train, car, plane, even on foot, carry some risk.
14 Airlines, railways, bus companies, shipping firms have a duty as passenger 'carriers' to maintain high standards.
15 But for passengers the time has come to realize that they too must exercise care.
16 In any case accidents will happen in this imperfect world, some of which are nobody's fault.

Exercise 192 Existential *there* [*SGE* 18.31–35]

Rewrite these quotations as they were originally written by adding *there* and making any other essential changes.

Example: In 1913 occurred one of those amazing events that make you feel truth really is stranger than fiction.

Answer: In 1913 there occurred one of those amazing events etc.

Example: A more extraordinary coincidence could hardly have been.

Answer: There could hardly have been a more extraordinary coincidence.

1 For, in a mysterious city referred to as London, lived a brother. (Shiva Naipaul: *An Unfinished Journey*)

2 Now and again appeared on the front steps of the house next door a good-looking woman. (Shiva Naipaul: *An Unfinished Journey*)

3 Some nicknames are obstacles to friendship. 'Honey' is one of them. (Paul Theroux: *The London Embassy*)

4 A month after Dostoyevsky died was enacted a scene such as he might have written into *The Devils*. (A N Wilson: *Tolstoy*)

5 A pleasanter place to buy a cottage for the summer could not be. (Lawrence Durrell: *The Greek Islands*)

19 From sentence to text

We often think of grammar as the grammar of sentences or clauses, but a longer 'text' is not just a collection of sentences. A group of sentences only form a meaningful text if they are connected by coherence of sense (eg: related vocabulary) and grammatical cohesion, which results from the use of place and time relators [*SGE* 19.3–14], pro-forms and ellipsis [*SGE* 19.15–20], conjuncts and other adverbials [*SGE* 19.21–25], coordinating and subordinating conjunctions [*SGE* 19.26–29] and the sequencing of the information in a suitable order [*SGE* 19.40–42]. In this chapter therefore the exercises are based on longer texts, rather than single sentences, and provide practice in a mixture of 'cohesive' devices.

Exercise 193 *A Brief History of Time*

Complete the following with these words:

after   already   but   did   equation   fate   half   however

in the end   it   mathematics   not   questions   so (2)   such as

therefore   these   this (2)   to   where   whether   which   without

I decided to try and write a popular book about space and time (1) .... I gave the Loeb lecture at Harvard in 1982. There were (2) .... a considerable number of books about the early universe and black holes, ranging from the very good, (3) .... Steven Weinberg's book, *The First Three Minutes*, (4) .... the very bad, (5) .... I will not identify. (6)..............., I felt that none of them really addressed the (7) .... that had led me to do research in cosmology and quantum theory: (8) .... did the universe come from? How and why did (9) .... begin? Will it come to an end and if (10)..............., how? (11) .... are questions that are of interest to us all. (12) .... modern science has become (13) .... technical that only a very small number of specialists are able to master the (14) .... used to describe them. Yet the basic ideas about the origin and (15) .... of the universe can be stated without mathematics in a form that people (16) .... a scientific education can understand. (17) .... is what I have attempted to do in this book. The reader must judge (18) .... I have succeeded.

Someone told me that each equation I included in the book would halve the sales. I (19) .... resolved (20) .... to have any equations at all. (21) ...., however, I (22) .... put in one equation, Einstein's famous (23)..............., E= mc^2. I hope that (24) .... will not scare off (25) .... of my potential readers. (Steve W Hawking: *A Brief History of Time*)

Exercise 194 Scurvy

Choose the best answers in the following:

1 Scurvy is a disease caused by vitamin C deficiency – (a) it (b) that (c) this (d) <u>which</u> itself is caused by a lack of fresh fruit and vegetables.

2 It was probably the biggest menace to crews on Pacific voyages (a) after (b) for (c) until (d) since   the nineteenth century,

3 as,(a) although (b) despite (c) however (d) seeing that   scurvy took a long time to kill them, it made them weak and was

4 (a) however (b) additionally (c) otherwise (d) thus   responsible for accidents, including shipwrecks.

5 There were cases of ships that, reaching home waters after months at sea, were unable to make port (a) although (b) because (c) even though (d) unless   there was no one on board strong enough to haul a rope.

6 The symptoms were various. First the gums swelled and the teeth became loose; (a) only (b) rather (c) then (d) still,   as the disease worsened it produced profound tiredness.

7 Men living exclusively on salted provisions (a) earlier (b) finally (c) similarly (d) sometimes   developed the symptoms within six weeks.

8 Though vitamins were not identified until the twentieth century, as (a) previously (b) early (c) recently (d) formerly   as 1593 it

9 (a) has been discovered (b) had been discovered (c) was to be discovered (d) would be discovered   that oranges and lemons were an effective remedy,

10 and the explorer James Cook (1728–79) had (a) a little (b) little (c) much (d) very much   trouble with scurvy among his crews on his long Pacific voyages.

11 (a) After all (b) Eventually (c) Finally (d) In the end,   in 1795 lemon juice was made compulsory in the Royal Navy.

12 Later, for a time, this was replaced with lime juice (a) although (b) however (c) whether (d) while   lemon is

13 (a) in case (b) in that case (c) in fact (d) by all means   better.

14 The American navy (a) at that time (b) meanwhile (c) on the contrary (d) nevertheless   had no such rule and laughingly described English sailors as 'limeys'.

Exercise 195 Young boy makes news

Here is a news item from *The Daily Telegraph* on 5 June 1991, but the paragraphs have been muddled. What order were they in in the paper?

1 With an instructor beside him he took off from San Diego, California, on 26 May and landed on Monday evening in North Carolina, home of Orville and Wright, the pioneers of flying.

2 Mr Art Greenfield, secretary of its Contests and Records Board, said he would not enter the flight as an aviation record because the boy was officially not solo.

3 Mr Ken Shanklin, 59, a plastic surgeon from California, said his grandson had broken the record, currently held by a nine-year-old, but the National Aeronautical Association had doubts.

4 Daniel Shanklin, from Texas, flew a single-engined Cessna for four hours a day for nine days, and is claiming the record for the youngest person to cross America by air.

5 But what worried Daniel was that he had not managed a smoother landing at the end of his feat. 'I wanted it to be the best,' he said.

6 The cockpit had to be adapted slightly, with extensions placed on the rudder pedals to accommodate his short legs, and he sat on a booster seat with a cushion.

7 A seven-year-old boy whose grandfather gave him flying lessons as a Christmas present has piloted a plane across the United States.

Exercise 196 Cousteau's undersea world

The words in italic are in the wrong places. Can you put them where they belong?

Now Jacques-Yves Cousteau invented the aqualung in 1943 in association with his colleague, Emile Gagnan, who designed the critical demand valve or regulator *and later the natural history of the marine environment.*

By enabling swimmers to move freely underwater, his invention proved of considerable strategic importance in occupied France during the Second World War. It was Cousteau's films of sunken wrecks *which enabled divers to breath air from gas canisters attached to their backs,* which brought the undersea world to the attention of millions of people *when used to plant submarine mines.*

However he has turned his efforts to campaigning for the conservation of Antarctica.

Exercise 197 Stress at work

The following phrases and sentences are missing from the passage. Put them where they belong.

(a) You may feel you have heard this before.

(b) Nor are ill-health, absenteeism, heavy drinking or insomnia.

(c) that is, too much work, too little time

(d) Another, by a clinical psychologist called Jenny Firth, looked at the effects of stress on medical students and doctors.

(e) this approach is counter-productive.

(f) It is just a question of using the immense power of your brain to take the load off your shoulders.

(g) And fatigue and stress are two of the biggest enemies of productivity and efficiency.

(h) and with high levels of absenteeism.

(i) for example

(j) too much to do, too little time to do it, and far too much pressure.

(k) that our lives are nothing but an endless grind; and that even this grind may not be enough to save us from failure.

(l) which is the key to efficiency.

(m) Another experiment showed that this deterioration can be much worse, if the fatigue is exacerbated by noise – which for most people it frequently is.

(n) It doesn't matter what you worry about

(o) until you stop pretending, you are unlikely to come up with a more intelligent solution to your problems.

Most people see work as a problem. Inside and outside the office, the complaints are almost invariably the same:(1) .... The problem is almost universal. But there is a solution. (2) ....

Most of us respond to a daunting workload by working harder – and by worrying. We worry that there are too many demands on our time and energy; (3) .... However hard we work, things never get any easier. But still we respond by working harder – and by worrying.

Unfortunately (4) .... Hard work – whether it is office work, housework, voluntary work or anything else – causes fatigue. Worry causes stress. (5) .... Simply trying harder, therefore, will not help you to get more done.

(6) .... But do you really accept it? It is easy to pretend to yourself that fatigue does not really affect you, just as it is easy to pretend that drinking does not really affect your driving. And (7) ....

So here, before we go any further are some facts. Fatigue does affect efficiency. Countless psychological studies have shown this. One study, (8) ...., showed that increasing a working day from eight hours to twelve hours can increase error rates by as much as eighty per cent. (9) .... Noise had alarming effects on subjects' alertness and judgement.

Similarly, the negative effects of worrying are well-documented. One company survey suggested that 75 per cent of senior managers found it difficult to sleep as a result of job worries. (10) .... She found that nearly a third of the fourth-year medical students showed signs of emotional disturbance – and roughly half of the junior doctors. (11) .... – worry is simply not good for you.

More detailed research, conducted in Holland, identified particular types of stress with particular symptoms. 'Overload' – (12) .... – is associated with high blood pressure, obesity and heavy smoking. 'Role ambiguity' in which people simply do not know what they are supposed to be doing – is associated with all sorts of psychological complaints – (13) ....

The implications are obvious. Psychological disturbance is not conducive to efficiency. (14) .... But if you are healthy and happy and not suffering from exhaustion, you are more likely to work well – (15) .... The best way of looking after your work is to look after yourself.

Punctuation [*SGE* 19.30–34]

Punctuation is a sort of written substitute for all those features of stress and intonation that we use in speech. It helps to make our message clear, and the wrong punctuation can sometimes not only make understanding difficult – it can actually give the wrong message.

Exercise 198 The meaning of punctuation

Punctuate the following items in two different ways each to show different meanings. Use capital letters, apostrophes, etc where necessary.

1 my brother who lives in Australia is retired

   (a) (I have only one brother) ....

   (b) (I have more than one) ....

2 do write soon should you have any problems let me know

   (a) (Write if you have problems) ....

   (b) (Write anyway) ....

3 if these boys were encouraged to play more football they wouldnt have time for other dangerous pursuits

   (a) (football is dangerous) ....

   (b) (football isn't dangerous) ....

4 this years exam papers were unusually difficult

   (a) (they are always fairly difficult) ....

   (b) (they are not usually difficult) ....

5 the island evidently did not evoke too many sentimental memories for charles and diana subsequently holidayed there

   (a) (they probably went together) ....

   (b) (Diana apparently went alone) ....

6 michael dobbss novel house of cards was adapted for television last year.

   (a) (*House of Cards* is an unusual work of some kind)

   ....

   (b) (it is a work of fiction) ....

7 an old bomb exploded in the capital yesterday killing a 15- year-old youth who was examining it and injuring his father

   (a) (the boy was attacking his father) ....

   (b) (the bomb claimed two victims) ....

8 the document has already annoyed the government which says the society is not really interested in the zoos problems

   (a) (it is claimed that the government does not care)

   ....

   (b) (it is claimed that the society does not care)

   ....

9 my neighbours dog has attacked our cat

(a) (the neighbour lives alone) ....

(b) (the dog belongs to a family) ....

10 the night porter serves sandwiches and drinks

(a) (you can get food and drink at night in this hotel)

....

(b) (the night porter is a bit of an alcoholic)

....

Exercise 199 *Among the Russians*

Punctuate the following passage, adding commas, full stops, quotation marks, capital letters, etc. as necessary.

even now i was unsure what drew me into this country i feared i belonged to a generation too young to romanticize about soviet communism yet nothing in the intervening years had dispelled my childhood estrangement and ignorance my mind was filled with confused pictures paradox cliche russia wrote the marquis de custine in 1839 is a country where everyone is part of a conspiracy to mystify the foreigner propaganda still hangs like a ground-mist over the already complicated truth newspapers until you know how to read them are organs of disinformation the arts are conservative or silent even in novels which so often paint the ordinary nature of things the visionaries and drunks who inhabit the pages of nineteenth century fiction have shrivelled to the poor wooden heroes of modern socialist realism it is as if a great lamp had been turned down. (Colin Thubron: *Among the Russians*, 1983)

Exercise 200 A final puzzle

Here is a children's puzzle. Can you punctuate this to make sense? (*Clue*: We are talking about what Geoffrey and Jan wrote.)

Jan whereas Geoffrey had had had had had had had had had had had their fellow authors approval.

KEY – Suggested answers

Note: In some cases other answers may be acceptable

Chapter 1 The English language

Ex 1

1 it did not *used* to be: this spelling, instead of it did not *use* to be, cannot be defended, but is often seen.

2 if it hadn't *have* been …: this is an unorthodox tense, quite often heard as an alternative for the more correct *if it hadn't been*

3 suggested she *take* up: an example of the subjunctive, which is increasingly being used in English today. Perfectly acceptable.

4 I *may* have followed: traditional grammar requires *might have followed* here, since clearly this is no longer a possibility. But the usage is common.

5 if he *were*: hypercorrection for *was*. Do not use the subjunctive in indirect questions.

6 As for *we* English: hypercorrection. After a preposition an object pronoun is needed (*for us*).

7 *us* spectators: the reverse mistake! *We … were kept*. But pronoun usage today is very confused.

8 *than* in the 1970s: traditional grammar requires *as many … as* in the 1970s. Again usage seems to be changing.

9 *less* words: Prescriptivists want *fewer* with a plural count noun, but *less* is very common.

10 *like* glass locks in: definitely a disputed usage. Prescriptivists cannot bear *like* to be used as a conjunction, but it has been so used for many years.

11 Writing …, a feeling: a misattached participle. Again a common

grammatical usage, but usually felt to be a failure of style.

12 breathe a little easier: disputed usage. Purists want an adverb here (*more easily*).

13 different … than: more disputed usage. Purists want *different from*.

14 a regular customer were … with their own branch, it may be …: two problems here. Prescriptivists object to a singular noun + *their*, though this is acceptable to grammarians, and increasingly popular as a way of avoiding the use of masculine pronouns, where men and women are referred to … Purists also object to *may* instead of *might* (see 4).

15 either impossible …, full of mistakes or both. Purists maintain that *either … or* can only refer to two choices, not three (as here). Grammarians don't mind.

16 None … were: perfectly all right, except to purists who wrongly maintain that *none* = no one and therefore needs a singular verb!

17 educations …: *education* is usually a noncount noun, but this plural usage is acceptable.

18 to actually carry out: this breaks a prescriptive rule that you mustn't 'split an infinitive', but it is perfectly acceptable.

19 No sooner are one set of perils …: purists always want grammatical concord (*no sooner is one set …*), but notional concord is acceptable here.

20 plus: purists do not like *plus* used as a conjunction, but this is a usage that is probably here to stay.

Chapter 2 A general framework

Ex 2

2(f) 3(j) 4(i) 5(h) 6(e) 7(d) 8(g) 9(b)
10(a)

Ex 3

1 was exhausted (verb + adj) 2 casting
long shadows 3 following it
4 immediately above 5 almost homely

Ex 4

2 subject 3 object 4 complement
5 object of preposition 6 complement
7 complement 8 complement 9 part of
NP 10, 11, 12 adverbials

Ex 5

2(a) 3(c) 4(a) 5(b) 6(c) 7(b) 8(b) 9(c)
10(b)

Ex 6

2 nouns 3 adjectives 4 pronouns
5 adverbs 6 prepositions 7 determiners
8 conjunctions

Ex 7

1 want 2 can 3 every 4 upwards 5 too
6 learn 7 obviously 8 must 9 how
10 friendly

Chapter 3 Verbs and auxiliaries

Ex 8

1 listen – imp 2 listen – bare infin
3 listen – subj 4 listen – *to*-infin 5 listen
– pres 6 stand – bare infin, get – imp
7 get – *to*-infin 8 work – bare infin, get –
subj, find – subj 9 get – pres 10 know –
bare infin, get – bare infin

Ex 9

1 gave 2 set 3 wrapped 4 led
5 populated 6 perched 7 descended
8 disappeared 9 dropped 10 rose
11 rounded 12 stood

Ex 10

simple past 1, 2, 4, 7, 8, 9, 10, 12
nonfinite participle 3, 5, 6, 11

Ex 11

waits – makes, hesitates, repeats, keeps,
corrupts; *weighs* – drives, broadens,
begins, comes, pays, tends; *wishes* –
catches, passes, washes

Ex 12

2 rested 3 said 4 began 5 thought 6 said
7 needed 8 rode 9 told 10 waved
11 pedalled 12 watched 13 thought
14 put 15 rode 16 was 17 led 18 kept
19 thought 20 revelled 21 darted
22 pulled 23 snapped 24 intended
25 jammed 26 jarred 27 catapulted
28 went

Ex 13

wished – watched, snapped; *weighed* –
waved, pedalled, revelled, pulled,
jammed, jarred; *waited* – rested, needed,
darted, intended, catapulted

Ex 14

2 lying 3 offered 4 mislaid 5 repaid
6 panicking 7 suing 8 whingeing
9 dyed 10 developed

Ex 15

1 Rioting has spread to the city centre.
2 A dream has come true for an
  octogenarian.
3 A boy has slept through a pit ordeal.
4 Tottenham have lost out …
5 Thousands have gone on strike …
6 Postal charges have risen again.
7 A madman has shot five people.
8 An MP has fought off a death threat
  from a mugger.
9 P&O profits have fallen …
10 A ferry has sunk …
11 Refugees have fled …
12 The last of the refugees have flown
  home.
13 The West Country has borne …
14 A gun victim has undergone …
15 A/The new pressure group has
  swung …
16 The coup leader has broadcast …
17 A tenor has hit back …

Ex 16

1 There is … 2 I am … 3 Do not …
4 We will … 5 It has … 6 I had …
7 Who would … 8 I have … I am …

Ex 17

1 Don't you? I do. 2 Can't you? I can.
3 Did you? I didn't. 4 Had you? I hadn't.
5 Have you? I haven't. 6 Has he? I
haven't. 7 Isn't he? I am. 8 Are you?

I'm not. 9 Don't you? We do. 10 Will you? We won't. 11 Would you? I wouldn't. 12 Haven't you? We have.

Ex 18
2 do you 3 doesn't do 4 don't 5 Does he
6 does he do 7 did he 8 did he do
9 doesn't 10 don't do 11 didn't do
12 don't

Ex 19
Your own answers, but notice 1/3/4/5/7/
8/9 need a bare infinitive 2/6/10/11/12
need *to*-infinitive

Ex 20
2(b) 3(e) 4(c) 5(i) 6(a) 7(g) 8(f)
9(j) 10(d)

Ex 21
might seem/had been doing/hadn't
chosen/had worked out/was born/died/
was/decided to make/had inherited/was/
managed to scrape/spent ploughing/
(spent) canoeing/(spent) skiing/gave
nonfinite: to plan/(to) carry out/making/
received/commanding

Ex 22
He ordered that all prison officers strictly
observe … insisted that they not let …
vital that visitors be searched … essential
that all sections of the prison be searched.
… recommended that extra staff be
recruited …

Ex 23
2 is built 3 are publicly advertised 4 be
informed 5 is given 6 be fully informed
7 be obtained 8 are directly affected 9 is
placed 10 are notified 11 be sent 12 (be)
told 13 be inspected 14 are kept 15 be
allowed 16 have been heard

Ex 24
2 … are raised by (a); 3 is conducted by
(e); 4 … be represented by (c); 5 is made
by (d)

Ex 25
2 sat/was sitting 3 are believed
4 approached 5 ran 6 was parked/had
been parked 7 shot 8 ran 9 fled 10 was
hit 11 is said 12 cordoned 13 was well

planned 14 had been targeted 15 was
later found 16 is not known

Chapter 4 The semantics of the verb phrase

Ex 26
State 5, 12, 13, 14
Habit 2, 4, 6, 10
Instantaneous 3, 9, 11
Past 1   Future 7, 8, 15

Ex 27
Event 3, 4, 6, 8, 12, 13, 15, 19, 20,
    21, 23, 24, 25
Habit 7, 10, 14, 17, 22
State 5, 9, 11, 18
Indirect speech 2
Attitude 1
Hypothesis 16, 26

Ex 28
2 feed 3 pick up/are picking up 4 eat
5 thrive/are thriving 6 emphasizes 7 is
shown 8 appears 9 do not attack 10 nest
11 nest 12 are adapting 13 says/say
14 are now asking

Ex 29
2 am watching 3 is giving 4 is making
5 know 6 make 7 know 8 are coming
9 enjoy 10 promise 11 ends 12 finishes
13 are interrupting 14 am missing
15 whisk 16 stand 17 make 18 looks
19 fold/am carefully folding 20 whisk

Ex 30
2 have been overworking 3 haven't been
sleeping 4 have been overeating 5 have
put on 6 Have you booked 7 has just
returned 8 has been going 9 have
sometimes thought 10 have been
11 have spent 12 have always wanted
13 have been teaching 14 have heard
15 have been saving 16 haven't saved
17 haven't had 18 have been 19 have
just moved 20 have made

Ex 31
2 has only recently started 3 is making
4 enjoys/is enjoying 5 has always found
6 likes 7 belongs 8 borrows 9 does not
look up 10 doesn't know 11 tries

12 says 13 is getting 14 likes 15 offers
16 declares 17 writes 18 find/have found
19 are forever making 20 has found
21 has already written 22 (has) received
23 have ever done 24 have always
wanted 25 says 26 has just been invited
27 feels 28 needs 29 is attending
30 means 31 says 32 am looking forward

Ex 32

2 wrote 3 have written 4 have become
5 published 6 have never been 7 have
been translated 8 have actually increased
9 died 10 fell 11 revived 12 were made
13 have more recently been followed
14 brought/have brought 15 honoured
16 was 17 has broken 18 has been
named 19 have enjoyed 20 has ever
been 21 has become

Ex 33

1 Julius Caesar was pursuing … when
  he first met …
2 When Julius Caesar met Cleopatra, he
  fell …
3 Philip II … was assassinated while he
  was planning …
4 Marco Polo began to write … while
  he 'was doing time' …
5 Columbus was looking for Asia, when
  he discovered …
6 When he returned to Spain, he
  received …
7 Captain Cook was making … when he
  was killed …
8 When Cook died, his crew took …
9 … Marat was sitting … when
  Charlotte Corday rushed in and killed
  him.
10 When she assassinated him, she was
  arrested …
11 Dr Livingstone was travelling …
  when Stanley found him.
12 When Stanley found him he said …

Ex 34

1 Scott had reached Melbourne when he
  received …
2 When Scott set up … Amunsden had
  not yet reached …
3 Scott's party set out … Amunsden's
  party had already left.

4 Scott's party had only got 2,000 feet
  above … when the Norwegians
  reached the Pole.
5 Scott did not know that Amundsen
  had beaten …
6 … Scott began … and sent … The
  other assault party had been sent
  back …
7 Scott reached the Pole … to discover
  Amundsen had raised the Norwegian
  flag …
8 They had covered … but they
  faced …
9 … they found that … oil had leaked
10 …Oates died. Evans had died four
  weeks earlier.
11 They were defeated before they had
  managed …
12 Scott … had been dead … months
  when they were discovered.

Ex 35

2 are going 3 will love 4 are you leaving
5 are flying 6 will be 7 are going
8 Won't you get 9 will certainly be
10 are visiting 11 will get 12 are you
staying 13 are only having 14 will
actually stay 15 will come 16 won't
17 are having 18 will just relax

Ex 36

I'll be 2 are you going to take … I'm
going to try 3 I'll lend 4 I'll phone
5 I'm going to try 6 will you do 7 I'm
going to take 8 We'll keep 9 Will you

Ex 37

2(a) 3(c) 4(a) 5(c) 6(a) 7(a) 8(b) 9(a)
10(a) 11(c) 12(c) 13(a) 14(b) 15(c)
16(a) 17(a) 18(a) 19(a) 20(c)

Ex 38

Past 7, 12, 17 Present 2, 4, 5, 8, 10, 11,
14, 16, 19, 21, 22 Future 1, 3, 6, 9, 13,
15 Future in the past 18, 20

Ex 39

Ability 10
Permission 14
Possibility 1, 7, 15
Obligation/necessity 2, 3, 4, 5, 6, 8, 13
Logical necessity 11
Tentative inference 9, 12

Ex 40

2(c) 3(b) 4(a) 5(b) 6(b) 7(a) 8(c) 9(c)
10(c) 11(b) 12(a) 13(a) 14 (b) 15(a)
16(b) 17(c) 18(c) 19(c) 20(b) 21(b)
22(b)

Ex 41

2 We could have bought tickets for Friday.
3 We thought you might have made ...
4 We couldn't have come on Friday.
5 We shouldn't have/oughtn't to have left it ...
6 We should have booked/ought to have booked ...
7 Mother may/could have arrived by then
8 She can't have/couldn't have telephoned yesterday ...
9 We will/shall have heard ...
10 ... she will have/must have forgotten ...
11 She can't have/won't have/wouldn't have forgotten.
12 needn't have apologized...

Ex 42

2 having to
3 didn't have to play football
4 were allowed to
5 to be able to
6 being able to play games well
7 haven't been able to continue playing tennis
8 have to

Ex 43

1(b) 2(d) 3(b) 4(a) 5(c) 6(c) 7(c) 8(c)

Ex 44

1 was sighted 2 dined/had dined 3 set sail/had set sail 4 realized 5 was sailing 6 wondered 7 went 8 was 9 had all vanished 10 had been 11 was held later/was later held 12 has never been solved

Ex 45

1 can't have 2 would have been found
3 must have got drunk etc 4 may have/might have/could have boarded etc
5 would they have done that 6 can't have been/cannot have been 7 must have exploded 8 may have decided

9 shouldn't have done/oughtn't to have done 10 must have caught the Mary Celeste, the rope must have/will have broken and everyone must have/will have drowned

Chapter 5 Nouns and determiners

Ex 46

1 one achievement/failure/success
2 employment/work 3 advertising/publicity/marketing 4 a bargain/saving/reduction 5 a fortune/an income 6 a new suit 7 Modern ammunition/equipment/weaponry is ... 8 a pass/permit 9 a good experience/time 10 one scene/view

Ex 47

2 glass/a glass 3 an experience/experience 4 a pleasure/pleasure 5 a painting/painting 6 a worry/worry 7 a noise/noise 8 Business/a business 9 a very special cheese/cheese 10 dinner/a dinner 11 a very active life/life 12 an ice/ice

Ex 48

2 detail/explanation 3 behaviour/conduct
4 damage/harm 5 importance/value/worth 6 storms/weather 7 bag/suitcase
8 computer/machine 9 fun/joy
10 courage/patience

Ex 49

2 no 3 no 4 Any 5 some 6 some
7 some 8 any 9 any 10 no
11 something 12 no

Ex 50

2 There are several more complaints about this one matter alone.
3 Both these two surgical dressings have to be changed every second day.
4 They needed three times that amount of food for all those people.
5 Take half a tablet every four hours.
6 Those first few days were worse than all the rest.
7 It's disgraceful because you now get half a packet at double the price.
8 Both Mary's last two husbands were twice her age.

9 She bought another ten new dresses the other day.

10 You could get several dozen little ones for the same price as one big one.

Ex 51

1 Few 2 a few 3 little 4 a little 5 A few 6 A little 7 little 8 few

Ex 52

1 the 2 the 3 a 4 a 5 the 6 A 7 a 8 the 9 a 10 the 11 the 12 an 13 the 14 a 15 the 16 a 17 The 18 the 19 the 20 the

Ex 53

1 – 2 – 3 The 4 The 5 – 6 the 7 The 8 the 9 the 10 the 11 the 12 the 13 a 14 – 15 A 16 – 17 the 18 the 19 A 20 the 21 – 22 the 23 – 24 the 25 the 26 – 27 a 28 – 29 the 30 a 31 the 32 the 33 – 34 – 35 – 36 a 37 – 38 the 39 – 40 – 41 a 42 an 43 the/– 44 the 45 a 46 the 47 a 48 the/– 49 the/– 50 the

Ex 54

2 after breakfast 3 to school 4 on foot 5 by car/by bus/by train 6 in the morning/in the afternoon/in the evening/at night 7 – home 8 at night, by day/during the day 9 by air 10 on the plane 11 an infectious disease such as – measles, – mumps or – whooping cough. 12 in hospital 13 on holiday 14 in (the) spring, (the) summer, (the) autumn or (the) winter?

Ex 55

the is needed in 3, 4, 6, 9, 11, 16, 17, 20, 21, 22, 24, 25, 26, 28, 29, 33, 34, 35, 36, 38, 39, 40, 41, 43, 45, 48, 49. Zero in all other places.

Ex 56

1 snowmen 2 bookshelves 3 scarves … handkerchiefs 4 plaice 5 dozen 6 stories … spacecraft 7 hundred 8 pound(s)

Ex 57

2 encyclopaedias 3 indexes and appendices 4 crises 5 memoranda/memorandums 6 prospectuses 7 stimuli

8 criteria

Ex 58

2 These belongings … were 3 This family need/This family needs 4 these binoculars but they aren't … 5 The police have … 6 What was the news … 7 There are a couple of people who want … 8 The PM's office has/have … 9 The outskirts … are 10 A majority of the strikers want … 11 Our MP's majority was … 12 Why are there remains … 13 The public has … in its name/The public have … in their name 14 The audience was/were

Ex 59

1 … my parents' insistence on taking the dog … 2 My uncle's education, … 3 My aunt's things … 4 … Bill's omission 5 Bill's loyalty 6 my grandmother's spectacles 7 My grandfather's advisers 8 My mother's disappointment

Ex 60

2 St Paul's Cathedral is in the City.

3 The Houses of Parliament are at Westminster.

4 The Travellers' Club is in Pall Mall.

5 Postmen's Park is near the General Post Office.

6 Cleopatra's Needle is on the Embankment.

7 The Royal Academy of Arts is in Piccadilly.

8 Madame Tussaud's is near Baker Street station.

9 The Museum of Childhood is in Bethnal Green.

10 The Tower of London is at Tower Hill.

11 Nelson's Column is in Trafalgar Square.

12 Traitors' Gate is at the Tower of London.

Chapter 6 Pronouns

Ex 61

1 ourselves … themselves … them 2 them … them … themselves 3 herself … it 4 me … yourself 5 ourselves …

ourselves ... us 6 himself ... him ... him
7 themselves ... myself 8 you ... you ...
myself ... yourself

Ex 62

1 ... crying over spilt milk 2 – 3 to
know what to do 4 – 5 to keep our
options open 6 – 7 – 8 if I'm late
9 when you talk like that 10 having
nothing to do 11 to tell you what to do
12 –

Ex 63

2(b) there's nothing for it 3(a) (to have)
   had it 4(d) have it both ways 5(e) live
   it up   6(h) have it in for (someone) 7(f)
   go it alone 8(g) rough it

Ex 64

2 All those late nights were the trouble.
3 I'm all in favour of his trying again.
4 I'm afraid that he is lazy.
5 We have to face the fact that he is not
   going ...
6 He appears to resent advice.
7 What really annoys me is all his talk
   of poverty.
8 I doubt if/whether he'll ask for a loan.
9 I'm not keen on the idea of lending
   him money.
10 If you hadn't helped, he would be in a
   worse mess.

Ex 65

2 Who did they get inside help from?
3 What were they looking for?
4 What clues have we got so far?
5 What help are we likely to get from
   the staff?
6 Which thief/Which of the thieves left
   his jacket behind?
7 Whose key did they use?
8 Who did this jacket belong to?/Whose
   jacket is this?/Whose is this jacket?
9 Which door did they enter by?
10 someone who/that had
11 someone to whom
12 anyone whose
13 everyone who/that has
14 everyone to whom
15 anything which/that could
16 someone whose

Ex 66

1 This 2 this 3 those 4 this and that
5 that 6 those 7 these 8 This 9 that
10 These 11 this 12 those

Ex 67

1 something 2 nothing 3 someone/
somebody 4 Everyone/everybody
5 everyone/everybody 6 Something
7 anyone's/anybody's 8 No one/Nobody
9 something 10 anyone/anybody
11 anything 12 No one/Nobody
13 everything 14 nothing

Ex 68

1 all 2 Half 3 half 4 all 5 Half 6 half
7 Neither 8 Both 9 Neither 10 either
11 both 12 both 13 Neither 14 Both
15 each

Ex 69

2 It 3 their 4 them 5 it 6 one 7 which
8 we 9 The 10 this/the 11 an 12 their
13 their/the 14 they 15 the 16 a
17 what 18 which 19 us 20 its 21 It
22 their 23 we/one 24 their 25 It
26 they 27 them 28 the 29 this/the
30 their

Chapter 7 Adjectives and adverbs

Ex 70

1 ashamed 2 afraid 3 an occasional
event 4 inner strength 5 an outdoor party
6 an only child 7 glad 8 the main worry
9 content 10 the maximum speed
11 ready 12 your elder brother

Ex 71

2 frightening 3 disappointed 4 annoyed
5 boring 6 is really interested
7 surprising 8 worrying 9 puzzling
10 are exhausted

Ex 72

2 our late chairman 3 the people present
4 certain people 5 people absent from the
meeting 6 the only proper thing 7 the
present addresses 8 is conscious of 9 his
subscription was late 10 her late husband
had always paid 11 a conscious effort
12 all the people concerned/involved
13 is certain that 14 a long and involved
business

Ex 73

2 glad of the opportunity 3 aware of the
difficulties 4 different from all my
previous jobs 5 worried about any aspect
of the work 6 subject to negotiation
7 good at coping 8 grateful for your
remarks 9 bored with my last job
10 answerable to the board

Ex 74

2 an impossible camera for a beginner
3 a similar model to the last one 4 an
easy camera to use 5 any different makes
from these 6 a more suitable camera for
a child 7 a big enough bag to carry spare
film in 8 any cheaper bags than these
9 as big an album as possible 10 a hard
customer to please

Ex 75

1 round – walks round in circles
2 also – also walks in straight lines
3 very – very long
4 sometimes – he rearranges the
 landscape and photographs the result
5 halfway – halfway up
6 out – make out
7 once – once described a ... walk ... as
 a ... sculpture
8 quite – quite the word
9 highly – highly talented
10 rather – rather a joker
11 fairly – fairly quickly
12 quickly – quickly creating great
 circles and other shapes on the walls
 and floors of art galleries
13 well – well over
14 technically – technically difficult
15 almost – almost anyone
16 previously – previously done this and
 called it art
17 together – gather together
18 too – too much

Ex 76

2 rightly 3 wrongly 4 hard 5 just
6 First/Firstly 7 Nearly 8 hardly 9 late
10 high 11 near 12 highly 13 Lastly
14 right

Ex 77

1 hard 2 last 3 first 4 in a cowardly way
5 early 6 late 7 high 8 in a leisurely way
9 near 10 justly

Ex 78

1 the highest 2 in the 3 higher 4 high
5 the highest 6 the highest of 7 higher
than 8 as high as 9 the highest 10 as
high as 11 higher than 12 the highest of

Chapter 8 The semantics and grammar of adverbials

Ex 79

single adverbs: everywhere, there,
around, somehow, suddenly, over, too,
now, out, just, always, very
noun phrases: all the time, one week, the
next week
prepositional phrases: on the stairs, in
the room, with his toe, for ten years
verbless clause: whenever possible
nonfinite clause: hearing his explanation
finite clause: if I could be bothered

Ex 80

2 'I don't play again until Thursday, so I
 can relax and practise a bit,'
3 said the defending snooker champion
 later at Sheffield's Crucible Theatre,
 where the championships are being
 held.
4 This may be the last time an IAAF
 competition is staged in London for
 some years.
5 According to her coach, Rosa Mota's
 most impressive performance was in a
 minor road race last summer.
6 She ran 10 km at Boulder, Colorado
 only two days ...
7 Hull saw Wolves skipper Ron
 Hindmarch clear the ball from near
 the line in the closing seconds ...
8 Nottingham Forest beat Chelsea 7-0 at
 City Ground yesterday.
9 Golfer Fred Couples of the USA led
 the field in the Tournois Perrier de
 Paris at la Boulie in Paris today.
10 The talented young Yugoslav tennis
 player hit 22 aces on clay to beat
 Becker at the French Open last year.
11 Bjorn Borg won the Wimbledon
 tennis champion ships five times
 between 1976 and 1980.
12 ... he returned to tennis in the Monte
 Carlo Open on 23 April 1991.

Ex 81

1(a) I badly need your help. (b) They organized the meeting badly.
2(a) I don't even try … (b) Even I don't try …
3(a) I just sat and waited … (b) … for just ten minutes.
4(a) Kindly explain … (b) … if you speak to me kindly.
5(a) I have only come … . (b) I think only you can help.
6(a) Possibly the guide told us/The guide possibly told us. (b) … we could not possibly get …
7(a) I really enjoyed it. (b) I enjoyed it really.
8(a) … simply try to explain … (b) try to explain simply …
9(a) I still don't have … (b) I don't still have …
10(a) he looked very much like … (b) I haven't thought about it very much at all …

Ex 82

2 … for some people to talk frankly. …
3 Frankly, I don't know …
4 … that truthfully described …
5 … and truthfully, I didn't want him any more.
6 Honestly, I don't mind/I honestly don't mind.
7 Dealing with feelings honestly …
8 … since it has been generally accepted …
9 The poor have generally been in favour …
10 … before it was shown generally.
11 … we do, generally speaking, dream in colour.
12 Literally all I had to do …
13 … we literally didn't have …
14 … literally explode.
15 … literally danced.
16 He personally wants to see you.
17 I didn't know her personally.
18 Personally, I think …/I personally think …

Ex 83

2 for example 3 As a result 4 Further
5 then 6 Hence 7 However 8 on the
contrary 9 thus 10 Anyhow 11 So
12 by contrast 13 In other words
14 though 15 In fact 16 On the other
hand 17 First 18 Thus 19 Secondly
20 Similarly

Ex 84

1 have still not studied
2 is merely one of those
3 entirely understandable
4 not suggested for a moment/not for a moment suggested
5 considering the evidence with great care
6/7 surely not too much to hope
8 reasonably open minds
9 After all, there are …/There are, after all, /… in the world, after all
10 which were once
11 very dubious indeed
12 first hit
13 the world's press in 1933
14 a strange animal in this remote lake
15 had circulated locally
16 unfortunately turned out
17 to track Nessie down
18/19 within four days he and his photographer found footprints on the shore
20/21 He even gave a talk about it on the BBC
22 But, sadly, the footprint/But the footprint had, sadly, been made
23 over the years numerous sightings/numerous sightings have been reported over the years
24 (allegedly of the animals)
25 produced in evidence
26 descended into the lake
27 a miniature sub with echo-sounding equipment/searched with echo-sounding equipment.
28 shown in the Houses of Parliament to/shown to MPs, scientists and journalists in the Houses of Parliament
29/30 large animals undoubtedly existed in the lake
31 strongly disagreed
32 published in 1991
33 painstakingly examines
34 is that, sadly, she does not and cannot exist

Chapter 9 Prepositions and prepositional phrases

Ex 85

1 interested in … What is Andrew interested in?
2 What is Andrew good at?
3 What is Andrew keen on?
4 What does Andrew worry about?
5 What did Andrew have to contend with?
6 What is Andrew suffering from?
7 What is Andrew hoping for?
8 What is Andrew fond of?
9 What does Andrew object to?
10 What does Andrew believe in?
11 What does Andrew depend on?
12 What does Andrew long for?

Ex 86

2 Contrary to 3 because of 4 except for
5 As for 6 apart from 7 instead of
8 Prior to 9 out of 10 along with
11 thanks to 12 irrespective of

Ex 87

2 With reference to 3 on account of 4 in addition to 5 in exchange for 6 for the sake of 7 in spite of 8 in comparison with 9 in touch with 10 by means of
11 by way of 12 on behalf of

Ex 88

1 on 2 across/around/of 3 from 4 from/out of 5 at/by 6 at 7 on 8 to 9 in
10 with 11 on/about 12 through
13 during 14 from 15 to 16 by 17 For
18 of 19 without 20 at 21 in 22 on
23 in 24 like 25 after (AmE – for)
26 from 27 In 28 of 29 by 30 for
31 between 32 in 33 at 34 on
35 outside 36 By 37 about 38 for 39 as
40 to 41 in 42 at 43 in 44 of 45 with
46 under 47 with 48 off 49 since
50 except

Ex 89

1 I only know them by sight.
2 He never arrives on time.
3 But for once he did.
4 … seem quite out of hand.
5 What I want above all is …
6 … you are right up to a point.

7 I didn't break it on purpose.
8 What are you doing at present?
9 I'm not doing anything in particular this evening.
10 I'll be with you in a minute.
11 No way. It is just out of the question.
12 After all, he's very old now.
13 Everything is in order.
14 By the way, have you seen Andrew lately?
15 If you go on trying, you'll manage in the end.

Ex 90

1(f) out of 2(k) over 3(i) in/at 4(n) on/of
5(h) without 6(a) in 7(e) like 8(l) in
9(g) of 10(j) for 11(c) with 12(b) at
13(m) of 14(d) at

Ex 91

2 on 3 to 4 against 5 to 6 for 7 to 8 for
9 at 10 with/for 11 for 12 on 13 with
14 on 15 on 16 of 17 with 18 with/about 19 for 20 to 21 from 22 of

Ex 92

1 … there have been no reports in the offical media of the growing tension …
2 … was described by Lambeth Palace as a misunderstanding or [a different meaning] … was described as a misunderstanding on the part of Lambeth Palace.
3 The third man has, on the advice of his lawyer, not made himself available.
4 He was forced, on Monday afternoon, to abandon …
5 Detectives arrested the girl's father after spending two days watching the flat he had rented.
6 Bend your legs when picking up heavy weights like groceries or children.

Chapter 10 The simple sentence

Ex 93

2 SV 3 SVOO 4 SVO 5 SVOA
6 SVOO 7 SVC 8 SVA 9 SVO
10 SVOA 11 SV 12 SVOC 13 SVA
14 SVA 15 SVOC

Ex 94

1 ... money to that dreadful man.
2 ... begging letters to people.
3 ... a proper letter to you.
4 ... a job for him.
5 ... work for him.
6 ... that loan to Tom.
7 ... a table for us.
8 ... a drink for you.
9 ... a menu to us.
10 ... a table by the window for me.
11 ... the salt to me.
12 ... a special pudding for us.

Ex 95

2 Would they allow me extra time to pay?
3 But they refused me this reasonable request,
4 saying I'd caused them a lot of trouble.
5 ... they'd promised me a discount.
6 ... on charging me the full price.
7 I envy them their self-confidence.
8 But it cost me a lot of money.

Ex 96

1 I felt really foolish.
2 It sounded excellent.
3 ... proved particularly successful.
4 ... looked sensible.
5 ... end up rich.
6 ... become thoroughly boring.
7 ... seems utterly mad to me.
8 ... is just selfish.
9 ... remained friendly.
10 ... turned out nice again.

Ex 97

1 brown 2 old 3 ready 4 open 5 flat
6 calm 7 delicious 8 bad 9 peculiar
10 true

Ex 98

1 taking photographs 2 Have/take a look!
3 do himself an injury 4 make
arrangements 5 giving him advice 6 do
him good 7 gives me lectures 8 done
anyone any harm 9 had a good cry
10 doesn't take an interest 11 He gives
me such funny looks. 12 have a talk
13 takes offence 14 make excuses for
15 we made a move

Ex 99

2 was 3 is 4 was 5 were 6 was
7 are 8 is 9 was 10 were 11 have
12 seems 13 is 14 watch 15 reaches
16 has 17 is 18 are 19 is 20 is 21 is
22 protest

Ex 100

2 they 3 use 4 has 5 is 6 them 7 costs
8 costs 9 answers 10 was/were 11 is/
goes 12 was/were

Ex 101

2 are they? 3 do you? 4 shouldn't they?
5 can you? 6 isn't it? 7 haven't there?
8 won't it? 9 is it? 10 haven't we?/ don't
we?

Ex 102

1 Yes they were. 2 Yes it has. 3 No we
can't. 4 No they wouldn't. 5 No they
haven't. 6 Yes it is. 7 Yes it did. 8 No it
wasn't. 9 No it doesn't. 10 Yes it will

Ex 103

1 Not long ago I flew to Egypt.
2 No longer do people go by sea nowadays.
3 Not since I went to Mexico have I been so impressed.
4 Nowhere will you find a more amazing building than that pyramid.
5 Not for the first time, I lost my wallet.
6 Little do you realize the trouble you can cause ...
7 Seldom have I heard such ...
8 Rarely do you discover the whole truth ...
9 Not once did the guide complain.
10 Hardly ever do you find such honesty.

Ex 104

1 they'll ever come 2 been waiting long
3 ... it's over yet 4 ... wait any longer
5 it's any better 6 knows much 7 either
8 ... far 9 ... is at all 10 ... anyone does

Ex 105

2(a) I advised him not to complain.
2(b) I didn't advise him to complain.
3(a) I definitely don't know what's happening.
3(b) I don't know definitely what's happening.

4(a) I don't even try …
4(b) Even I don't try …
5(a) Once, he didn't arrive on time.
5(b) He didn't once arrive on time.
6(a) I don't particularly like oysters.
6(b) I particularly don't like …
7(a) I really don't understand.
7(b) I don't really understand.
8(a) That's simply not acceptable.
8(b) That's not simply acceptable – it's
   very welcome!

Chapter 11 Sentence types and discourse functions

Ex 106

1 Didn't you get my message?
2 Don't you ever consider other people?
3 Doesn't some of this worry you?
4 Aren't you going to say you're sorry?
5 Haven't you (got) any feelings?
6 Couldn't you have let me know?
7 Won't your parents be worried?
8 Can't you see how they feel?
9 Mightn't it be better to go and see them?
10 Shouldn't you try and explain?
11 Wouldn't it be a good idea (for you)
   to tell your father?
12 Can't we (both) forget this now?

Ex 107

1 hadn't you? 2 won't you? 3 had you?
4 would you? 5 will you? 6 will you?
7 aren't I? 8 shall we? 9 shall we?
10 is there?

Ex 108

1 When were the first Olympic Games
   in modern times inaugurated?
2 What other events besides running
   constitute athletics?
3 What do field events include?
4 What does the word decathlon mean?
5 How often are the Olympic Games
   now held?
6 Which country hosted the 1988
   Olympic Games?
7 Who became the youngest ever player
   to win the men's singles
   championship at Wimbledon – and
   when?
8 How old was he at the time?

9 How many people managed to finish
   the London Marathon in 1990?
10 Which is older – cricket or football?
11 Whose motor racing win at Asheville,
   North Carolina in 1988 set a record?
12 Why was this achievement special?

Ex 109

1 Who can I borrow one from?
2 Who can I discuss it with?
3 What do the letters WHO stand for?
4 What are you getting at?
5 What are you worrying about?
6 What have I got to look forward to?
7 Who do you think I bumped into?
8 Which of his parents … he takes after?
9 Which shall I get rid of?
10 Who are you waiting for?

Ex 110

1 What delicious food! Isn't this food
   delicious?
2 What slow service! Isn't the service
   slow?
3 What good-looking waiters! Aren't
   the waiters good-looking?
4 How quickly you eat! Don't you eat
   quickly?
5 What expensive vegetables! Aren't
   the vegetables expensive?
6 What a lot they charge! Don't they
   charge a lot?
7 How very fresh everything is! Isn't
   everything fresh?
8 How I love food!
9 How I dislike dieting!
10 How I wish I could come here more
   often.

Ex 111

1 The police fear that there is a
   gangland feud.
2 A hoaxer who claimed that there was
   a bomb on a plane has been jailed for
   thirty years.
3 The Colony's police have been given
   a surprise pay award.
4 A man who took out a bank loan is
   said to have had 'a secret plan'.
5 Six people died in a [car] crash
   [yesterday].
6 A cash machine was ripped from the

wall [of a bank, in a raid].

7 Heathrow [airport] is going to have a fifth terminal.

8 Six people appeared in court [yesterday] after a battle in the streets of a city.

9 A body has been found washed up [on a beach].

10 A prison inmate who swapped clothes [with a visitor] escaped.

11 Somebody was stabbed on a train.

12 A missing couple have been found safe.

13 Thirty people reached the top of the world [the summit of Mount Everest] in the same day.

14 A high-tech spy camera is guarding an [old] bridge [against large speeding lorries].

15 There are/will be no nuclear weapons on ships of the Royal Navy.

Chapter 12 Pro-forms and ellipsis

Ex 112

1 the instructions 2 the form 3 each child 4 none of your answers 5 some of the questions 6 fewer questions
7 Neither question *13* nor question *14*
8 many questions 9 both parts of question *11* 10 a woman 11 that question 12 this information

Ex 113

1 one 2 those 3 ones 4 one 5 that 6 one 7 that 8 those 9 ones 10 those 11 that 12 those

Ex 114

1 One of these little statues has a chair …

2 … a dress …

3 One talk began …

4 some other young people

5 … witnessed a will on the back of an envelope.

6 … to look after the people who are.

7 One member of the family was in a Test team …

8 Only one person in five of those who start off doing general medicine …

9 … never a woman/person for half

measures

10 another visa

Ex 115

2 (b) … the matter with it … buy a new one

3 (f) … to hear them

4 (c) … getting one … which one would be best

5 (a) looking at some … ones that take …

6 (e) show you it. Borrow it … buy one. Ones with …

Ex 116

2 (a) 3 (a) 4 (a) 5 (c) 6 (c) 7 (c) 8 (a) 9 (a) 10 (c) 11 (c) 12 (c)

Ex 117

1 that 2 so 3 it 4 it 5 that 6 it 7 that 8 so 9 so

Ex 118

1 I think so. 2 I hope not. 3 It seems so.
4 So I heard. 5 … even so … 6 It appears not 7 So would I. 8 Nor do I.
9 Maybe not, but … 10 So people say.
11 perhaps so. 12 I don't think so/I think not. 13 if not, what about … 14 So it is.

Ex 119

Of course a baby's need for sleep is greater than an adult's. That's different.

But the effects of too much sleep are not dissimilar to the effects of too little – tiredness, irritability and so on. Most healthy adults sleep between six and a half and eight and a half hours a night. Less than 5 per cent sleep more than nine and a half or less than five and a half. But some celebrated short sleepers can manage with a mere five. How do they manage?

Studies indicate that most of us could cut down on our sleep – though we cannot perhaps cut down to five hours – if we practised. A team of experimental 'sleep slimmers' gradually reduced their sleep by two hours, and research suggests that short sleepers improve the quality of their sleep.

Short sleep, it is claimed, is the best you can have, and of course if you are not in bed when other people are, think of all the things you could do.

Ex 120

1 (to) bring the letter. 2 John's job is going perfectly well. 3 have you finally spent my book token today? 4 realize he'd been to the Lake District. 5 so they don't just stay 6 I won't try to pronounce it. 7 No, we weren't together when we saw these. 8 I am interested about to the same extent as Jo is interested.

Ex 121

1 So we/the president/the committee deleted the offending words ... but perhaps we were wrong to do so. [*to do so* cannot substitute for a passive verb *were deleted*]

2 If you have retired (or are just about to) *or* If you are retired (or just about to be) [*are retired* here = verb + adjective, whereas (*are*) *just about to* ... needs a verb]

3 ... if they are not efficiently enforced and do not work better ... [We cannot derive *do not* from *are not*]

4 ... but which instead developed a taste ... [*introduced* is a passive participle here (= which were introduced), but *developed* is an active past tense]

5 ... decay, unless they are prepared to risk ... [The precedent set by the new decision is surely not expected to encourage owners to protect ... or to risk. Rather the sentence must mean that the new decision will encourage owners to protect their buildings, in the knowledge that *otherwise* they will face larger bills]

Chapter 13 Coordination

Ex 122

4 So that we don't offend people, we need to be aware of these differences.

8 Because his girl-friend ..., a famous murderer ...

10 Although she was ... Ethel le Neve ...

11 Whenever she ..., she ...

12 That the couple were Crippen and le Neve, the captain was convinced. [The other sentences cannot be changed.]

Ex 123

1 They enjoy ... yet will be glad ...

2 Other people recognize [that they will have to retire], but fear boredom [once they no longer] ...

3 Others ... look forward ... but [when they do] find [they long for ... and miss the stimulus (they had)]

4 [If people stop ... and have ... or feel (they are)] they may rapidly decline.

5 Most retired people will be ... [if they stimulate ...] and will be mentally [if they take ...]

6 ... they walk, play golf, work in their gardens.

7 Other people want ... so go to classes ...

8 They learn ... or study ... art [they have never explored] and suddenly find ...

9 [... because they discover ... and cannot find ...]

10 No ellipsis

11 No ellipsis

12 She had not had time ... [while she brought up ... and pursued ...]

Ex 124

1 Either we must protect the world's wildlife, or some species of animal will die out.

2 Both the panda and the black rhino are in danger of extinction.

3 Some species have been nearly wiped out by man either for food or (for) sport.

4 I personally don't like either snakes or bats.

5 Many people neither understand nor appreciate what the problem is.

6 People both admire tigers as beautiful animals and fear them as man-eaters.

7 Neither rhinoceroses nor tigers are the most valuable animals in the world.

8 Elephants are found in both Africa and Asia.

9 The African elephant is neither the largest nor the heaviest mammal in the world.

10 Some species spend most of their time either eating or sleeping.

Ex 125

Driving through the Outback in an ancient Land-rover enabled us to to enjoy the changing scenery and (to) appreciate the desert's changing moods. I do not think I have ever felt so close to nature or in a sense so carefree. Occasionally, when the desert's silence fell upon us, we would consider our isolation and vulnerability, gaze in wonder at the vast empty plain, and watch the birds of prey circling overhead.

The road itself was narrow but smooth. So the driving was easy except when we had to pull aside for one of the 'road-trains' – huge linked lorries which stir up great clouds of red dust and are definitely lacking in road manners!

The other hazard of driving in the Outback is the wildlife, resilient to the extreme environment, but not to the motor car. At dusk unsuspecting kangaroos, cows and buffalo would wander on to the road, attracted by the glare of car headlamps. It was curiosity which would often lead the kangaroo to its untimely end, and the car to the nearest garage.

With rusting cars and dead animals lying abandoned at the roadside, you experience moments of anxiety. So when you finally reach Ayers Rock, the largest monolith in the world – you get a wonderful sense of achievement.

But this is not the end. You start photographing it from every angle, gazing at it in wonder, touching it or walking round it. Finally, you climb it.

Ex 126

2 Neither John nor Mary look after themselves properly. [Acceptable colloquially]
6 Both John and Mary are …
7 Neither John nor Mary likes/like going round alone.
10 Neither John nor Mary went …
11 Neither John nor Mary is/are yet thirty.
15 Both John and Mary are good friends of mine.

Ex 127

2 … are wasting *their time*
3 … and *(that) they must train* their lips to make no movements.
4 nor *should* efficient reading *be attributed* to good ones.
5 Slow readers are using *habits more suitable to young children,* or at least …
6 … can *slow the reading process.*
7 … the same as *quick reading,* and must not be …
8 but sometimes *we read* to find specific information.
9 and more careful reading *may be more suitable* for …
10 and *reading 550-700 words a minute is generally considered* exceptionally fast.
11 and *that will help* everyone to improve a bit.

Ex 128

1(b) 2(a) 3(b) 4(b) 5(b) 6(a) 7(a) 8(b) 9(c) 10(a) 11(a) 12(b)

Chapter 14 The complex sentence

Ex 129

1 New traffic lights have been developed
2 The flat-lensed signals can be washed out
3 It is claimed
4 The new signals will look similar at a distance, + but close up the driver will notice a pattern of holes.
5 it will look a lot blacker.
6 The main change is in the lens
7 The lenslets make the best use of available light + and form an intense light beam … and a more diffuse beam

Ex 130

1 With nothing to declare, you …
2 Rather than do something illegal, you should …
3 All being well, you will not …
4 … are carrying dutiable goods without realizing it.
5 It is best for people to declare anything they …

6 By going through the red channel, they ...

7 Despite knowing they are wrong to do so, some people go through the 'Nothing to Declare' channel.

8 Besides looking for drugs, the Customs officers are also looking for smuggled pets.

9 Because of the danger of rabies, smuggling pets is a serious offence.

10 If caught trying to smuggle anything illegal, people face ...

11 If not prepared to risk this, they ...

12 If asked to take something through Customs ...

Ex 131

1 Whether sensible or not, ...

2 Though understandable, ...

3 Wherever possible, ...

4 Particularly when on holiday, ...

5 If obtainable in your country, ...

6 You'll feel safer with your money and passport in a money belt.

7 While on holiday, ...

8 When in a climate you are not used to, ...

9 Whenever possible, ...

10 Do not point your camera ... as if about to photograph them.

11 Never wave your arms around as though about to hit somebody.

12 Although sometimes understandably annoyed, never, never shout!

Ex 132

1 If given a book, my grandparents were likely ...

2 My mother, having learnt to read, would read to us. ...

3 When lent my first book by a rich old neighbour, I thought ...

4 Then one day the old lady, stopping me in the street, asked me ...

5 Not having even thought of reading it, I had used it as ...

6 To have been told that one day I would be a writer would have astonished me.

7 While still at the village school, I read several famous English 'classics' bought at a jumble sale.

8 Then, reaching the age of 12, I was sent ...

9 Made here to read novels by Sir Walter Scott, I have managed ...

10 But, not put off reading, I developed a passion ...

11 Then one day, walking through the town, I discovered ...

12 Not knowing what to choose, I started with ...

Ex 133

2 As soon as I retire, I shall go round the world.

3 I shall let my house while I am away.

4 Even if I live to be a hundred, there won't be time to do everything I want to do.

5 I can hardly wait until I'm sixty.

6 I hope I keep my health.

7 I shall go round the world unless it is too late.

8 You should retire yourself before you are too old.

9 Suppose our health fails, what would we do?

10 I do wonder what will be happening in ten years' time.

Ex 134

2 ... was asking that I should take her seat.

3 ... whether they are princes or peasants ...

4 ... had signed petitions demanding that it should not be shown.

5 Still do, if the truth is (to be) known.

6 ... ordered that Potohar Plateau ... should be transformed ...

7 I would much rather that he was safely on dry land and (that) the search and rescue forces were not engaged/should not be engaged ...

8 When Christmas comes, ...

9 Let it never be forgotten though, that ...

10 ... insisted that ... her music should be turned off ...

11 ... asked that the woman's name should not be published.

12 ... asked his parents that the boy should not be allowed to come back.

Ex 135

2 ... regrets that you should have made ...

3 ... don't understand why you should be embarrassed.

4 ... natural that you should have considered ...

5 ... anxious that this shouldn't affect ...

7 ... a scandal should they do so/if they should do so.

8 ... glad you should have felt able to come to the decision you did.

9 ... preferable that people should make up ...

10 ... shame some of the committee should be so ...

[*Should* is not possible in 1 or 6]

Ex 136

1 has dreamt/has dreamed; began 2 died; had achieved/could achieve 3 occurred; flew 4 had flown; flew 5 flew; were 6 became; flew 7 had flown; had made 8 led/had led; were broken 9 broke out; had already occurred 10 was achieved; flew 11 was first flown; has been regularly used 12 had flown/had been flying; set; cruises

Ex 137

1 Patrick asked her if the man had mentioned a wife. Jenny replied that he had said nothing about that, nor about a girl-friend or she would have remembered. Patrick then asked if the man had given his name, and Jenny said he had but she had forgotten it straightaway, although she remembered thinking that it could not be right. She said that anyway the man had said he would be back.

2 Patrick said that unless she felt like another drink, he suggested they should move, because with Saturday shopping there might be a bit of traffic and he wanted to be there on the dot.

3 JLR Sebastian said he assumed she was nothing to do with books or anything like that, and he asked her what she was to do with. Jenny said she taught in a hospital, so she supposed she was a bit to do with books. JLR Sebastian said that was splendid, and asked her what her field was. Jenny said she hadn't really got one, because she just went in in the mornings during the week and taught some of the younger long-stay children. She said that she had at one time taught in a proper ... And then her voice trailed off.

4 Jenny said she was sorry, but she was just popping round to the hospital, because one of the little girls had had a minor operation the day before, so she thought she would look in for a few minutes. Actually, she said, she was going for a breath of air. Patrick said that was fine, and asked if she wanted him to go with her. But she said she didn't, because she would be there and back in a second.

Ex 138

2 *Barman*: Have you come to live round here? My wife's out shopping at the moment, but will be only too delighted to give you the benefit of her local knowledge any time. Meanwhile the dry cleaners in the block tried to get away with losing my topcoat for me last winter.

3 He's the best-looking man I've ever met.

4 If they/we are just going to stay here all the evening talking I'll get very hungry.

5 *Tom*: Please don't tell anybody. I don't want my/the neighbours to find out.

Us: Of course we won't say anything to anyone. But it might be better to apologize. Shall I help you write a letter?

Tom: No, thank you. I think you should mind your own business.

Ex 139

1 *The friend*: Where do you come from?
Levi: A country called England.
Friend: Oh yes, England. Wouldn't that country be/Isn't that country near Kabul?

2 *He*: Shall I go after them?

Nina: No, better not. It may not be opening time yet. It would be best for us to wait for Olga.

3 *Waiter*: Would you like your coat checked, Sir, or a drink, or a menu, or perhaps the wine list?

4 *Interviewer*: Do you play chess? Can you read music? How good are you at crosswords?

5 *He*: Do you have a copy of *The Faerie Queene* by Edmund Spenser?

Bookstall assistant: No, we don't/ haven't.

He: Not in any edition? Do you realize that *The* Faerie Queen is one of the jewels in the crown of English poetry?

Bookstall assistant: There isn't much call for poetry at Heathrow. But, sir, you could if you wished, sir, try the other bookstalls ... though your chances of success are slim.

6 Will you come up and see me, because I've an idea. I'm writing a show and I want you to appear in it. Are you prepared to leave Paris?

7 *Interviewer*: Have you ever been in danger?

Lewis: Not so far.

I: What have you learned in your travels?

L: I'm gradually coming to the conclusion ...

I: Does this depress you?

L: I can't say that it does actually.

8 *Noonan*: Wouldn't you rather go somewhere else? To your sister's perhaps? Or to my wife, who would/ will take care of you and put you up for the night.

Woman: No. I don't feel I can move even a yard at the moment. Would you mind awfully if I stay/stayed just where I am until I feel better? I don't feel too good at the moment, I really don't.

N: Then hadn't you better lie down on the bed?

Woman: No, I'd like to stay right where I am, in this chair. A little later perhaps, when I feel better, I'll move.

Ex 140

1 I/We didn't expect him to be. 2 I/We hoped he wouldn't. 3 He didn't seem to be. 4 We don't believe he is. 5 I/We don't suppose he has. 6 I/We don't consider he should. 7 I/We don't imagine they can. 8 I wouldn't have thought it was. 9 It doesn't look as though he will. 10 I/We don't feel there is.

Chapter 15 Syntactic and semantic functions of subordinate clauses

Ex 141

2 nominal (object) 3 adverbial 4 relative 5 nominal (object) 6 relative 7 nominal (appositive) 8 nominal (object) 9 reduced relative 10 adverbial 11 nominal (object) 12 nominal (object) 13 adverbial 14 comparative 15 comparative 16 comparative 17 nominal (complement) 18 adverbial

Ex 142

1 that this animal ... was living in some nearby hills – extraposed subject

2 why we were camping ... among the Boran tribesmen – complement of subject

3 that George was returning much earlier [than expected] – direct object of *mean*

4 what had happened – direct object of *told*

5 that her behaviour showed [that she ... her litter] – object of *recognized;* that she was defending her litter – direct object of *showed*

6 Whatever trick I tried [to make them ... milk] – subject of *resulted*

7 that one usually sees only two cubs with a lioness – extraposed subject

8 what may be left over ... of the pride – complement of preposition *on*

9 that [when the cubs ... under some shady bush] he was able to sit ... [watching ... molested them] – object of *meant;* that no snakes or baboons molested

them – direct object of *to see*

10 that they only required three-hourly feeds – direct object of *showed*

11 that she should continue to love the little rascals [even though … from herself] – complement of adjective phrase *very touched*

12 how happy she was – direct object of *showed*

13 that we could not keep forever three fast-growing lions – in apposition to *the fact*

14 that two must go – direct object of *decided;*
that it would be better [that the two big ones … should be the ones to leave] – direct object of *decided;*
that the two big ones should be the ones to leave – extraposed subject

15 that [if she had only ourselves as friends] she would be easy to train – direct object of *felt*

Ex 143

1 We do not know whether/if it was the need for food or perhaps some natural disaster.

2 Perhaps it is easier to understand what, in historical times, inspired … the unknown.

3 Do we understand whether it was trade or the desire … or perhaps a mixture of motives.

4 Who can explain why some people … journeys?

5 Is it perhaps the case that they are seeking adventure or a challenge?

6 Can we who have never travelled in space imagine what are the emotions of space travellers/what the emotions of space travellers are as they … on the earth?

7 Doesn't everybody know when Christopher Columbus discovered America?

8 Columbus didn't ask himself whether/if he could have been mistaken …

9 Do you know where he actually made landfall?

10 Do you think (that) it was what we now call the Bahamas?

11 Can you say which is the remotest

place on earth?

12 Tell me who first sailed round the world.

13 Do you remember how long Magellan's fleet took on the voyage?

14 I can't remember where Magellan was killed.

15 Well, do you know who made the second … world?

Ex 144

1 whether 2 whether … whether
3 whether/if 4 whether 5 Whether
6 Whether 7 whether 8 whether/if 9 if
10 whether

Ex 145

1 Talking 2 to act 3 to cause 4 to save/ saving 5 to endanger 6 being 7 to protect 8 culling 9 swimming
10 Providing 11 expecting 12 to distinguish 13 swimming 14 swimming
15 killing 16 to become 17 to preserve
18 endangering

Ex 146

1 Nobody nowadays can hope to visit …

2 It is a rare pleasure to find …

3 And to see the enormous crowds …

4 It would be foolish for any of us to imagine …

5 … nothing left to preserve.

6 … measures to protect …

7 … solution is for governments to set up …

8 (with armies of officials) to direct visitors …

9 Another possibility, to rely on the price mechanism …

10 … pay more to see the more popular … attractions.

11 – to repair some of the damage

12 … the only ones to benefit …

13 … happier for them not to be overrun.

14 … wake up one day to find it is too late.

Ex 147

1 While I was on my way … recently, I had … experience.

2 I reached Paddington Station just as my train was leaving.

3 I had to wait half an hour before the

next train left.

4 I walked all along … until I found …

5 Once I had put my case on the rack, I settled …

6 When the train stopped at Peterborough a young man got in.

7 As soon as he sat down, he began …

8 I couldn't go on reading after this young man …

9 It was all right once I had given up …

10 He too had caught the wrong train after he had missed …

11 He had spent two years … before he had decided …

12 When I told him …, it turned out that …

13 We reached York while we were deep …

14 The moment the train stopped he jumped out.

15 Alas he left the train before he had told me his …

Ex 148

1 If this is justice – rhetorical

2 If Aristotle were alive today – hypothetical

3 …if people think you're dead – open

4 If anything can go wrong – open

5 If you don't like the heat – open

6 If you ask me – rhetorical

7 … if I didn't want to know – hypothetical

8 If there is one thing … know – open

9 … if you enquire – open

10 … if I hadn't wanted to know – hypothetical

Ex 149

1 If people were not curious …, archaeology would not exist.

2 If the ancient Egyptians had not believed … they would not have built …

3 If they had not been clever at … the Great Pyramid would not be accurately lined up …

4 If there had been coinage when the pyramids were built, the workmen might not have been paid with food.

5 If the Egyptians had not put …, we would not know much/so much

about …

6 If the pyramids had not been plundered …, later explorers would have found …

7 If the first European visitors had been archaeologists they might have made detailed notes.

8 If the sands had not buried some treasure, part of a wooden boat would not have been safely excavated …

9 If the Valley of the Kings had not also been partly protected by sand, Tutankhamun's tomb would have been found before 1922.

10 If Tutankhamun's tomb had been found by grave robbers, the wonderful treasures would not now be in the Cairo Museum.

11 If archaeologists did not work carefully … they would not continue to teach us about the past.

Ex 150

1 Should you see …, let me know.

2 Were I to see one, I should …

3 Were I to meet …, I'd inform …

4 Were you not so sceptical, you might learn.

5 Had you been with me last night, …

6 Had you not told me, I …

7 … hoaxes, were we to investigate them.

8 Had I not examined …

Ex 151

1 Although employers naturally want to recruit the right people, some of their methods …

2 Though they need to find out about us, do they …

3 While I don't mind filling in a questionnaire, I object to …

4 Even if some personal information may be necessary, I don't want …

5 Much as I wanted the last job I applied for, I refused …

6 Relevant as the questions may have been, they struck me as unpleasant.

7 Whatever the consequences could have been for me, I still wasn't …

8 So my application was a waste of time, except that I did get practice …

9 Even though I really disliked the questionnaire, I enjoyed the interview.

10 Perhaps I'll make up the answers next time, only don't tell anyone.

Ex 152

1 Because they are convinced that exercise is good for you, doctors are urging ...

2 Such a lot of men in particular die of heart disease, they ought to be warned.

3 Many people damage their hearts because they eat too much fat.

4 Some doctors set a bad example, so that people ...

5 Since we are always being told to change our habits, some people don't listen.

6 Some marathon runners train so hard that they experience real pain.

7 Some runners are so obsessive that they injure themselves.

8 As they take no exercise, other people become unfit.

9 Such people often also overeat, so they put on weight.

10 Because some people really dislike exercise, they make excuses.

11 Some people say they lead such busy lives that they don't have time.

12 Some older people take up running in order to strengthen their bones.

13 Serious runners plan their diet carefully, for violent exercise can damage muscles.

14 Have a check-up with your doctor in case you have a heart condition.

15 Choose your running shoes carefully so as not to damage your feet.

16 You don't have to run in order to keep fit – cycling or swimming will do.

Ex 153

1 Once these are sold, you are unlikely ...

2 Acceptable

3 I thought that you, as an active supporter of the arts in Britain, would be ...

4 While I was waiting around ... a ... ten-year-old ...

5 Acceptable

6 It is open for lunch and dinner, but booking is advised ...

7 When he was asked much later on ... a wide silent smile ...

8 Acceptable

9 One of the wealthiest men in the world, he has foreign investments estimated at over $100 billion.

10 Once you are inside, the house ...

11 Acceptable

12 Acceptable

Ex 154

1 Monaco is bigger than the Vatican City, but not as big as Nauru. Nauru is smaller than ...

2 ... that Hong Kong is more densely populated than any other territory in the world, but actually it is less densely populated than Macao. Bangladesh of course is not as densely populated as either.

3 India's current population is not as big as China's, but ... by 2050 it will be bigger than China's.

4 ... was not as big as Tokyo in 1985 ... it could be bigger than any other city ...

5 ... lower in West Germany than ... more than twice as fast as the world's average.

6 ... there are not as many females in the world as males ... there may be more women than men

7 ... live longer than their parents did ... as high as Japan's ... live as long as women do ... fewer men than women can expect to reach eighty.

Ex 155

1 ... that a surface to air missile ... plane – nominal (appositive to *the possibility*)

2 lightning and pilot error ... ruled out – nominal (object)

3 if any of the bodies ... bomb blast – nominal (object)

4 that they could not find ... engine – nominal (extraposed subject)

5 That is extremely strange – nominal (object of *said*)
   We have no idea [what it implies] –

nominal (also object of *said*)
what it it implies – nominal
(appositive to *no idea*)

6 the implication ... missile – nominal
(object of *said*)
that the right side of the plane ...
explosion – nominal (appositive to *the implication*);
that it might have been caused by a
missile – nominal (appositive to *the theory*)

7 how the wing came to be detached –
nominal (object of preposition *on*)

8 that it disintegrated – nominal
(appositive to *the possibility*)

9 that it would have broken up in small
pieces – nominal (extraposed subject)

10 that his team ... the site – nominal
(object of *confirmed*)

11 who joined the investigation yesterday
– relative

12 where the black box will go ...
examination – nominal (object of
preposition *about*)

13 In our view ... involved – nominal
(object of *said*)
that the examination should be done
... involved – nominal (complement
of *necessary*)
where nobody is involved – relative
(to *country*)

14 if it were the United States – adverbial
(of condition)
because the Americans are players in
this – adverbial (of reason)

15 Boeing 767s were well constructed
and well proved – nominal (object of
said)

16 that the aircraft ... altitude – nominal
(complement of *was*)

17 which began ... bombs – relative (to
the investigation)
that the left-hand engine ... mid-air –
nominal (object of *confirmed*)

Chapter 16 Complementation of verbs and adjectives

Ex 156

1 fooling around 2 settled down
3 dropped out 4 cried off 5 gives up
6 come on 7 fell through 8 ringing up

9 wait up 10 taking off 11 touched down
12 own up 13 went ahead 14 bear up
15 wear off 16 Hold on 17 look back
18 stands out 19 come about 20 caught
on 21 give in 22 pass away

Ex 157

1 The tickets haven't been paid for,
have they?

3 The car had better be seen to [or we'll
have ...]

5 This problem really ought to be
looked into further.

7 Some of the problems have already
been referred to.

8 Some of the proposals were strongly
objected to.

9 The car has been really well cared for.

10 That missing money is never going to
be accounted for.

11 Have these library books been
finished with?

12 These boxes are not to be interfered
with.

13 These rules must be adhered to.

14 The house seems to have been quite
well looked after.

15 Some things are argued over for ages
– with no result.

16 The problem has been disposed of
now.

19 David can be relied on to help.

20 Why am I always being laughed at?
[No passives for 2, 4, 6, 17 or 18]

Ex 158

1 running it in 2 take them in 3 confide
in her 4 invested in them 5 cashed them
all in 6 rely on her 7 turn on him
8 move them on 9 insist on it 10 pass it
on to 11 win them over 12 get over it
13 stood by him 14 putting them across
15 come across it 16 keep them out
17 takes after him 18 turn it down
19 look them up 20 put it off

Ex 159

1(c) 2(i) 3(h) 4(g) 5(b) 6(k) 7(d) 8(f)
9(j) 10(e)

Ex 160

1 Please answer. Well, stop criticizing.
Why can't you help? I'm asking whether

you are still borrowing from the bank. You really should stop spending the way you do. At your age I saved regularly. You seem to spend a fortune on rubbish.

That's not true. I don't accept that. I need a lot of things – a car for a start.

Oh, come. You don't need a car. You mean you want a car. I think you should write to your bank manager and …

2 I arrived hot and tired. I'd been driving all day and then had a job trying to park. After I'd unpacked, washed and changed, I lay on the bed reading until it was time for dinner. Next morning I went out looking for a bank, because I needed to change money. But I couldn't find a bank anywhere.

Ex 161

1 Have these repairs been costed in advance? 3 When my brother was measured for a new suit, he was told by the tailor that [all the rest in active] 6 The hostages are being held in dreadful conditions. 9 A new washer needs to be fitted to that tap/That tap needs to have a new washer fitted. 12 Was Billie-Jean King's record equalled by Navratilova's? [passives not possible for 2, 4, 5, 7, 8, 10, 11]

Ex 162

2 I wish I were …
3 I wish I could …
4 I wish I understood …/knew… /felt …
5 I wish I didn't waste so much money/ watch so much TV/worry so much
6 I wish I had had …/had saved …/had worked …
7 I wish I hadn't watched …/hadn't bought …
8 I wish I had (got) …
9 I wish I didn't have so many problems/so much to do/such difficult hair
10 I wish I had been to …
11 I wish people would't keep …
12 I wish that one day I could …

Ex 163

1 criticizing 2 to pay 3 to do 4 doing 5 listening 6 to be 7 worrying 8 trying

9 to do 10 to speak up 11 to do 12 trying 13 making 14 being 15 to understand 16 to do 17 to realize 18 stopping 19 trying 20 to succeed

Ex 164

1 him to apply 2 he should apply 3 him to apply/that he should apply 4 he would think about it 5 him to think about it/him that he should think about it 6 him write in 7 that he should write in 8 to lend him the car 9 him to borrow the car 10 him borrow the car 11 never to lend 12 that her mind was made up 13 her to change her mind 14 his/him asking 15 him ever to ask again

Ex 165

2(a) 3(c) 4(i) 5(d) 6(g) 7(b) 8(e) 9(j) 10(h)

Ex 166

1 Some progress is supposed to have been made.
2 The chairman is considered to be an expert.
3 Some members are rumoured to be unhappy.
4 The findings are understood to be fair.
5 The recommendations are presumed to be radical.
6 Tempers are believed to have run high.
7 The discussions were reported to have been tough.
8 The results are said to be far-reaching.
9 Some proposals are thought to have been dropped.
10 Some members are known to disagree.

Ex 167

1 She reminds me of my cousin. 2 I congratulated her on passing her exam. 3 Don't keep plying people with drinks. 4 They accused me of borrowing … 5 Please introduce me to your parents. 6 I must write and thank her for … 7 But you just can't prevent them from ruining … 8 Have you compared it with prices in other shops? 9 … it is sexist to compliment a woman on her appearance. 10 … to try and treat them to a meal.

Ex 168

us – 2, 4, 6, 9, 12
to us – 1, 3, 5, 7, 8, 10, 11

Ex 169

1 careful to pay her bills 2 quick to spot
a mistake 3 relieved to hear that David
… 4 mad to have thrown/to throw up
your job 5 keen to start my own business
6 disappointed not to have heard …
7 unable to telephone 8 She is usually
easy to contact 9 She was impossible to
get hold of 10 The papers are ready to be
signed/to sign 11 You would be most
unwise
to lend … 12 We were pleased to be
able to help

Chapter 17 The noun phrase

Ex 170

2 example 3 Association 4 report
5 monopoly 6 cloud 7 interests
8 investigation 9 report 10 forecasting
11 Office 12 task 13 weather 14 way
15 language 16 translations 17 *Which?*
18 style 19 science 20 forecast
21 phrases

Ex 171

1 that abstract science whose professors
   never seem able to agree …
2 the first by-election whose result has
   been claimed…
3 Not possible – because the *of* belongs
   with the verb *convince (you) of*. That
   is, the meaning is – for plot reasons
   which it takes a good scriptwriter to
   convince you *of*.
4 a tour whose function is to
   introduce …
5 one hundred million dollars whose
   value you must maintain …
6 designs whose meaning is not
   understood.

Ex 172

2 which/that 3 which/that/ – 4 that/
which 5 which 6 who 7 whom 8 – /
that/which/ 9 which 10 – /that/which
11 who 12 which 13 which 14 that/
which 15 whose 16 whose 17 where

Ex 173

1 Travellers on the Trans-Siberian
   railway, which stretches from Moscow
   to the Pacific Ocean, take 8 days 4
   hours 25 minutes on the journey,
   during which there are 97 stops.
2 The Indian-Pacific railway, whose
   reputation is perhaps less fearsome
   than the Trans Siberian, crosses
   Australia from Perth … the Pacific.
3 It covers a distance of 2,720 miles, of
   which 297 … are dead straight, which
   is the longest … the world.
4 These journeys appeal to a certain type
   of traveller, who is not in a hurry and
   to whom the journey, not the arrival,
   matters.
5 G Sowerby and T Cahill, who was his
   co-driver and navigator, in 1987 drove
   a four-wheel drive pick-up truck from
   Ushuaia to Prudhoe Bay (Alaska),
   which is a distance of 14,739 miles, in
   just under 24 days, which is a record
   time for the journey. [note that *in 1987*
   has been moved]
6 They were however surface freighted
   over the Darien Gap, which is between
   Colombia and Panama, where the
   Trans-American highway does not
   exist.

Ex 174

1 Any suggestion that we are not all
   equal makes some people very angry.
2 Many people do not accept the
   explanation that accidents …
3 Is it a fact that there are more
   scientists …?
4 I don't understand the theory that there
   are a lot of black holes …
5 There is also the idea that the universe
   …
6 Is there any hope that we can rid the
   world …?
7 Everyone remembers Neil Armstrong's
   remark when he stepped on the moon
   that/it was one small step …
8 I am not sure whether I agree with
   Shakespeare's observation that all the
   world is a stage.

Ex 175

1 a new technique to cure sleeplessness

2 a new technique ... based on thought-jamming 3 a simple word ... repeated under the breath three or four times a second 4 technique being tested ... Cambridge 5 millions suffering from sleeplessness 6 a kind of 'memory traffic control' called 'the central executive' 7 information entering the brain 8 nothing particularly interesting 9 ways to provide a steady flow ... brain 10 other tasks to do 11 a method to induce sleep 12 the imaginary sheep being counted 13 the only thing (for most people) to do 14 tests specially designed ... the theory 15 those tested 16 work to be done

Ex 176

2 the end of the week 3 research by psychologists 4 irritation of a social kind 5 a weakening of the ... system 6 four days after a row 7 the latest study into the effects ... 8 the effects of mental well-being 9 the effects [ ] on physical health 10 Evidence of/about/for such effects 11 a number of serious diseases 12 emotions of anger 13 the death of a spouse 14 a similar effect for the common cold 15 a hundred clerical staff from/at/in a tax office 16 a tax office in the north ... 17 the north of England 18 a diary of/about their health ... they had 19 what sort of day 20 four days before contracting the cold 21 a marked drop in diary entries ... their spouses 22 friendly relations with their spouses 23 an increase in the number ... 24 the number of social annoyances 25 a definite link between mood and infection

Ex 177

1 It's my belief that the fire ...
2 Their correspondence lasted for twenty years.
3 Is there ever a hyphen in the word cooccur?
4 Their behaviour was really bad, which ...
5 These people are inhabitants of one ...
6 All the competitors must ...
7 Were there any survivors of the crash?
8 The organization of the event was brilliant.

9 Those children's education was not very good.
10 You need more practice. [AmE practise]
11 The hostages' release was wonderful.
12 I don't like your continual criticism.
13 Can we make arrangements to meet?
14 What are the stars and stripes symbols/a symbol of?
15 Perhaps the club needs more publicity.
16 Where is the cat's food?
17 It's a hotel where you can have dinner in the garden.
18 Office relocation usually upsets the staff.
19 I was out of breath.
20 You didn't raise any objection.

Ex 178

1(c) the wheel clamp, the police device for immobilizing illegally parked cars, when ...
2(e) ... the new rich, those richer than himself, ...
3(g) the Bushes' spaniel, Millie ...
4(f) ... gang warfare, them or us ...
6(b) Australia's new plastic banknote, the latest word in anti-fraud know-how ...
7(d) ... a peculiar phenomenon, the willingness of academics to pay tribute to the leaders of bloodthirsty regimes.

Ex 179

1 It was an entertaining play.
2 He gave an amazing performance.
3 I admire Edward Fox's beautifully timed acting.
4 Not possible [*arriving late people]
5 Some plays contain rather surprising language.
6 One really shocked man left.
7 Not possible [*the talking ... children]
8 The opening scene was brilliant.
9 Not possible [*we ate got ice-creams]
10 Not possible [*the demanded prices]
11 We always have reserved seats.
12 The play had a rather complicated plot.
13 There was an unrelated twist at the end of the play.
14 That was certainly an unexpected

ending.

Ex 180

1 a drug addict 2 life insurance 3 eye strain 4 a news bulletin 5 a banana skin 6 a measles outbreak 7 garden chairs 8 tooth decay 9 armholes 10 a clothes brush 11 an egghead 12 a two-car family 13 a post office 14 a bus stop 15 a baby-sitter 16 a ten-storey office block 17 a package holiday 18 arms control 19 a dress shop 20 junk food

Ex 181

2 the whole skein 3 human kind 4 a striking resemblance 5 the British scene 6 a better opportunity 7 fishing rods 8 shot guns 9 hunting boots 10 activist organizations 11 field sports 12 country habits and perspectives 13 relationships between human kind and the animal world 14 hunting, shooting and fishing as a pastime 15 a weakness for the chase 16 intermittent harassment of hunts and their supporters 17 fox-hunting since the war 18 the involvement of possibly two million people 19 both sides of the argument 20 the access to the media 21 methods of behaviour 22 a weakness for the chase 23 the weaknesses 24 literature and a culture 25 those 26 the extent 27 the money and the access to the media 28 concerned with animal welfare, and ranging across the whole skein ... the animal world 29 barred by those ... from the British scene 30 to press their arguments to successful conclusions.

Chapter 18 Theme, focus, and information processing

Ex 182

1(b) 2(c) 3(a) 4(c) 5(b) 6(d)

Ex 183

1 After an hour or two I had extracted from my interlocutor the admission ... getting me across.
2 The Revolutionary Guards beat up and detained for one day, Mr Edward Chaplin, a British diplomat, in apparent retaliation ... charges.

3 In his contribution to *Late Picasso*, ... David Sylvester argues (that) these pictures lay naked the horror of growing old.
4 We cannot deduce from an election ... won by a distance any very confident pointers ... four years hence.
5 Wild horses would not have dragged from me the truth.

Ex 184

1(b) 2(b) 3(a) 4(d) 5(b) 6(d) 7(c) 8(a)

Ex 185

2 Very 3 fifty 4 families/themselves 5 Chris/Christy 6 left 7 1976 8 Peardon/ Pearson 9 in 10 landscape 11 two 12 without

Ex 186

1 Object – I can do without that sort of remark.
2 Complement – It is not objective.
3 Complement (of object) – I call it unkind.
4 Predicate – but they did criticize.
5 Adverbial – I must have seemed a child to them.
6 Object – These people would bring in three or four cars at a time for servicing.
7 Adverbial – They'd grumble ... about some £10 item on the bill.
8 Predicate – They were always grumbling.
9 Complement – They probably were millionaires.
10 Complement – They were not generous.
11 Object – Nobody can defend this particular law.
12 Adverbial – Nobody is arguing about the need for a libel law.
13 Predicate – ... that it is needed.
14 Adverbial – The law cannot be ... defended in its present state.
15 Complement – ... though it may be unsatisfactory ...

Ex 187

1 Staring up at him, row upon row, smug, self-satisfied and hostile sat the new generation of Communists, ...

2 ... Then out came the spades, sand mats and towing ropes, and the whole dreary business of 'un-sticking' would start again.

3 Across the valley, dark against the setting sun, rose the first of the ranges of hills which lay between us and the coast.

4 Across the bay stretched a chain of sand islands and black jagged rocks, sheltering the harbour from the westerly gales sand islands and black jagged rocks, sheltering the harbour from the westerly gales and squalls of the Adriatic.

5 Round us at other tables sat the collection of Egyptian pashas, Greek millionaires ... the war.

6 Out of the fire and smoke rose cries of terror.

7 Every so often along the seafront could be seen the bare white ribs of a boat ... Noah's Ark.

8 In 1925 Ragamah was a simple farm, and there was enacted the agreement that unified Arabia.

9 Opposite me sat two retired factory workers whose ... maps.

10 Above it hung a bar by which the Chairman could haul up his ageing body and near the tap was a red button for emergencies.

Ex 188

1 Nowhere have I seen a more wonderful building.

2 No longer are there regular passenger liners ...

3 No inversion – Nowhere I have seen surpasses the Taj Mahal.

4 No inversion – Neither my sister nor I likes/like the heat.

5 ... And neither do I.

6 No sooner had we arrived than the storm broke.

7 Not since I was a child have I experienced ...

8 No inversion – I neither knew nor cared what would ...

9 Not only did Tom arrive late, but he started complaining.

10 Never again will I invite him.

11 No inversion – No good will come of this.

12 No good will this do you.

Ex 189

1 Perhaps it's boredom or a longing for excitement that makes people experiment with drugs.

2 I think it's mainly among the young that we find drug-taking.

3 What we need to make people realize is that drug-taking is self-destructive.

4 What some people think is that all drugs ...

5 They say it's the glamour of doing something illegal that attracts people.

6 What surprises me is that any people become 'couriers' when some governments have such tough laws ...

7 I suppose it is the hope of easy money that tempts them.

8 What many people don't realize is that ordinary drug-takers ...

9 What the drug barons deliberately do is involve 'small people'.

10 What the Customs people are looking for is travellers who ...

11 It's often the small people, not the big people, who get caught.

12 What most governments want is to stop ...

Ex 190

1 To persuade him won't be easy. 4 That we are quite likely to fail seems clear. 7 What you say will probably make no difference. [All the other sentences are awkward or impossible]

Ex 191

2 an outcry about the safety of carriage doors

3 a young man who had been drinking for most of the journey

4 rather more than he should have

5 a claim that the railway is responsible for his death

6 accusations of negligence

7 yet another investigation into safety standards

8 a duty to ensure that doors and windows are not faulty

9 more than is good for them

10 a lot of nonsense about human rights

11 the idea that there is always someone
to blame for an accident/someone who
should pay compensation to the
victims or their families
12 no absolute human right to survive a
journey
13 journeys by train, car, plane, even on
foot
14 a duty to maintain high standards
15 the time to realize that they too must
exercise care
16 accidents, some of which are
nobody's fault

Ex 192
1 ... there lived a brother.
2 Now and again there appeared on the
front steps ... a good-looking woman.
3 There are some nicknames that are
obstacles to friendship.
4 A month after Dostoyevsky died there
was enacted a scene ...
5 A pleasanter place ... there could
not be.

Chapter 19 From sentence to text

Ex 193
1 after 2 already 3 such as 4 to 5 which
6 However 7 questions 8 Where
9 it   10 so 11 These 12 But 13 so
14 mathematics 15 fate 16 without
17 This 18 whether 19 therefore 20 not
21 In the end 22 did 23 equation 24 this
25 half

Ex 194
2(c) 3(a) 4(d) 5(b) 6(c) 7(d) 8(b) 9(b)
10(b) 11(b) 12(a) 13(c) 14(a)

Ex 195
7/ 4/ 1/ 6/ 3/ 2/ 5

Ex 196
Jaques-Yves Cousteau ... in association
with his colleague, Emile Gagnan, who
designed the critical demand valve or
regulator, *which enabled divers to breath
air from gas canisters attached to their
backs.* By enabling swimmers ..., his
invention proved of considerable strategic

importance ... during the Second World
War *when used to plant submarine mines.
However* it was Cousteau's films of
sunken wrecks *and later the natural
history of the marine environment* which
brought the undersea world to ... people.
Now he has turned his efforts to ...
Antarctica.

Ex 197
1(j) 2(f) 3(k) 4(e) 5(g) 6(a) 7(o) 8(i)
9(m) 10(d) 11(n) 12(c) 13(h) 14(b)
15(l)

Ex 198
1(a) My brother, who lives in Australia,
       is retired.
 (b) My brother who lives in Australia
       is retired.
2(a) Write soon should you have any
       problems. Let me know.
 (b) Write soon. Should you have any
       problems, let me know.
3(a) If these boys were encouraged to
       play more football, they wouldn't
       have time for other dangerous
       pursuits.
 (b) ... they wouldn't have time for
       other, dangerous, pursuits.
4(a) This year's exam papers were
       unusually difficult.
 (b) ... were, unusually, difficult.
5(a) The island evidently did not evoke
       too many sentimental memories,
       for Charles and Diana
       subsequently holidayed there.
 (b) ... too many sentimental memories
       for Charles, and Diana
       subsequently holidayed there.
6(a) Michael Dobbs's novel *House of
       Cards* was adapted ...
 (b) Michael Dobbs's novel, *House of
       Cards*, was adapted for television
       last year.
7(a) An old bomb exploded in the
       capital yesterday, killing a 15-
       year-old youth who was examining
       it and injuring his father.
 (b) An old bomb exploded in the
       capital yesterday, killing a 15-
       year-old youth who was examining
       it, and injuring his father.

8(a) The document has already annoyed the government which, says the society, is not really interested in the zoo's problems.

  (b) The document has already annoyed the government, which says the society is not really interested in the zoo's problems.

9(a) My neighbour's dog has attacked our cat.

  (b) My neighbours' dog …

10(a) The night porter serves sandwiches and drinks.

  (b) The night porter serves sandwiches, and drinks. [(a) is still a bit ambiguous and might be better reworded – He serves drinks and sandwiches.]

Ex 199

Even now I was unsure what drew me into this country I feared. I belonged to a generation too young to romanticize about Soviet Communism. Yet nothing in the intervening years had dispelled my childhood estrangement and ignorance. My mind was filled with confused pictures: paradox, cliché. 'Russia,' wrote the marquis de Custine in 1839, 'is a country where everyone is part of a conspiracy to mystify the foreigner.' Propaganda still hangs like a ground-mist over the already complicated truth. Newspapers, until you know how to read them, are organs of disinformation. The arts are conservative or silent. Even in novels, which so often paint the ordinary nature of things, the visionaries and drunks who inhabit the pages of nineteenth century fiction have shrivelled to the poor wooden heroes of modern socialist realism.

It is as if a great lamp had been turned down.

Ex 200

Jan, whereas Geoffrey had had 'had had', had had 'had'. 'Had had' had had their fellow authors' approval.

Acknowledgements

We are grateful to the following for permission to reproduce copyright material:

the Trustees of the Elsa Conservation Trust for an adapted extract from *Born Free* by Joy Adamson; the author's agent on behalf of the author for an adapted extract from 'One of Virtues' by Stan Barstow in *Further Recollections, Ten Stories on Five Themes* (Edward Arnold, 1989); the author, Ted Botha for an adapted extract from his article 'Off the Rails' in *The Sunday Telegraph* 4.92; Guiness Publishing Ltd for adapted extracts from *The Guiness Book of Records 1991*. Copyright © Guiness Publishing Limited 1990; the author's agent on behalf of the author for an adapted extract from *A Brief History of Time* by Stephen Hawking (1988); Ewan MacNaughton Associates for extracts from articles 'Divers fail to solve riddle of flight 19' and 'Boy 7, flies plane across US' by Quentin Letts in *The Daily Telegraph* 5.6.91, 'Met office taken to task for 'foggy' forecasting' by Virginia Marshall in *The Daily Telegraph* 6.6.91, 'A word that beats counting sheep' by Robert Matthews in *The Sunday Telegraph* 17.2.91, 'Cold Comfort from a bust up' by Robert Matthews in *The Sunday Telegraph* 26.5.91 and 'More is less' by Geoffrey Beattie in *The Sunday Telegraph Magazine* 29.5.88. © The Telegraph plc, 1991, 1991. © The Sunday Telegraph, 1991, 1991. © The Sunday Telegraph Magazine, 1988; MFPA (Mouth and Foot Painting Artists), 9 Inverness Place, London W2 3JF, for an adapted extract from an MFPA Leaflet; the author's agent on behalf of the author for an adapted extract from 'The Man of the House' by Frank O'Connor in *Further Recollections, Ten Stories on Five Themes* (Edward Arnold, 1989); Penguin Books Ltd for adapted extracts from *I Can't Stay Long* by Laurie Lee (1977). Copyright © Laurie Lee, 1975. (First published by Andre Deutsch, 1975) and *Eastern Approaches* by Fitzroy Maclean (1991). Copyright © Fitzroy Maclean, 1991; Reed International Books for adapted extracts from *The Royal Geographical Society History of World Exploration* (Paul Hamlyn Publishing, 1991) and *Among the Russians* by Colin Thubron (William Heinemann Ltd, 1983); Times Newspapers Ltd for an adapted extract from *The Times* Leader 27.11.82. © Times Newspapers Ltd, 1982.

Whilst every effort has been made to trace the owners of copyright material, in a few cases this has proved impossible and we take this opportunity to offer our apologies to any copyright holders whose rights we may have unwittingly infringed.